STRATEGIC PLANNING
FOR
PUBLIC SERVICE
AND
NON-PROFIT ORGANIZATIONS

THE BEST OF LONG RANGE PLANNING

Series Editor: Professor Bernard Taylor, Henley Management College

The aim of this series is to bring together in each volume the best articles on a particular topic previously published in *Long Range Planning* so that readers wishing to study a specific aspect of planning can find an authoritative and comprehensive view of the subject, conveniently in one volume.

Titles in *The Best of Long Range Planning* **Series:**
Strategic Planning — The Chief Executive and the Board (Number 1)
Edited by Bernard Taylor

Entrepreneurship — Creating and Managing New Ventures (Number 2)
Edited by Bruce Lloyd

Making Strategic Planning Work in Practice (Number 3)
Edited by Basil Denning

Planning for Information as a Corporate Resource (Number 4)
Edited by Alfred Collins

Developing Strategies for Competitive Advantage (Number 5)
Edited by Patrick McNamee

Strategic Planning for Human Resources (Number 6)
Edited by Sheila Rothwell

Strategic Service Management (Number 7)
Edited by Denis Boyle

Strategic Management in Major Multinational Companies (Number 8)
Edited by Nigel Freedman

Turning Strategy into Action (Number 9)
Edited by Ken Irons

Creating Shareholder Value through Acquisitions and Divestment (Number 10)
Edited by Christopher Clarke

Strategic Management in Japanese Companies (Number 11)
Edited by Toyohiro Kono

Strategic Planning for Public Service and Non Profit Organizations (Number 12)
Edited by John M. Bryson

Each volume will contain 10 – 12 articles, and about 120 pages. In due course they will provide a comprehensive and authoritative reference library, covering all important aspects of Strategic Planning.

A Related Journal

LONG RANGE PLANNING★

The Journal of the Strategic Planning Society and of the European Strategic Planning Federation.

Editor: Professor Bernard Taylor, Henley — The Management College, Greenlands, Henley-on-Thames, Oxon RG9 3AU, UK.

> The leading international journal in the field of strategic planning, which provides authoritative information to senior managers, administrators, and academics on the concepts and techniques involved in the development and implementation of strategies and plans.

★Free sample copy gladly sent on request to the Publisher.

STRATEGIC PLANNING
FOR
PUBLIC SERVICE
AND
NON-PROFIT ORGANIZATIONS

Edited by

JOHN M. BRYSON
Strategic Management Research Center;
Hubert H. Humphrey Institute of Public Affairs

PERGAMON PRESS

OXFORD · NEW YORK · SEOUL · TOKYO

U.K.   Pergamon Press Ltd, Headington Hill Hall,
            Oxford OX3 0BW, England

USA   Pergamon Press, Inc, 660 White Plains Road,
            Tarrytown, New York 10591-5153, NY., USA

KOREA   Pergamon Press Korea, KPO Box 315, Seoul 110-603,
            Korea

JAPAN   Pergamon Press Japan, Tsunashima Building Annex,
            3-20-12 Yushima, Bunkyo-ku, Tokyo 113, Japan

First edition 1993

Library of Congress Cataloging-in-Publication Data

Strategic planning for public service and non-profit
organizations / edited by John M. Bryson.
p. cm. -- (The Best of long range planning ; no. 12)
Originally published: Strategic planning for public and
nonprofit organizations / John M. Bryson. 1st ed. 1988.
1. Strategic planning. 2. Corporations, Nonprofit--
Management. 3. Public administration. I. Bryson,
John M. (John Moore), 1947–. II. Bryson, John M.
(John Moore), 1947– Strategic planning for public
and nonprofit organizations. III. Series.
HD30.28.S73434 1993   658.4′012--dc20   92-35238

British Library Cataloguing in Publication Data

A catalogue record for this book is available from the
British Library.

ISBN 0 08 040672 6

Printed in Great Britain by BPCC Wheatons Ltd, Exeter.

Contents

Page

INTRODUCTION: Strategic Planning for Public Service and Non-Profit Organizations
John M. Bryson   1

PART 1   THE STRATEGIC PLANNING PROCESS

A Strategic Planning Process for Public and Non-Profit Organizations
John M. Bryson   11

PART 2   STRATEGIC PLANNING IN LOCAL GOVERNMENT

Making Strategic Planning Work in Local Government   23
Robert W. Rider

Planning for Strategic Performance in Local Government   33
Robert McGill

PART 3   STRATEGIC PLANNING IN STATE ENTERPRISES

Why Planning in State Enterprises Doesn't Work   43
Mansour Javidan and Ali Dastmalchian

Strategic Management of Public and Non-Market Corporations   51
Jean Ruffat

PART 4   STRATEGIC MANAGEMENT OF PROJECTS

Planning Development Projects: Lessons from Developing Countries   65
Dennis A. Rondinelli

How NASA moved from R&D to Operations   75
John L. Hunsucker, Shaukat A. Brah and Daryl L. Santos

PART 5   STRATEGIC PLANNING IN NON-PROFIT AND VOLUNTARY ORGANIZATIONS

Strategic Planning for the World Wildlife Fund   87
G. J. Medley

PART 6   MANAGING PARTICIPATION

Participative Planning for a Public Service   99
Timothy Grewe, James Marshall and Daniel E. O'Toole

Futures Research — Working with Management Teams   107
David Sims and Colin Eden

PART 7   ADDITIONAL TOOLS

Foresight Activities in the U.S.A.: Time for a Re-Assessment   119
Leonard L. Lederman
Washington, D.C.

Realistic Planning for Transportation — A Flexible Approach   129
Ata M. Khan

Strategic Planning for Public Service and Non-Profit Organizations

John M. Bryson, Associate Professor of Planning and Public Affairs; Associate Director of the Strategic Management Research Center at the University of Minnesota

I Foreword

This volume of *The Best of Long Range Planning* is about strategic planning for public and non-profit purposes — for governments, public agencies of all sorts, nonprofit or voluntary organizations, that do what governments might otherwise have to do, and communities. The authors address several issues:

☆ What does strategic planning for public and non-profit purposes look like?

☆ How does strategic planning differ from other kinds of planning, and how can these different approaches be reconciled?

☆ How can strategic planning for public and non-profit purposes be tailored to fit differing circumstances, including those facing governments, state enterprises, non-profit organizations, public projects, and public services?

☆ How can participation by the key stakeholders be managed?

☆ How should various planning tools be used in strategic planning?

Strategic Planning for Public Purposes

Interest in strategic planning for public purposes has heightened in recent years for two main reasons. First, political leaders, and managers in governments, public agencies, nonprofit or voluntary organizations, and communities, face difficult challenges. Turbulence and upheaval surround them. Furthermore, the pace of change is increasing as the world becomes increasingly interconnected and changes can echo unpredictably and often dangerously in other places. Second, in spite of the increased difficulty of controlling their environments, organizational and community leaders and managers are being held publicly accountable for the performance of their organizations and communities. Political leaders and managers need management approaches which will help them to manage in this rapidly changing environment. Strategic planning provides some of the concepts, procedures, and tools which they need.

Strategic planning can be applied to a wide range of public and nonprofit situations. The historical roots of strategic planning for public purposes run deep, since the management of war, foreign policy, and international relations has almost always taken place in the context of broad strategies. This book focuses on the more recent applications of strategic planning concepts, procedures, and tools to:

★ public agencies, departments, or divisions;
★ governments involved in a broad array of functions, such as cities, counties, or states;
★ nonprofit or voluntary organizations providing what are basically public services;
★ specific functions such as transportation, health, or education which bridge organizational and governmental boundaries;
★ entire communities, urban or metropolitan areas, regions, or states.

The examples presented in this book illustrate these applications.

1

Because strategic planning is designed to assist with the management of complex and changing situations, it is likely to become part of the standard repertoire of management in public and nonprofit organizations. Nevertheless, politicians and managers must be careful in their use of the concepts, procedures, and tools of strategic planning, since specific applications must be tailored to specific circumstances. The chapters in this book describe a variety of different approaches and some of the problems which occur in their application.

Strategic planning in relation to other kinds of planning

Strategic planning is defined as "a disciplined effort to produce fundamental decisions and actions that shape and guide what an organization is, what it does, and why it does it." Strategic planning is designed to help leaders and decision makers think and act strategically. The best examples of strategic planning include:

 ★ a process tailor-made to pursue specific purposes in specific circumstances;
 ★ effective and targeted gathering of information;
 ★ extensive communication with, and participation by, the key stakeholders;
 ★ the accommodation of divergent interests and values;
 ★ an assessment of the future implications of present decisions and actions;
 ★ focused analysis, a creative exploration of alternative solutions, and orderly decision making;
 ★ effective implementation, monitoring, and evaluation.

Strategic planning tends to differ from the more traditional long-range planning in the following ways:

1. Strategic planning typically focuses on strategic issues and their political context, while long-range planning emphasizes goals and objectives without clearly acknowledging the politics of planning. Strategic planning thus is better suited when competing interests are involved, while long-range planning may work well in an atmosphere of consensus and clear authority.

2. Strategic planning emphasizes an assessment of the organization's internal and external environment. Long-range planning tends to rely more on extrapolation of current trends.

3. Strategic planning is more likely to result in a "vision of success" for the organization.

4. Strategic planning is more action-oriented, because it emphasizes the need to build a capability to respond to a range of possible futures, rather than assuming that a projected 'most-likely' future will happen.

Strategic planning differs from comprehensive physical planning for communities in a number of ways as well:

1. Comprehensive planning is focused on a preferred future which is extrapolated from a narrow set of trends (e.g., population, land use, and traffic forecasts) and the preferences of those involved in the process. A plan for moving from the present to the desired state is outlined, except that the specific actors and actions necessary to achieve the desired future are rarely named.

2. Comprehensive planning typically focuses on an agenda for action that is far narrower than the agenda of the government as a whole. Comprehensive planning attends to transportation, land use, public facilities, parks, housing, and some other functions, but rarely to the full agenda of the government. Comprehensive planning thus is less useful to decision makers than strategic planning, which considers the full range of government's roles, focuses on the most relevant issue areas, and then develops strategies and action steps to deal with those issues. Comprehensive planning is likely to remain necessary for statutory reasons, and is desirable because of the need for plans in the areas it covers, but it should not take the place of strategic thinking which should provide a framework for comprehensive planning, and the action orientation that flows from effective strategy development.

The Role of Policy Boards

An organization's policy-making or governing board has an important role to play in strategic planning for public and non-profit purposes. It is responsible for defining the organizations' purpose and mission, articulating the strategic issues, and seeing that the issues are resolved effectively by management. In order to fulfill this role, an effective policy board (Carver, 1990; Bryson, 1988):

 ★ focuses most of its attention on its policy-making role;
 ★ has a mission statement that clearly states its purposes as a policy-making body;
 ★ disciplines itself to focus on policy making;
 ★ establishes a set of policy objectives for the organization, the function, or the community it oversees;
 ★ controls managers primarily through the questions which board members ask; the general form of these questions is "How does this recommendation (proposal, strategy, budget) serve these purposes, values, or policies?"

* concentrates its resources in order to be more effective in policy making;
* has staff who help its members become better policy makers;
* relies on good communications e.g. newsletters, press announcements, and videos, to transmit information to the media, employees, and other key stakeholders;
* holds periodic 'retreats' or 'away days' to develop strategic plans and work programs for subsequent years.

Unfortunately, few public or nonprofit organizations or communities are governed by effective policy-making boards. A strategic issue that often arises therefore is how to use strategic planning to make the governing boards more effective policy-making bodies. The articles in this book include examples of success and failure in doing this.

Participation

Strategic planners usually rely on 'stakeholder analyses' to determine who should be involved, and what role they should play in the strategic planning process. A stakeholder may be defined as "any person, group, or organization that can place a claim on an organization's attention, resources, or output, or is affected by that output". In a stakeholder analysis, all of the various claimants are listed and their "stakes" in the process are discussed: what they want and what they have to contribute. Based on this analysis, a participation strategy can be formulated which appropriately involves the relevant stakeholders.

In traditional democratic theory, there are two basic arguments for public participation. The first is to achieve informed and implementable decisions. The second is to educate and involve the public. Stakeholder analyses can be used to promote participation based on both of these rationales.

Public participation is likely to vary depending on whether the strategic planning process is focused on an organization, a program, or a community:

1. If the focus is on an organization, the participants are more likely to be insiders than outsiders. Insiders are more likely to believe they have the necessary information, that the policy board represents the public, and that extensive involvement would be too time-consuming and expensive. The absence of public participation is similar to the practice in corporate planning for corporations.

2. If the focus is on a program, then more public involvement is likely. This would be equivalent to extensive consumer involvement in marketing research. For example, planning for transportation, parks, and community services typically involves substantial public participation.

3. Finally, if the focus is on a community, extensive public involvement is likely. It is important, however, not to treat all citizens alike, because different groups of citizens are likely to have different interests. Stakeholder analyses can assist with the development of different approaches which are adapted to various groups and their interests. Community strategic planning appears to be very different from private sector corporate planning. There does not seem to be an equivalent in business except perhaps for development of a new town, which is owned by a company, or a group of companies.

Future Directions

Strategic planning is likely to become standard practice for governments, public agencies, non-profit or voluntary organizations, and communities. For this practice to enhance the effectiveness of these bodies, however, action is required:

1. These bodies need more experience with strategic planning, so that they can become more proficient. The chapters in this book describe such experience and suggest valuable lessons.

2. Political leaders, and managers need to understand the ways in which strategic planning must be tailored to specific situations.

3. The politics involved in strategic planning for public purposes must be embraced and worked with, rather than simply decried. Politics is the "name of the game" when it comes to strategic planning for public purposes. Politicians and managers need to use strategic planning to produce positive results rather than destructive conflict.

4. More work is needed on how to improve the formulation of strategic issues and strategies. It is in these two areas that the strategic planning process often breaks down.

5. More work is needed on how to resolve the many ambiguous, and often conflicting goals and objectives in the public sector.

6. We need to understand better how to link different strategic planning tools together as part of the strategic planning process.

7. In contrast to corporate strategic planning, which assumes a competitive model, much public sector strategic planning must emphasize cooperation and collaboration. We need more examples of how to work collaboratively to achieve public purposes.

The best public and non-profit decision makers and planners are now, and probably always have been, those who are best at strategic analysis and action. The chapters in this book describe approaches to the improvement of strategic thinking and action for those who wish to sharpen their skills and improve their strategic planning efforts, so that important public and non-profit purposes can be achieved.

References

(1) Bryson, J. M. *Strategic Planning for Public and Nonprofit Organizations*, San Francisco: Jossey-Bass, 1988.

(2) Carver, J. *Boards That Make a Difference*, San Francisco: Jossey-Bass, 1990.

II Summaries

Part 1 The Strategic Planning Process

A Strategic Planning Process for Public and Non-profit Organizations
John M. Bryson
LRP Vol. 21, No. 1, Feb 1988.

John Bryson describes a strategic planning process for public and nonprofit organizations and illustrates how it might be applied in practice with short illustrative cases (one involving a local government, and the other focusing on a public nursing service). The process includes eight steps:

1. Development of an initial agreement about the strategic planning effort.
2. Identification and clarification of political & statutory mandates.
3. Development and clarification of mission and values.
4. External environmental assessment.
5. Internal environmental assessment.
6. Strategic issue identification.
7. Strategy development.
8. Developing a description of the organization in the future, or its "vision of success."

Bryson argues that strategic planning can help government, non-profit, and community leaders do the following:

★ think strategically;
★ clarify future direction;
★ make today's decisions in light of their future consequences;
★ develop a coherent and defensible basis for decision making;
★ exercise maximum discretion in the areas under their control;
★ solve major organizational or community problems;

★ improve performance;
★ deal with rapidly changing circumstances;
★ build teamwork and expertise.

He goes on to suggest the important elements for initiating an effective strategic planning processes. Organization, or communities, that wish to engage in strategic planning should have:

1. A strong process sponsor(s) to authorize and legitimize the process.
2. A "champion" to push the process along.
3. A strategic planning team.
4. An expectation that there will be disruptions and delays, because 'they come with the territory.'
5. A willingness to be flexible regarding what constitutes a strategic plan, because the form of the plan should fit its purpose.
6. An ability to pull information and people together at key points for important discussions and decisions.
7. A willingness to construct and consider arguments geared to very different evaluative criteria, since effective strategies must be acceptable to many different stakeholders who often hold quite different assumptions and expectations regarding the purpose of the exercise.

Part 2 Strategic Planning in Local Government

Making Strategic Planning Work in Local Government
Robert W. Rider
LRP Vol. 16, No. 3, June 1983

The introduction explained some of the differences between strategic planning and other types of planning. In this article, Rider goes further and argues that local governments should consider fitting together various planning "building blocks" — of which strategic planning is one — into an overall framework which provides a context for political decision making and meets various legal requirements for consistency among, for example, policies and plans, capital budgets, and land use decision. The other building blocks include the comprehensive plan (for U.S. local governments), where this plan and the strategic plan primarily serve the legislative body's needs, the chief executive's planning needs and style, the agency plans, and the neighborhood organizations and plans.

While some of the specifics of Rider's argument apply mainly to the U.S., most of his argument is more generally applicable. He believes that strategic planning is more important than comprehensive planning, because it focuses on issues, is more relevant to political decision makers, and is more likely to result in agreed-upon, implementable strategies in shared-power settings. Comprehensive planning, he argues, should flow from the sort of political agreements that strategic planning helps facilitate, rather than try to force such agreements, which is likely to be a fruitless exercise in any case. Plans that are necessary for legal reasons will still need to be prepared (for example, to assure that the capital program is consistent with the land use plan), but if those plans (and the planners who make them) attempt to pre-empt political decision makers' prerogatives, those decision makers are likely to find ways to disregard or undercut the plans (and planners).

Rider also emphasizes that consistency for consistency's sake is not useful. Inconsistences, to the extent they need to be resolved, should become the basis for "thinking about options, the interchange of ideas, and the process of negotiation." The idea is to promote coordination through "directed interaction" rather than through rigid, legalistic central control, which is unworkable in any event when political power is shared among different individuals and groups. The process of planning is what is important, not specific plans.

Planning for Strategic Performance in Local Government
Robert McGill
LRP Vol. 21, No. 5, Oct 1988

Ronald McGill emphasizes the need to develop performance measures if local authorities (or by extension, other government bodies, or communities) are to make progress in dealing with important problems. He begins by drawing a distinction between public administration and business management. He argues that public administration refers to "the non-trading sector of government," in which political decision making must predominate, because of the absence of market discipline, and the regular budgeting cycles provide one of the most important expressions of political decision making. He notes the need to use the budgeting cycles for strategic purposes, and shows how Renfrew District Council in Scotland has done so.

McGill believes that budgeting, because it has to happen on an annual basis, can be used to force strategic decision making. But he argues that budgeting should be tied to a three-tiered set of strategic performance criteria. The first tier consists of *outcome or social impact*, measures over three to five years. Assuring performance against these measures is in large part the policy makers' job, as the measure is typically tied directly to the government's mission, or reason for being. The second tier consists of *output* measures tied to specific programs which are designed to support agreed strategies to achieve desired outcomes. These measures have a one-to-three-year time horizon.

Achieving performance against these measures is a management responsibility. Finally, the third tier consists of specific *operational* performance indicators which are the responsibility of individual departments. These indicators have a quarterly to one-year horizon. Budgeting should follow a review and evaluation of existing strategies in relation to level 1 and 2 indicators. McGill describes the experience of Renfrew District Council which has followed this process for several years in its efforts to tackle issues related to poverty. He also describes how the approach could be applied to other kinds of issues.

Part 3 Strategic Planning in State Enterprises

Why Planning in State Enterprises Doesn't Work
Mansour Javidan and Ali Dastmalchian
LRP Vol. 21, No. 3, June 1988

While most authors in this volume present an optimistic case for strategic planning for public purposes, Mansour Javidan and Ali Dastmalchian provide more sobering evidence of strategic planning in practice. Based on their survey of the chief executive officers of 65 provincially controlled corporations in Canada, they find that strategic planning often is more "ceremonial" than real. Strategic planning is often used primarily to justify, or provide "window dressing" for budgets and financial plans, which are seen as the "real" planning documents. Indeed, financial objectives dominate most of the plans produced, with far less attention given to marketing and human resource objectives.

Not surprisingly, the exercises seem to produce little real change in practice. The companies are far more reactive, than proactive. It seems that, in the authors' words, "No change will take place unless they absolutely have to introduce one." In addition, there seems to be little connection between strategic planning and action planning and control activities.

One of the reasons is that the boards of directors "seem to play a minimal role in actual formulation of corporate plans at most companies." With little buy-in at the top, probably not much can be expected. Beyond that, the authors note problems due to vague organizational objectives, lack of market exposure, and limited top management authority.

They conclude with a set of prescriptions for top management at state-owned enterprises. They suggest that top management should:

1. determine if there is a need for strategic planning.

2. communicate the rationale and the need for strategic planning.
3. prepare line managers for strategic planning.
4. move beyond "motherhood" goals.
5. emphasize the need for detailed action plans.
6. examine the fit between strategic thrusts and the organizational reward system.
7. examine the link between the planning and the budgeting system.
8. emphasize the need for monitoring and evaluation of accomplishments.

Strategic Management of Public and Non-Market Corporations
Jean Ruffat
LRP Vol. 16, No. 2, Apr 1983

Jean Ruffat presents a conceptual framework for improving the accountability of public and non-market corporations. The importance of the task is highlighted by Ruffat's assertion that one-third of the world's gross product is generated by non-market corporations, and that over half of all productive investments are made by these corporations.

Ruffat argues that there are three main stakeholder groups: users or customers of services; employees; and taxpayers and budget authorities. Unfortunately, each group typically acts as if the main purpose of the corporation is to cater to its own needs and interests. As a consequence, all stakeholders are not satisfied simultaneously. Management's main function is to address the competing claims by, and contributions from, all of the stakeholder groups in such a way that from a corporate standpoint the yields to each stakeholder are optimized in relation to the costs expended in achieving those yields. The accommodation of these divergent interests is a challenge and Ruffat presents an accountability framework to help with the task. To operationalise the framework may be difficult, but having the ideas behind the framework in mind should help public managers and policy makers to improve the performance of non-market corporations.

Part 4 Strategic Management of Projects

Planning Development Projects:
Lessons from Developing Countries
Dennis A. Rondinelli
LRP Vol. 12, No. 3, June 1979

Projects are a basic means of implementing national and sectoral development plans in the developing world, and thus are a crucial element of formulating and implementing effective strategies for achieving national and sectoral goals. Dennis

Rondinelli distils a series of important lessons about how to improve the project planning and implementation process based on twenty-five years of experience. Subsequent experience probably has only reinforced the wisdom embodied in the chapter. A particular advantage of the chapter is that with little translation the lessons may also be applied to the developed world.

The lessons Rondinelli offers include the following:

★ Projects should be viewed as complex administrative activities requiring an integrated management framework.
★ Informal as well as formal sources of project identification should be recognized and stimulated.
★ Project design should be linked more realistically to objectives, needs, and conditions in developing countries.
★ The project appraisal, selection, and approval processes should be simplified.
★ A broader array of institutional forms and managerial arrangements should be considered for projects than the matrix form used most frequently in developed nations.
★ Project management skills should be broadened from narrow programming and coordination function to include leadership capabilities.

How NASA Moved from R & D to Operations
John L. Hunsucker, Shaukat A. Brah and Daryl L. Santos
LRP Vol. 22, No. 6, Dec 1989

Hunsaker, Brah, and Santos address two issues that are important for successful strategic management. One is the management of organizational transitions, which is always necessary when an organization moves from one kind of strategy to another. The second is the institutionalization for the long haul of an activity developed first in a research and development mode. The requirements for successful research and development are quite different from those for successful long-term operations. This article thus has a significance far broader than the unique organization and program — NASA and the space shuttle — on which it is focused.

The authors argue that transition management involves four phases:

★ The creativity phase, in which the nature of the transition is articulated and processes and structures are put in place to manage the change.
★ The control phase, in which the initial implementation of the strategy occurs.
★ The integration phase, in which residual problems are worked out and employee commitment and support are nurtured.
★ The stabilization phase, in which the transition is completed and ongoing operations begin.

They argue that a four-step analysis is useful in the creativity phase. The analysis consists of developing answers to four questions typical of any strategic analysis:

* Where are we now?
* Where do we want to be?
* How do we get there?
* How badly do we want to get there?

Part 5 Strategic Planning for Non-Profit and Voluntary Organizations

Strategic Planning for the World Wildlife Fund
G. J. Medley
LRP Vol. 21, No. 1, Feb 1988

There are few case examples in the literature of strategic planning by non-profit and voluntary organizations. George Medley helps to fill this gap with his story of strategic planning at the World Wildlife Fund in the United Kingdom. The organization began strategic planning in 1978 when Medley became director, after a successful career in business. The process which they followed included several steps, and has since been repeated on an annual basis. The steps are as follows:

1. Deciding on the purpose (or mission).
2. Identification of key areas — those areas where success would contribute to the overall success of the organization, and failure would have a significant adverse impact on the organization. Examples include: marketing, public awareness, fund status, innovation.
3. Identification of strengths, weaknesses, opportunities, and threats in each key area.
4. Deciding on strategies in each area.
5. Development of departmental action plans to achieve each of the strategies where it might contribute.
6. Consolidation of the action plans into a working plan for the organization as a whole.
7. Development of departmental budgets to meet the objectives.
8. Consolidation of the departmental budgets into an overall organizational budget.
9. Implementation, including quarterly departmental reviews of progress against budgets.

The performance of WWF U.K. in such areas as net funds (the equivalent of profitability) and productivity have been outstanding. Net funds increased five times from 1978 to 1981, while productivity (net funds per employee) increased six times. Medley attributes much of this success to the annual round of strategic planning and subsequent implementation efforts.

Part 6 Managing Participation

Participative Planning for a Public Service
Timothy Grewe, James Marshall and Daniel E. O'Toole
LRP Vol. 22, No. 1, Feb 1989

Timothy Grewe, James Marshall and Daniel O'Toole make the point that the literature includes little in-depth discussion of how to manage a strategic planning process. The literature contains numerous broad conceptual overviews of strategic planning, but little on tools, techniques, and procedures for managing the participation of groups of people over the course of a strategic planning exercise. The process must be managed effectively so that the participants feel involved, the information they have to offer is elicited, the resulting products reflect their input, and they are committed to implementation actions.

The authors outline a process, along with a set of specific activities, tools, and guidelines or considerations, to help fill this gap. Without this kind of guidance, people who are convinced of the desirability of strategic planning may be not be able to follow through on their desire to use it simply because they do not understand the mechanics of how to apply strategic planning concepts in practice.

They conclude that participation in the process may be at least as important as the content of the plan. Participation can lead to the following desirable outcomes:

1. Participants can form a common vision of the future and its implications for the organization.
2. Participants can improve their group problem-solving skills.
3. Participants can recognize that continuous planning is a management necessity.

Futures Research — Working with Management Teams
David Sims and Colin Eden
LRP Vol. 17, No. 4, August 1984

While participation may produce many benefits, it also involves significant challenges. One of the biggest is how to develop a shared sense of the precise nature of the complex strategic issues that typically confront a public or nonprofit organization on the one hand, and a shared sense of the complexly interrelated activities that typically are necessary to address these issues, on the other hand. The mechanics and norms of typical group meetings often limit, rather than enhance, participation. Individuals find themselves restricted to making short, assertive speeches that don't come close to reflecting their real understanding of the issues, and don't facilitate the kind of collegial dialogue necessary to develop real understanding and to incrementally build commitment to new or revised strategies.

David Sims and Colin Eden outline an approach to building shared understandings and commitments called "cognitive mapping." In my own view, this approach is one of the most promising recent developments for enhancing strategic thought and action by public and non-profit groups. There are computer programs to facilitate the development of these maps, but very effective maps can be constructed manually. These maps help group members clarify the concepts that comprise important issues areas, the interrelationships among concepts, and actions that might be taken to produce desirable outcomes. The maps help the groups engage in the kind of constructive dialogue necessary to make real progress in complex issue areas. Even simple maps, such as those the authors present based on their work with three British public housing managers, can enhance group effectiveness.

Part 7 Additional Tools

Foresight Activities in the U.S.A.:
Time for a Re-Assessment?
Leonard L. Lederman
LRP Vol. 17, No. 3, June 1984

An important component of strategic planning for public and non-profit organizations is reconnaissance and careful thought about current realities and future possibilities and their potential impact on the organization and its short and long-run effectiveness. Lederman reviews the foresight activities of U.S. private corporations and Federal government agencies in the early 1980's and finds wide variation in the then-current practice across corporations and between corporations and the Federal government. Unfortunately, public sector foresight activities tend to have a relatively short-term and narrow focus and do not involve top management as much as private-sector efforts. The likelihood of being blindsided by future events therefore is enhanced. While many state and local governments in the U.S. have improved their efforts, there is little evidence that anything has changed on the Federal level.

Governments in other countries vary widely in the effectiveness of their own foresight activities. Some do better than U.S. governments, others not as well. Lederman's findings probably are equally applicable, however, to all governments:

Foresight activities are likely to be effective to the extent that:

1. They are supported by and involve top management of the organization.
2. They are the responsibility of a top official of the organization and are directed by a line officer or manager.
3. Line managers and staff in many parts of the organization actively participate.
4. The activities are used in the decision-making and operations of the organization.

Realistic Planning for Transportation
Ata M. Khan
LRP Vol. 22, No. 5, August 1989

Major capital investments — such as large transportation projects — typically require reasonably effective forecasting efforts. Ata Kahn argues that the linkage between forecasting efforts and effective planning depends on use of flexible approaches to each, rather than rigid insistence on particular forecasting methodologies and immutable master plans. As the demands for participation increase in public-sector (and, for that matter, in non-profit) planning efforts the needs for such a flexible approach will increase.

Kahn argues that planning for major projects that have significant long-term impacts should proceed through at least four steps: The first is a preliminary analysis, in which the problem is defined, alternative strategies are explored, and a choice of approach is made. The broad strategic direction of the project is set in this step, along with the justifications for the project. The second step consists of a very detailed analysis and refinement of the preferred concept developed during the first step. The third step involves partial implementation, in which the solution is tried out on a small scale to see how it will work in practice and what changes are necessary before full-scale implementation. The fourth step is full implementation. The author also discusses a variety of different forecasting methods that will help produce the kind of information and flexibility that the four-step process requires.

PART ONE

The Strategic Planning Process

A Strategic Planning Process for Public and Non-profit Organizations

John M. Bryson

A pragmatic approach to strategic planning is presented for use by public and non-profit organizations. Benefits of the process are outlined and two examples of its application are presented—one involving a city government and the other a public health nursing service. Requirements for strategic planning success are discussed. Several conclusions are drawn, namely that: (1) strategic planning is likely to become part of the repertoire of public and non-profit planners; (2) planners must be very careful how they apply strategic planning to specific situations; (3) it makes sense to think of decision makers as strategic planners and strategic planners as facilitators of decision making across levels and functions; and (4) there are a number of theoretical and practical issues that still need to be explored.

I skate to where I think the puck will be.
Wayne Gretzky

Men, I want you to stand and fight vigorously and then run. And as I am a little bit lame, I'm going to start running now.
General George Stedman
U.S. Army in the Civil War

Not all of the readers of *Long Range Planning* may be familiar with either Wayne Gretzky or George Stedman, but their two quotes capture the essence of strategic planning (often called corporate planning in Britain). Wayne Gretzky is perhaps the world's greatest offensive player in professional ice hockey. He holds the single-season scoring record for players in the National Hockey League—by such a wide margin that many consider him the greatest offensive player of all time. His quote emphasizes that *strategic thinking and acting, not strategic planning per se,* are most important. He does not skate around with a thick strategic plan in his back pocket. What he does is to think and act strategically every minute of the game, in keeping with a simple game plan worked out with his coaches and key teammates in advance.

Let us explore Gretzky's statement further. What must one know and be able to do in order to make—and act on—a comment like Gretsky's? One obviously needs to know the purpose and rules of the game, the strengths and weakneses of one's own team, the opportunities and threats posed by the other team, the game plan, the arena, the officials, and so on. One also needs to be a well-equipped, superbly conditioned, strong and able hockey player—and it does not hurt to play for a very good team. In other words, anyone who can assert confidently that he or she 'skates to where the puck will be' knows basically everything there is to know about strategic thinking and acting in hockey games.

Wayne Gretzky is respected primarily for his extraordinary offensive scoring ability. But defensive abilities obviously are important, too. Whereas Gretzky is a great offensive strategist, General George Stedman of the U.S. Army in the Civil War was an experienced defensive strategist. At one point he and his men were badly outnumbered by Confederate soldiers. A hasty retreat was in order, but it made sense to give the lame and wounded —and the General, too!—a chance to put some distance between themselves and the enemy before a full-scale retreat was called. The General and his men then would be in a position to fight another day.

Stedman had no thick strategic plan in his back pocket, either. At most he probably had a general battle plan worked out with his fellow officers and recorded in pencil on a map. Again, strategic

John M. Bryson is Associate Professor of Planning and Public Affairs in the Hubert H. Humphrey Institute of Public Affairs and Associate Director of the Strategic Management Research Center at the University of Minnesota, MN 55455, U.S.A.

thinking and acting were what mattered, not any particular planning process.

How does this relate to public and non-profit organizations today? The answer is that strategic thought and action are increasingly important to the continued viability and effectiveness of governments, public agencies and non-profit organizations of all sorts. Without strategic planning it is unlikely that these organizations will be able to meet successfully the numerous challenges that face them.

The environments of public and non-profit organizations have changed dramatically in the last 10 years—as a result of oil crises, demographic shifts, changing values, taxing limits, privatization, centralization or decentralization of responsibilities, moves toward information and service-based economies, volatile macroeconomic performance, and so on. As a result, traditional sources of revenue for most governments are stable at best or highly unpredictable or declining at worst. Further, while the public may be against higher taxes, and while transfers of money from central to local governments are typically stable or declining, the public continues to demand a high level of government services. Non-profit organizations often are called on to take up the slack in the system left by the departure of public organizations or services, but may be hard-pressed to do so.

To cope with these various pressures, public and non-profit organizations must do at least three things. First, these organizations need to exercise as much discretion as they can in the areas under their control to ensure responsiveness to their stakeholders. Second, these organizations need to develop good strategies to deal with their changed circumstances. And third, they need to develop a coherent and defensible basis for decision making.

What is Strategic Planning?

Strategic planning is designed to help public and non-profit organizations (and communities) respond effectively to their new situations. It is *a disciplined effort to produce fundamental decisions and actions shaping the nature and direction of an organization's (or other entity's) activities within legal bounds.*[1] These decisions typically concern the organization's mandates, mission and product or service level and mix, cost, financing, management or organizational design. (Strategic planning was designed originally for use by *organizations*. In this article we will concentrate on its applicability to public and non-profit organizations. Strategic planning of course can be, and has been, applied to projects, functions —such as transportation, health care or education —and communities.)

What does strategic planning look like? Its most basic formal requirement is a series of discussions and decisions among key decision makers and managers about what is *truly* important for the organization. And those discussions are the *big* innovation that strategic planning brings to most organizations, because in most organizations key decision makers and managers from different levels and functions almost *never* get together to talk about what is truly important. They may come together periodically at staff meetings, but usually to discuss nothing more important than, for example, alternatives to the organization's sick leave policy. Or they may attend the same social functions, but there, too, it is rare to have sustained discussions of organizationally relevant topics.

Usually key decision makers need a reasonably structured process to help them identify and resolve the most important issues their organizations face. One such process that has proved effective in practice is outlined in Figure 1. The process consists of the following eight steps:

1. *Development of an initial agreement concerning the strategic planning effort.* The agreement should cover: the purpose of the effort; preferred steps in the process; the form and timing of reports; the role, functions and membership of a strategic planning coordinating committee; the role, functions and membership of the strategic planning team; and commitment of necessary resource to proceed with the effort.

2. *Identification and clarification of mandates.* The purpose of this step is to identify and clarify the externally imposed formal and informal mandates placed on the organization. These are the *musts* confronting the organization. For most public and non-profit organizations these mandates will be contained legislation, articles of incorporation or charters, regulations, and so on. Unless mandates are identified and clarified two difficulties are likely to arise: the mandates are unlikely to be met, and the organization is unlikely to know what pursuits are allowed and not allowed.

3. *Development and clarification of mission and values.* The third step is the development and clarification of the organization's mission and values. An organization's mission—in tandem with its mandates—provides its *raison d'être*, the social justification for its existence.

Prior to development of a mission statement, an organization should complete a stakeholder analysis. A *stakeholder* is defined as any person, group or organization that can place a claim on an organization's attention, resources or output, or is affected by that output. Examples of a government's stakeholders are citizens, taxpayers, service recipients, the governing body, employees, unions, interest groups, political parties, the financial community and other governments.

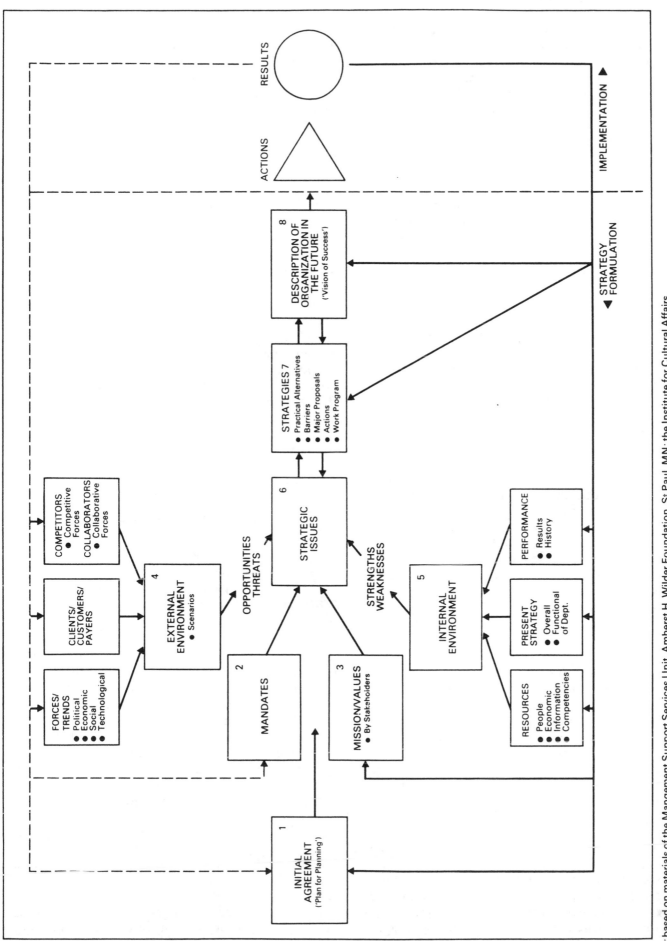

Sources: based on materials of the Mangement Support Services Unit, Amherst H. Wilder Foundation, St Paul, MN; the Institute for Cultural Affairs, Minneapolis, MN; and the Office of Planning and Development, Hennepin County, MN.

Figure 1. Strategic planning process

In the simplest form of stakeholder analysis, the organization identifies its stakeholders and their 'stakes' in the organization, along with the stakeholders' criteria for judging the performance of the organization. The organization also explores how well it does against the stakeholders' criteria. Once a stakeholder analysis is completed, the organization can develop a mission statement that takes key stakeholder interests into account.

4. *External environmental assessment.* The fourth step is exploration of the environment outside the organization in order to identify the opportunities and threats the organization faces. Political, economic, social and technological trends and events might be assessed, along with the nature and status of various stakeholder groups, such as the organization's customers, clients or users, and actual or potential competitors or collaborators.

5. *Internal environmental assessment.* The next step is an assessment of the organization itself in order to identify its strengths and weaknesses. Three assessment categories include—following a simple systems model—organizational resources (inputs), present strategy (process) and performance (outputs). Unfortunately, most organizations can tell you a great deal about the resources they have, much less about their current strategy, and even less about how well they perform. The nature of accountability is changing, however, in that public and nonprofit organizations are increasingly held accountable for their outputs as well as their inputs. A stakeholder analysis can help organizations adapt to this changed nature of accountability, because the analysis forces organizations to focus on the criteria stakeholders use to judge organizational performance. Those criteria are typically related to output. For example, stakeholders are increasingly concerned with whether or not state-financed schools are producing educated citizens. In many states in the United States, the ability of public schools to garner public financing is becoming contingent on the schools' ability to demonstrate that they do an effective job of educating their students.

The identification of strengths, weaknesses, opportunities and threats—or SWOT analysis—in Steps 4 and 5 is very important because every effective strategy will build on strengths and take advantage of opportunities, while it overcomes or minimizes weaknesses and threats.

6. *Strategic issue identification.* Together the first five elements of the process lead to the sixth, the identification of strategic issues. *Strategic issues* are fundamental policy questions affecting the organization's mandates; mission and values; product or service level and mix, clients, users or payers, cost, financing, management or organizational design. Usually, it is vital that strategic issues be dealt with expeditiously and effectively if the organization is to survive and prosper. An organization that does not address a strategic issue may be unable to head off a threat, unable to capitalize on an important opportunity, or both.

Strategic issues—virtually by definition—embody conflicts. The conflicts may be over ends (what); means (how); philosophy (why); location (where); timing (when); and who might be helped or hurt by different ways of resolving the issue (who). In order for the issues to be raised and resolved effectively, the organization must be prepared to deal with such conflicts.

A statement of a strategic issue should contain three elements. First, the issue should be described succinctly, preferably in a single paragraph. The issue itself should be framed as a question the organization can do something about. If the organization cannot do anything about it, it is not an issue—at least for the organization. An organization's attention is limited enough without wasting it on issues it cannot resolve.

Second, the factors that make the issue a fundamental policy question should be listed. In particular, what is it about mandates, mission, values or internal strengths and weaknesses and external opportunities and threats that make this a strategic issue? Listing these factors will become useful in the next step, strategy development.

Finally, the planning team should state the consequences of failure to address the issue. A review of the consequences will inform judgments of just how strategic, or important, various issues are. The strategic issue identification step therefore focuses organizational attention on what is truly important for the survival, prosperity and effectiveness of the organization—and provides useful advice on how to achieve these aims.

There are three basic approaches to the identification of strategic issues: the direct approach, the goals approach and the scenario approach.[2] The *direct approach*—in which strategic planners go straight from a view of mandates, mission and SWOTs to the identification of strategic issues—probably will work best for most governments and public agencies. The direct approach is best when one or more of the following conditions prevail: (1) there is no agreement on goals, or the goals on which there is agreement are too abstract to be useful; (2) there is no pre-existing vision of success and developing a consensually based vision will be difficult; (3) there is no hierarchical authority that can impose goals on the other stakeholders; or (4) the environment is so turbulent that development of goals or visions seems unwise, and partial actions in response to immediate, important issues seem most prudent. The direct approach, in other words, can work in the pluralistic, partisan, politicized and relatively fragmented worlds of most public organizations—as long as there is a 'dominant coalition'[3] strong enough and interested enough to make it work.

The *goals approach* is more in line with conventional planning theory which stipulates that an organization should establish goals and objectives for itself and then develop strategies to achieve those goals and objectives. The approach can work if there is fairly broad and deep agreement on the organization's goals and objectives—and if those goals and objectives themselves are detailed and specific enough to guide the identification of issues and development of strategies. This approach also is more likely to work in organizations with hierarchical authority structures where key decision makers can impose goals on others affected by the planning exercise. The approach, in other words, is more likely to work in public or non-profit organizations that are hierarchically organized, pursue narrowly defined missions and have few powerful stakeholders than it is in organizations with broad agendas and numerous powerful stakeholders.

Finally, there is the *scenario*—or 'vision of success'[4]—*approach*, whereby the organization develops a 'best' or 'ideal' picture of itself in the future as it successfully fulfills its mission and achieves success. The strategic issues then concern how the organization should move from the way it is now to how it would look and behave according to its vision. The vision of success approach is most useful if the organization will have difficulty identifying strategic issues directly; if no detailed and specific agreed-upon goals and objectives exist and will be difficult to develop; and if drastic change is likely to be necessary. As conception precedes perception[5] development of a vision can provide the concepts that enable organizational members to see necessary changes. This approach is more likely to work in a non-profit organization than in a public-sector organization because public organizations are more likely to be tightly constrained by mandates.

7. *Strategy development.* In this step, strategies are developed to deal with the issues identified in the previous step. A *strategy* is a *pattern* of purposes, policies, programmes, actions, decisions and/or resource allocations that define what an organization is, what it does and why it does it. Strategies can vary by level, function and time frame.

This definition is purposely broad, in order to focus attention on the creation of consistency across *rhetoric* (what people say), *choices* (what people decide and are willing to pay for) and *actions* (what people do). Effective strategy formulation and implementation processes will link rhetoric, choices and actions into a coherent and consistent pattern across levels, functions and time.[6]

The author favours a five-part strategy development process (to which he was first introduced by the Institute for Cultural Affairs in Minneapolis).

Strategy development begins with identification of practical alternatives, dreams or visions for resolving the strategic issues. It is of course important to be practical, but if the organization is unwilling to entertain at least *some* 'dreams' or 'visions' for resolving its strategic issues, it probably should not be engaged in strategic planning.

Next, the planning team should enumerate the barriers to achieving those alternatives, dreams or visions, and not focus directly on their achievement. A focus on barriers at this point is not typical of most strategic planning processes. But doing so is one way of assuring that strategies deal with implementation difficulties directly rather than haphazardly.

Once alternatives, dreams and visions, along with barriers to their realization, are listed, the team should prepare or request major proposals for achieving the alternatives, dreams or visions directly, or else indirectly through overcoming the barriers. For example, a major city government did not begin to work on strategies to achieve its major ambitions until it had overhauled its archaic civil service system. That system clearly was a barrier that had to be confronted before the city government could have any hope of achieving its more important objectives.

After the strategic planning team prepares or receives major proposals, two final tasks must be completed. The team must identify the actions needed over the next one to two years to implement the major proposals. And finally, the team must spell out a detailed work programme, covering the next 6 months to a year, to implement the actions.

An effective strategy must meet several criteria. It must be technically workable, politically acceptable to key stakeholders, and must accord with the organization's philosophy and core values. It must also be ethical, moral and legal.

8. *Description of the organization in the future.* In the final (and not always necessary) step in the process the organization describes what it should look like as it successfully implements its strategies and achieves its full potential. This description is the organization's 'vision of success'. Few organizations have such a description or vision, yet the importance of such descriptions has long been recognized by well-managed companies and organizational psychologists.[7] Typically included in such descriptions are the organization's mission, its basic strategies, its performance criteria, some important decision rules, and the ethical standards expected of all employees.

These eight steps complete the strategy formulation process. Next come actions and decisions to implement the strategies, and, finally, the evaluation of results. Although the steps are laid out in a linear, sequential manner, it must be emphasized that the process is iterative. Groups often have to repeat steps before satisfactory decisions can be reached and actions taken. Furthermore, implementation typically should not wait until the eight steps have been completed. As noted earlier, strategic thinking *and* acting are important, and all of the thinking does not have to occur before any actions are taken.

To return to Wayne Gretzky and George Stedman, one can easily imagine them zooming almost intuitively through the eight steps—while already on the move—in a rapid series of discussions, decisions and actions. The eight steps merely make the process of strategic thinking and acting more orderly and allow more people to participate in the process.

The process might be applied across levels and functions in an organization as outlined in Figure 2. The application is based on the system used by the 3M Corporation.[8] In the system's first cycle, there is 'bottom up' development of strategic plans within a framework established at the top, followed by reviews and reconciliations at each succeeding level. In the second cycle, operating plans are developed to implement the strategic plans. Depending on the situation, decisions at the top of the organizational hierarchy may or not require policy board approval, which explains why the line depicting the process flow diverges at the top.

The Benefits of Strategic Planning

What are the benefits of strategic planning? Government and non-profit organizations in the United States are finding that strategic planning can help them:

☆ think strategically;

☆ clarify future direction;

☆ make today's decisions in light of their future consequences;

☆ develop a coherent and defensible basis for decision making;

☆ exercise maximum discretion in the areas under organizational control;

☆ solve major organizational problems;

☆ improve performance;

☆ deal effectively with rapidly changing circumstances;

☆ build teamwork and expertise.

While there is no guarantee that strategic planning will produce these benefits, there are an increasing number of case example and studies that indicate it can help as long as key leaders and decision makers want it to work, and are willing to invest the time,

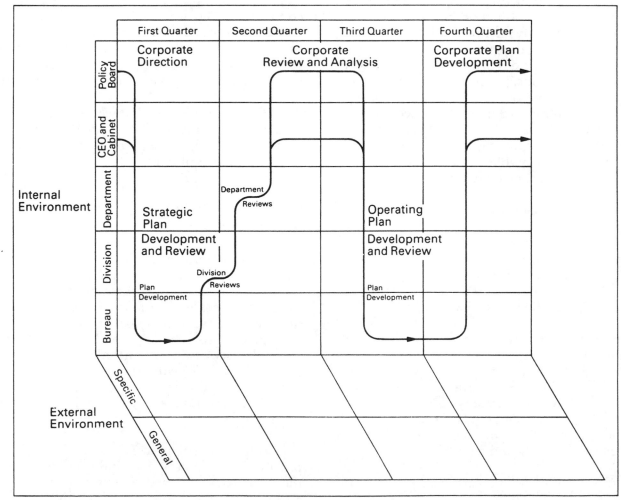

Figure 2. Annual strategic planning process

attention and resources necessary to make it work.[9] In the next two sections we will turn to two cases in which the strategic planning process outlined above produced desirable results. The author served as a strategic planning consultant in each case.

Case No. 1—Suburban City

Suburban City is an older, middle-class, 'first ring' suburb of a major metropolitan city in the American Midwest. Suburban City is regarded among city management professionals as one of the best-managed cities in the state. The city has 227 employees and an annual budget of $25·6m. The assistant city manager was the leader of the strategic planning team. The city manager was a strong supporter and member of the team. The team performed a stakeholder analysis, developed a mission statement, identified strategic issues, and developed strategies to deal with its most important issues. They are now implementing their strategies.

The following strategic issues were identified:

☆ What should the city do to enhance and improve its vehicular and pedestrian movements throughout its hierarchy of transportation facilities?

☆ What should the city do to improve its image as a place to live and work?

☆ What should the city do to attract high quality housing that meets the needs of a changing population and maintains the integrity of the existing housing stock?

☆ What should the city do to maintain its physical facilities while responding to changing demands for public services?

☆ What should the city do to restore confidence in its water quality and supply?

Strategies were developed to deal with all these issues, but we will consider the strategies stemming from the last two. The first step in responding to changing demands for public services was to undertake a major survey of households and businesses in the city to uncover preferences for services. Now that the survey is complete, city staff are rearranging and reorganizing services and delivery mechanisms to respond effectively.

Suburban City residents became worried, to the point of panic, when the city's water supply was found to be contaminated by uncontrolled seepage from a creosote plant. The city immediately closed down the affected wells and began a major cleanup effort. The water *quality* problem was cleared up, but the public *perception* that the city had a serious water quality problem persisted. City staff undertook a public education effort to deal with this misperception, and another effort was undertaken

to deal with the remaining—and real, not just perceived—problem of a water *quantity*.

The strategic planning team did not go on to draft a 'vision of success' for the city. One reason why this was not done was that the team had had real difficulty developing a mission statement that all could support. The difficulty was not over content, interestingly enough, but over style. The city manager felt that a mission statement should give a person 'goose bumps', and the team had trouble drafting a mission statement that did. Finally, the city manager relented and supported a mission statement that had less of a physiological effect.

An interesting result of the city's strategic planning effort has been the recognition by members of the city council that they have not been an effective policy-making board. As a result, they hired a nationally known consultant on effective governance to help them become better policymakers. The city manager and assistant city manager are convinced that as the council becomes more effective, strategic planning for the city also will become more effective.

Case No. 2—Public Health Nursing Service

Public Health Nursing Service (Nursing Service) is a unit of the government of a large, urban county in the same state as Suburban City. The county executive director decided to explore the utility of strategic planning for the county by asking several units of county government, including Nursing Service, to undertake strategic planning.

Nursing Service is required by statute to control communicable diseases, and it also provides a variety of public health services at its clinics throughout the county. In 1984 Nursing Service had over 80 staff members and a budget of approximately $3·5m.

The strategic planning team was led by the director of the service, who was a major supporter of the process. Other sponsors, though not strong supporters, included the county's executive director and the director of the department of public health, of which Nursing Service is a part. The department's health planner was an active and dedicated promoter of the process.

The director, deputy director and staff of Nursing Service saw strategic planning as an opportunity to rethink the service's mission and strategies in light of the rapidly changing health care environment. They were concerned, however, that they had been selected as 'guinea pigs' for the executive director's experiment in strategic planning. Nursing Service has always lived with the fear that it would be taken over, put out of business or otherwise circumvented by the county government's huge medical centre, a famous hospital that was considering entering the home health care field (Nursing Service's main 'business') at the same time that Nursing Service began its strategic planning process. Nursing Service was afraid that any information or arguments it created as part of its process might be used against it by the executive director and county board to benefit the medical centre. A number of reassurances from the executive director were necessary before Nursing Service would believe it was not being 'set up'.

As a result of the process, Nursing Service identified a number of strategic issues. The principal issue was what the mission of Nursing Service should be given the changing health care environment. After rethinking their mission, the Nursing Service team rethought their first set of strategic issues. The team identified a new set of strategic issues concerning how the new mission could be pursued. Those issues were:

☆ What is the role of Nursing Service in ensuring the health of the citizens of the county?

☆ How should Nursing Service deal with the growing health care needs for which there is inadequate or no reimbursement of services?

☆ What is the role of Nursing Service (and the county) in ensuring quality in community-based health care?

☆ What is the role of Nursing Service (and the county) in ensuring community health planning and health system development?

Nursing Service went on to develop a set of strategies designed to deal with these issues. The set includes:

☆ Differentiation and clarification of line and staff functions of Nursing Service's supervisors and administrators.

☆ Development of a process for programme development and change.

☆ Development of an organizational structure which will allow the agency to respond most effectively and efficiently to the needs of communities as well as individuals and families.

By the end of 1987 these strategies should be fully implemented. The strategies do not necessarily deal with the strategic issues directly. Instead, they focus primarily on overcoming the barriers to dealing with the issues. Once the agency is organized properly and has programme development and change procedures in place, it will be better able to address the health care needs of the citizens of the county.

Nursing Service also developed a 'vision of success'

for itself. The Service's idealized scenario of itself envisages an agency thoroughly responsive to community, family and individual health care needs.

Ironically, it was Nursing Service's strategic planning efforts that in part forced strategic planning on the county board. Nursing Service prepared its strategic issues and then was asked to make a presentation to the county board on the issues and desirable strategies to address them. The issues ultimately concerned the county government's role in the health care field and the board's willingness to pay for meeting the health care needs of the county's residents. County board members realized they were completely unprepared to deal with the issues raised by Nursing Service. The board also realized that they might soon be faced with similar vexing issues by other departments engaged in strategic planning. The board felt a need to think about the county government as a whole, and about how to establish priorities, before they were presented with any more policy questions for which they had no answers. The board decided to go on a retreat in order to clarify the county government's mission, to identify strategic issues and to agree on a process for resolving the issues. They identified eight key issues, including issues prompted by Nursing Service's questions concerning the county's role in health care.

Also ironically, partway through Nursing Service's planning efforts, the county board forced the county's executive director to resign. Nursing Service then saw the strategic planning process as a real opportunity to think through its position so that it could have the most impact on the thinking of the new executive director.

What it Takes to Initiate and Succeed with Strategic Planning

The two case histories and the growing body of literature on strategic planning for the public and non-profit sectors help us draw some conclusions about what appears to be necessary to initiate an effective strategic planning process. At a minimum, any organization that wishes to engage in strategic planning should have: (1) a process sponsor(s) in a position of power to legitimize the process; (2) a 'champion' to push the process along;[10] (3) a strategic planning team; (4) an expectation that there will be disruptions and delays; (5) a willingness to be flexible about what constitutes a strategic plan; (6) an ability to pull information and people together at key points for important discussions and decisions; and (7) a willingness to construct and consider arguments geared to very different evaluative criteria.

The criteria for judging the effectiveness of strategic planning for governments and public agencies probably should differ from those used to judge effectiveness in the private sector. The nature of the public sector prevents exact duplication of private sector practice.[11] The more numerous stakeholders, the conflicting criteria they often use to judge governmental performance, the presssures for public accountability and the idea that the public sector is meant to do what the private sector cannot, all militate against holding government strategic planning practice to private-sector standards. Until governments and public agencies (as well as non-profit organizations) gain more experience with strategic planning, it seems best to judge their strategic planning efforts according to the extent to which they: (1) focus the attention of key decision makers on what it important for their organizations, (2) help set priorities for action, and (3) generate those actions.

Conclusions

Strategic planning for public and non-profit organizations is important and probably will become part of the standard repertoire of public and non-profit planners. It is important, of course, for planners to be very careful about how they engage in strategic planning, since every situation is at least somewhat different and since planning can be effective only if it is tailored to the specific situation in which it is used.[12] The process outlined in this article, in other words, represents a generic guide to strategic thought and action, and must be adapted with care and understanding to be useful in any given situation.

To assert that strategic planning will increase in importance raises the question of who the strategic planners are. It is likely that within the organization they may not hold job titles that include the word 'planner'; instead, they may be in policy making or line management positions.[13] Since strategic planning tends to fuse planning and decision making, it makes sense to think of decision makers as strategic planners and to think of strategic planners as facilitators of decision making across levels and functions in organizations (and communities). The specific blend of technical knowledge and process expertise that the persons with the formal job title of planner should bring to strategic planning exercises, of course, will vary in different situations. The more the key decision makers already have the necessary technical knowledge, the more the planners will be relied upon to facilitate the process than to provide technical knowledge.

Finally, research must explore a number of theoretical and practical issues in order to advance the knowledge and practice of strategic planning for governments, public agencies and non-profit organizations. In particular, more detailed strategic planning models should specify key situational factors governing their use; provide specific advice on how to formulate and implement strategies in different situations; be explicitly political; indicate how to deal with plural, ambiguous or conflicting goals or objectives; link content and process; indicate how collaboration as well as competition should be handled; and specify roles for the strategic planner. Progress has been made on all of those fronts[14] (to which, it is hoped, this article and the book from which it is drawn attest), but more is necessary if strategic planning is to help governments, public agencies and non-profit organizations, as well as communities and functions, fulfill their missions and serve their stakeholders effectively, efficiently and responsibly.

Acknowledgement—This article is based on a chapter in John M. Bryson, *Strategic Planning for Public and Nonprofit Organisations*, Jossey-Bass, San Francisco (1988).

References

(1) J. B. Olsen and D. C. Eadie, *The Game Plan: Governance With Foresight*, p. 4, Council of State Planning Agencies, Washington, D.C. (1982).

(2) B. Barry, *The Strategic Planning Workbook for Nonprofit Organizations*, The Amherst H. Wilder Foundation, St Paul, MN (1986).

(3) J. D. Thompson, *Organizations in Action*, McGraw-Hill, New York (1967).

(4) B. Taylor, Strategic planning—which style do you need?, *Long Range Planning* **17**, 51–62 (1984).

(5) R. May, *Love and Will*, Norton, New York (1969).

(6) P. Bromiley, Personal communication (1986).

(7) T. J. Peters and R. H. Waterman, Jr, *In Search of Excellence: Lessons from America's Best-Run Companies*, Harper & Row, New York (1982); E. A. Locke, K. W. Shaw, L. M. Saari and G. P. Latham, Goal setting and task performance: 1969–1980, *Psychological Bulletin* **90**, 125–152 (1981).

(8) M. A. Tita and R. J. Allio, 3M's strategy system—planning in an innovative organization, *Planning Review*, September, pp.10–15 (1984).

(9) J. M. Bryson and R. C. Einsweiler (Eds), *Strategic Planning for Public Purposes—Concepts, Tools and Cases*, The Planners' Press of the American Planning Association, Chicago, IL and Washington, D.C. (1988).

(10) P. Kotler, *Marketing Management*, p. 200, Prentice-Hall, Englewood Cliffs, N.J.; R. M. Kanter (1976), *The Changemasters*, p. 296, Simon & Schuster, New York (1983).

(11) P. S. Ring and J. L. Perry, Strategic management in public and private organizations: implications and distinctive contexts and constraints, *Academy of Management Review* **10**, 276–286 (1985).

(12) J. M. Bryson and A. L. Delbecq, A contingent approach to strategy and tactics in project planning, *Journal of the American Planning Association* **45**, 167–179 (1979); K. S. Christensen, Coping with uncertainty in planning, *Journal of the American Planning Association* **51**, 63–73 (1985).

(13) J. M. Bryson, A. H. Van de Ven and W. D. Roering, Strategic planning and the revitalization of the public service, in R. B. Denhardt and E. T. Jennings, Jr (Eds), *The Revitalization of the Public Service*, pp. 55–75, Extension Publications, University of Missouri, Columbia, MO (1987).

(14) B. Checkoway (Ed.), *Strategic Perspectives on Planning Practice*, Lexington Books, Lexington, MA (1986).

PART TWO

Strategic Planning in Local Government

Making Strategic Planning Work in Local Government

Robert W. Rider, Department of General Planning, Hawaii

Since decisions are made through the political process in local government, planners are being advised to modify their style of planning. Planners acknowledge the need to modify the practice of planning, but reforms are introduced within the framework of the comprehensive plan which continues to serve as the principal planning instrument. This results in internal conflicts within the planning process. In this paper a proposal is made for a planning system which is composed of a series of interacting building blocks. The planning process is molded to fit the management function and capability of those involved in the decision process. Plans are developed as management tools and the planning process accommodates the multiple centres which interact to produce a community's policies and strategies.

Two closely related issues, which are central to the evolution of the practice of planning in local government, are treated in this paper. The first issue relates to the practice of planning as it is currently being conducted in the United States. With experience, planners are modifying the traditional comprehensive plan to account for the complexities of the decision-process in local government. However, retention of the comprehensive plan as a principal tool of planning affects the style of planning and pulls planners in unproductive directions. It hampers planners' efforts to design a planning process for an environment in which decisions are made through the interaction of multiple centers of power.

The second issue is the existence of practical alternatives for enhancing the effectiveness of planning in local government by making planning an integral part of the management function. Public administrators who have a management function must become a force in the evolution of the planning process if that function is to be adequately served by this process. At the same time, planners must integrate their planning into the dynamic decision-making process to retain or enhance their relevance. An approach is set forth for integrating planning into the levels of management which contribute to the general process of forming government strategies.

Paradox of Planning in Local Government

Planners have set aside the traditional rational model of planning for a multi-dimensional model which allows for a variety of planning styles, and stresses the need to integrate planning into a dynamic and complex decision-process.

In his study of corporate planning, Quinn found that the processes used to arrive at a firm's strategy are typically fragmented, evolutionary, and largely intuitive. Formal planning systems have a role, but strategies tend to emerge from a series of 'strategic subsystems', each of which attacks a specific class of strategic issues and is blended incrementally and opportunistically into a cohesive pattern that becomes the company's strategy.[1]

Ansoff has suggested that planning systems evolve to deal with increasingly complex problems. In corporate planning formal systems currently deal with the technological-economic environment of the firm. However, socio-political problems are becoming priority concerns of management and the need to arrive at a proper match between a firm's management capability, technology and market thrust involves the emergence of a concept of strategic management. Ansoff sees a continuing

The author is on the staff of the Department of General Planning, City and County of Honolulu, State of Hawaii. He has experience in planning within state and county governments. His address is 48–286 Heeia Street, Kaneohe, Hawaii 96744.

trend toward a comprehensive management system, but that trend no longer embraces the goal of handling all planning problems within a single framework. Instead, the requirement for integration is slackening with a shift toward 'loosely coupled systems'.[2]

The evolution of thought in the field of corporate planning suggests a number of valuable insights into planning systems which can be employed in local government. Like their corporate counterparts, public planners see their task not merely as one of introducing formal planning systems, but to assist decision-makers to arrive at specific choices. To do so, planners cannot be content with plans based on extrapolations from past and present experience. They must assist decision-makers to cope with rapid changes in the environment and unforeseen impacts of prior decisions. That is, they must undertake strategic planning.

Yet, public planners must acknowledge that decision-making within local government is a political process. Ansoff observes that in such an environment decisions are typically incremental and adaptive, determined by interactions of political influence and shocks from the environment. Moreover, strategic leadership is likely to be missing and the ability of management in government to employ creative thinking, effect shifts in strategy and implement programs to deal with issues is limited.[3] This is the paradox of government planning. While planners can recognize a clear need to introduce planning in the decentralized decision process of local government, the very nature of that process tends to make it incompatible with concepts of strategic planning or planning which is based on techniques of central coordination.

In such an environment Rondinelli suggests that adapting the practice of planning to the decision-making process requires the formulation of 'intervention strategies' in contrast to techniques of central coordination and control.[4] Taylor[5] and Michael[6] observe that in this context planning is a learning process in which the planning system is developed, not to predict and control, but to cope with change and uncertainty. Friend, Power and Yewlett note that planning within local governments is an inter-organizational process characterized by a 'continuing process of mutual adjustment'. In this process a comprehensive plan has only a marginal influence.[7] Planners face the very practical problem of how to pursue these ideas within the context of the political process.

Practice of Planning

In their everyday practice of planning, city planners are well aware of the complexity of their task.[8] However, the comprehensive plan (general or master plan) remains the prevailing planning instrument in local government. Comprehensive plans are assuming new forms as planners adjust to the political environment in which they operate. The detailed end-state plan is being replaced by a plan that is more general, has a shorter time horizon and tends to be viewed as a 'statement of policy'. To Beal and Hollander this means the plan is 'an expression of community intentions and aspirations'. In their view the plan, as an 'instrument of policy', has the advantages of facilitating public participation in the planning process, demanding the involvement of public officials, providing stability and consistency, and serving as a guide to decision making.

The interest in growth management and court decisions mandating some form of planning as a basis of growth controls have been among the factors contributing to the continued development and evolution of comprehensive plans. An additional factor has been state legislation requiring the preparation of comprehensive plans by local governments and the consistency of public investment and zoning decisions with those plans.[9] The requirement that such decisions be consistent with the plan is a logical extension of viewing the plan as a 'policy statement'. Many planners view this requirement as essential to give comprehensive planning a new vitality. The plan is formally adopted by the legislative body of local government and given legal status to 'demand' the attention of government officials and fulfill the plan's role as a commitment to prior decisions. For example, in an interview of the 'top people' in city planning, Einsweiler found that the new trend in central city planning 'focuses as much on strategies as on goals' and treats the city 'as a series of related public and private functional systems'. Yet the planners ranked their 'legal powers', in the sense that plans are binding on decisions, as the most important influence on the effectiveness of planning.[10]

Unfortunately, the attempt to develop the plan into a legal instrument conflicts with the reality of the political process within which government officials must cope with complex decision problems involving a high degree of uncertainty. In this process decision-makers seek to retain flexibility and commitments emerge incrementally from a continuous process of exploration.[11] Policies which emerge from this process are largely the result of social interaction. They emerge from unplanned responses to unforeseen circumstances, or as Lindblom observed, 'they are better described as happening than as decided upon'.[12]

Planners recognize that policies emerge from an interactive process and view their plans as a 'basis for debate, discussion, and conflict resolution'.[13] The desire to have their plan become an element of an interactive process whose outcome is uncertain, while, at the same time, requiring that future decisions be consistent with a previously prepared set of policies contained in a comprehensive plan, introduces a degree of confusion in the planning process.

This confusion is reflected in the observation of Beal and Hollander that the plan should be flexible and departures from the plan 'should always be possible', but 'not necessarily easy'. The commitment to flexibility is half-hearted and uncertain. At the same time, the plan's role as a guide to future decisions is compromised by the acknowledgment that elected officials 'may be reluctant to commit themselves too far into the future'.[14] Vasu's study of the planning profession suggests that this confusion is grounded in the planners' continuing commitment to an ideology of comprehensive rational planning while recognizing that they function in a pluralistic society.[15]

The attempt by planners to be relevant to the governmental decision process while clinging to the comprehensive plan as their principal planning instrument is causing operational problems. For example, a central motive for making the plan a legal instrument is to resolve problems attributed to the use of discretion in the application of flexible zoning techniques. However, if a plan is designed to incorporate only broad 'policy' statements to avoid the problems associated with specificity, then the 'policies' are open to a wide range of interpretations. As a result, discretion must be used in making an interpretation and the concept of consistency loses its relevance. Greater specificity may be introduced into the plan to avoid this problem, supported perhaps by complementary actions to suppress flexibility, as by making amendments more difficult to achieve. But then an entirely new set of even more significant problems is encountered as the plan assumes the characteristics of a control mechanism.[16]

The requirement of consistency also implies a distinction between planning and implementation that does not exist in a turbulent environment. The management function must embrace the implementation process which provides constant feedback to the planning program to account for unanticipated events. The concept of consistency in an environment of continuous interaction has limited value. But in spite of the problems, planners view a requirement of consistency as a means to strengthen the comprehensive plan and enhance their relevance.

As a legal instrument the comprehensive plan is designed to compel actors in the decision process to pay attention to its contents. But unless that content offers a means for assisting management within government to cope with complex decision problems, government officials will take countermeasures to neutralize the plan's influence (as by making it increasingly general) so decisions may be made outside of the formal planning process. If for some reason they are prevented from doing so, then the formal process may become a serious barrier to the introduction of desirable change which will eventually result in its replacement by a new system. This will, however, involve a traumatic experience for political leaders and citizens.

Nature of the Problem

The practical problem planners must face is not how to compel government officials to pay attention to the plan, but how to relate planning to the dynamics of the decision process. The difficulty is that this must be accomplished in a pluralist environment where power is distributed among interest groups. Contemporary planners use their ingenuity to search for means to minimize discretion exercized in the decision-making process. But discretion is essential to decision-makers in the political process, particularly where complex decision problems must be confronted. The planner must function in a decision process that accommodates multiple power centers, but planners lack a consistent framework for making a complementary accommodation in their formal planning process.

The aim of this paper is to set forth a framework in which the planning process is viewed as a series of interacting building blocks which are an integral element of the management function and decision process of local government. The building blocks represent major independent, but interacting forces which shape government strategy. Three such forces are singled out for treatment as part of the formal planning process of local government. These are the decision-making processes of the city council (the legislative body), the strategy-making process of the chief executive and the process for making decisions having localized geographical impacts. The latter process involves the issue of the role of neighborhood organizations as independent decision-making units.

The attempt here is not to provide a detailed prescription for local government, but a framework for breaking-down the planning process into components that are designed to match existing management capability. The result is not only a planning process that is better understood by those involved in it, but a planning process that has brighter prospects for becoming operational in the sense of being an integral part of the decision-making process.

Formulation of Strategies

Comprehensive plans have been traditionally centered on issues of physical development which are of such dominant concern to local governments. The task planners and public administrators must face is one of transforming the comprehensive plan into an operational element of the process of policy formation. Planners are struggling with this problem. For example, Judith Getzels and Charles Thurow report on a number of attempts to link policies to capital budgets. That linkage, however, is not clearly developed.[17]

To accomplish this task planners must keep in mind that policies evolve from a series of decisions and existing policies are continually in the process of being modified as issues are addressed. The task of preparing a comprehensive plan containing 'policy statements' must be replaced, in part, with the task of making explicit policies, to the extent this is possible, by examining past decisions.

The insertion of existing policies in the plan is complemented by intended actions to be carried out by local government. The plan is viewed as a forum for the review and negotiation of the city council's intentions for directing the community's development. Intended actions incorporated into a plan may either support existing policies, as proposed actions to attract new private capital into an existing industrial area, or modify existing policy, as a proposal for public investments which will encourage higher densities. The existing policies and intended actions are blended into strategies which give a degree of cohesiveness and direction to government actions.[18]

Actions relating to the city's development are typically designed to influence the character and rate of growth of areas which perform specific functions, as industrial, residential and natural resource areas. These areas, referred to here as activity centers,[19] may be used as a means for organizing government's strategies concerning the physical dimensions of the community (as density, rate of expansion and mix of activities). These strategies may include private and public investment decisions which have a potential for significantly altering the physical dimensions of one or more activity centers. Such decisions may involve, for example, investment in major public facilities, regional shopping centers, or precedent setting residential developments.

Strategies may also be concerned with how effectively activity centers are functioning in terms of meeting the community's needs. Government's strategies for activity centers may consist of a blend of actions designed to influence the physical dimensions of these centers and remove bottlenecks in the production of social goods and services.

Thus, strategies may not only be concerned with the rate of expansion of residential centers, but whether these centers are meeting the range of housing needs which exist within the community. Similarly, maintaining or improving the competitive advantage of industrial and commercial centers may become a part of the strategy for an activity center. The strategies may also embrace interrelationships between activity centers as when, for example, economic forces cause shifts in the location of economic activity which, in turn, results in some residents losing their accessibility to jobs.

The content of strategies will vary depending on how problems are perceived within the community and how this perception changes over time. Communities confronting problems associated with the rapid growth of some activity centers tend to formulate different strategies than communities preoccupied with the need to stimulate redevelopment and offset the physical and economic deterioration of industrial centers. In either case, strategies will be enriched as actions are defined to address the complex problems that government must cope with in existing and developing activity centers. Proposed actions will be undertaken, where possible, incrementally and in response to the perceptions among interest groups of what constitutes the problem and its solution. If a degree of comprehensiveness is achieved, it is achieved opportunistically and through a series of limited actions.

The Strategic Plan

Strategies in the process of being formulated by local government are set forth in a strategic plan. This title is given to the plan to direct attention to specific characteristics which distinguish it from the comprehensive plan. The primary characteristics of the comprehensive and strategic plans are outlined in Table 1. The intent is not to dismantle the comprehensive plan but to direct its evolution in a manner that gives the city council a management tool to assist its members to think through various options and formulate new ones as conditions warrant rather than constrain the council to a predetermined choice. Thus, the plan is not legally binding on future decisions and there is no requirement that these decisions must be consistent with the plan. Any negotiation that accompanies the insertion of an intended action in the plan will be subject to continuing renegotiation as conditions change, new options come to light and power shifts with the formation of new coalitions. This avoids the unfortunate circumstances in which planners, who consider an adopted plan a statement of policy, look with suspicion upon proposals not consistent with the plan and defend it against change. In the process of strategic planning, as adapted to the circumstances of government, the planner's task is not to defend the plan but to facilitate thinking about options, the interchange of ideas, and the process of negotiation.

Also, unlike many comprehensive plans, the strategic plan does not have a rigid set of elements. Strategies in the plan are modified as actions evolve

Table 1. Primary characteristics of comprehensive and strategic plans

Plan characteristics	Comprehensive plan	Strategic plan
Timing	5–20 years, usually complemented by formal amendment process	1–5 years with recognition that life span of strategies depends on political and economic forces
Purpose	Current thrust is for a legally binding plan; decisions and plans must be consistent with adopted policies and maps	Serves as management tool; used to assist management think through options; no clear hierarchy of plans
Flexibility	Discretion seen as a problem; seeks to minimize discretion	Discretion seen as essential to address complex issues; boundaries placed on discretion through interaction, role definition, performance rules
Orientation	Generally focused on physical development, use of land; but may be focused on strategies for activity centers	Focused on strategies for functioning of activity centers; concerned with production of social goods
Comprehensiveness	Includes entire city and major urban systems	Strategies evolve as needed; may focus on selected activity centers and issues
Format	Tends to have a standard format for all areas	Format of plan may vary by area depending on issues
Goals	Includes goals for the city	Does not include goals; goals may be placed in another document
Method	Tends to be based on forecasts derived from extrapolation of past and current trends	Designed to deal with discontinuities in the environment and unforseen impacts of decisions
Evolution of plan	Format is often prescribed by city charter or higher level of government; process and format difficult to change	Management reviews and adapts process and format as required for effective operation; change is accepted as part of process

to address new problems and they may include a different range of actions for each of the various activity centers.

The plan's focus is on what government is doing and intends to do rather than on motives. Unlike many comprehensive plans, no attempt is made to devise a set of community goals for incorporation into the plan. The basic thrust of the strategic plan is to make policies and intended actions explicit so the opportunity for review and interaction may be expanded. However, this does not preclude the city council from developing a set of goals in a separate goals document.[20] To make goals acceptable to the many interest groups in the community they must be very general and, as a result, will lack operational value.

Finally, the plan provides a framework for a process of continuous problem analysis such as 'problem and program planning' advocated by Weaver and Babcock in which planners focus on immediate problems and the 'big picture' is seen only dimly.[21] The strategic plan is focused on the next 1–5 years in contrast to comprehensive plans which are usually given a long-range perspective (as from 5 to 20 years). However, each policy or action in the plan will have a different life span depending on the stability of forces affecting it. Where strategies have long-range implications they may be supported by supplementary analysis.[22]

The strategic plan forms a basis for broad regulations governing activity centers. These regulations may take the form of performance standards which allows the private sector greater discretion when making investment decisions within activity centers. At the same time, a more specific neighborhood planning process, to be discussed in the following text, may treat land use issues having localized impacts.

Though strategic planning is not yet a well developed concept in local government, elements of strategic planning are emerging as these governments seek to evolve more effective planning systems (such as eliminating the details of land use and focusing on strategies for activity centers, and preparing annual plans which help shape budget priorities). A common starting point for the introduction of change is the preparation of a growth management program or an attempt to make the capital budget an implementing tool of development policies. However, while the introduction of change permits elements of a strategic plan to emerge, the overall system may not offer a favorable environment for the evolution of strategic planning.

For example, a much discussed process in the city of Atlanta requires the annual adoption of a Comprehensive Development Plan consisting of plans for 1, 5 and 15 years. The annual comprehensive plan is intended to be a 'policy guide' to the capital budget. An initial search for usable project selection criteria led planners to propose that existing policies be identified as the basis for their 1, 5 and 15 year capital budget.[23] Such pragmatic attempts to grapple with policies and priorities may result in a fruitful evolution of the process. Unfortunately, as may be the case with Atlanta, this evolution is often hampered by overly rigid (as where specific processes are spelled out in a city charter) and cumbersome systems designed more to promote control over capital budgets than to serve as a flexible management tool.

The Chief Executive

The process by which the chief executive (CE) formulates strategies constitutes another major building block in the planning system. Though the CE does not establish policy, he is continuously defining strategies which have a powerful influence on policy. While the importance of the CE has long been recognized,[24] comprehensive plans are often oriented more toward the city council which adopts them (often in response to a legal requirement). The CE must cope with an array of complex problems and any prepackaged comprehensive solution is likely to be viewed with a healthy scepticism and have only minimal involvement of the CE in its preparation.[25]

Planning from the perspective of the CE is a highly personalized affair and the planning program must be sensitive to the CE's management style. The program must be designed to assist in the task of defining the CE's priorities and evolve strategies in accordance with those priorities. The task of providing central direction is complicated by a decentralization of power and a process in which a loose federation of agencies struggle with their clients to arrive at a viable set of priorities.

Planners have not been very successful in providing direction to a diverse group of government agencies through their comprehensive plans. Even so, they continue to seek ways to strengthen the central planning function and limit the exercise of discretion.[26] Experience suggests that coordination must be achieved through a process of directed interaction among agencies as opposed to seeking their compliance with a centrally prepared plan.

The specific form of interaction must be compatible with the situation existing within each local government. One possibility is for the CE to appoint a planning group chaired by the chief operating officer (such as the managing director or city manager) and composed of selected agency heads, including the budget and planning chiefs.[27] This group may be assigned such tasks as detecting problems before they evolve into a crises by monitoring the supply and demand for critical services, developing strategies to address specific politically sensitive issues, developing joint public–private sector programs, forming interdepartmental teams to address issues, advising the CE on the implementation of plans and changes in the environment which impact on strategies, and formulating priorities and goals for the administration. This group sifts through the massive flow of data for strategic information the CE can act on.

The strategies which evolve from the interaction of agencies, the CE's planning group and the CE are incorporated into the city's strategic plan, as they might be amended by the city council. The strategic plan must be complemented by financial strategies defined in a financial plan, the development of which must be a primary responsibility of the CE's planning group.

Within this process planners act as technical advisers to the planning group and the CE, but they may also assume an advocacy role as issues of equity surface in the debates over strategies. Rather than try to compel compliance with a centrally prepared plan, planners seek to influence decisions as a participant in an interactive process which serves as a primary building block for strategies.

Agency Plans

Plans prepared by government agencies, often referred to as functional plans, are a part of the CE's strategy formulating process. Traditionally these plans have been regarded as being subject to the constraints of a comprehensive plan, or developed as an element of that plan. Consistency with the comprehensive plan generally means, in practical terms, that the capital improvement program must conform to the land use plan. However, the capital budget is, in reality, likely to be the force which shapes the land use plan as major projects are debated in the political process and the community is subject to financial and economic forces beyond its control.

Experience suggests that great care must be taken to align the managerial and technical capabilities of agencies when preparing plans. The imposition of a requirement for formal plans often results in a mass of data which is only vaguely related to decisions. Although prepared from a study of corporate planning. Wheelwright and Banks provide some insight into the evolution of planning systems.[28] At an initial stage the system is largely numbers-oriented and does not involve program managers, but as it matures and program managers become involved, there is more communication, more emphasis on the process and more simplified plans.

Barkdoll's review of the Food and Drug Administration planning experience also stressed the importance of the planning process as opposed to the plan. He also highlighted the need for multiple forms of communication, simplicity and change in the process as experience is gained.[29] On the other hand, Gremillion, McKenny and Pyburn found that the Program, Planning and Budgeting System was a useful management tool for the National Forest System. This appears to have been due to the ability to measure the goods and services being produced.[30]

The experience of planners suggests that to be useful, the content of plans must reflect the environment in which program managers operate. That is, they must reflect the degree of management control over program outputs, the extent to which technical relationships between inputs and outputs can be specified, and the degree to which program impacts can be accurately predicted. In government programs there is typically a low level of control or achievement in all three areas. As a result, the planning process is likely to be primarily an internal and relatively flexible management tool through which strategic issues are identified and plans continually reassessed. The plan provides a framework for negotiation and testing options.

Planners are constantly concerned with the problem of coordinating the plans of agencies. These plans will be blended into coherent strategies as political pressures and external forces permit. The CE will act as opportunities make the forging of new strategies politically and financially feasible. Strategies are not formed by making agency plans subservient to a centrally prepared plan but through the interaction between the CE's priorities and the political realities which serve to shape agency plans and budgets.

Neighborhood Organizations

How government interacts with residents of a community is another important building block in the process of strategy formulation. Neighborhood organizations often have limited political power and rely heavily on administrative regulations to achieve their aims. They will tend to weave their strategies around the planning instrument put into operation by government. If, for example, planners put a detailed long-range land use plan into operation neighborhood organizations will strive to make the future land use pattern resemble the existing situation. The plan is viewed as a means to limit change. However, since the strategic plan is part of the process for making management decisions, rather than a specific prescription, it is not readily co-opted by any one group.

The response of neighborhood organizations to the strategic planning process may heavily depend on implementation tactics. The focus of the strategic plan, which is on activity centers rather than the use of specific parcels of land, tends to reduce central planning for neighborhoods. This may be made attractive if it is accompanied by an enhancement of the neighborhood organization's role in localized development decisions. Such a role may evolve through the organization of formal neighborhood boards or councils and the development of a negotiating and mediating role for these organizations with respect to decisions having impacts on the neighborhood.

Also, the implementation of strategic planning may be conducted in a manner that does not raise anxiety levels. For example, strategic planning may initially focus on a few troubled areas undergoing change. These areas may serve as testing grounds for a gradual shift toward some form of strategic planning.

The Neighborhood Plan

The implementation tactics for strategic planning may strengthen the role of neighborhood organizations by assisting them to devise their own planning instrument, the neighborhood plan, to replace the traditional centrally prepared land use plan. A neighborhood plan would be subject to the constraints of the strategic plan. However, the neighborhood plan need not be consistent with the strategic plan. Inconsistencies are accepted as a starting point for negotiation. The community organization may view its plan as one means for expressing positions which may alter existing policy.

Some local governments are encouraging the preparation of neighborhood plans. However, caution must be exercised since many community organizations may feel the cost of preparing and maintaining a plan is not worth the benefits. In addition to a range of interests among community organizations in preparing formal plans, there is a diversity of problems and priorities. In some neighborhoods, residents may be preoccupied with transportation issues; in others, crime and unemployment may be primary issues. Community organizations should be free to put into a plan what they consider to be of interest, not what planners want addressed.

The neighborhood plan need not be a 'balanced plan' but may address only a few points of interest.[31] Community organizations must experiment and evolve a style that enables them to express their concern in a manner that can be interpreted by government agencies. By prescribing a format for these plans, government eliminates innovation and experimentation as well as predetermine the agenda.

The neighborhood plan is a tool which residents may use to require public and private investors to show the impact of their investments on the neighborhood and how they affect those values which the neighborhood residents give priority. Using their plan as a starting point, neighborhood organizations may negotiate with developers who are having an impact on their area, with the city government concerning the capital budget, and with other community organizations to form coalitions as a means of enhancing their ability to influence strategic decisions. If a neighborhood organization also develops the capacity to mediate in disputes concerning unneighborly acts it has the potential for playing a relatively significant role in the community. The decentralization of the planning and land regulatory function that potentially accompanies strategic planning sets the stage for this role.

Observations

The planning process as presented in this paper consists of a series of interacting building blocks for the development of priorities and formulation of strategies. Planning is molded to the management capabilities and orientation of actors in the decision process in order to serve as a useful management tool. A variety of planning instruments and forms of communication are utilized in this process. Strategy formulation is viewed as a process of experimentation and negotiation.

The proposed planning process acknowledges the existence of, and accomodates, multiple centers of power. Rather than attempt to coerce these power centers into complying with a central plan, the planning process is built around, and facilitates, the interaction which occurs in the political process. The planning process, with its focus on strategies for activity centers and a negotiating role for neighborhood organizations, also sets the stage for allowing decisions of private investors a greater role in determining the course of urban development.[32]

Planning in government is a complex business. It is essential to keep the planning process flexible and prevent it from becoming prematurely locked into a rigid design. The process must be allowed to evolve incrementally as experience is gained and as actors in the process negotiate for additional roles (as a mediating role for neighborhood organiz-

ations). The opportunity for a gradual evolution of the system will be greatly enhanced if the planner is not committed to a single planning instrument, or the need to create a comprehensive set of 'policies' in one grand flourish; and is willing to give up the illusion of control for the task of interacting in the decision process.

References

(1) J. B. Quinn, Strategic change: 'logical incrementalism', *Sloan Management Review*, **20**, 7–21, Fall (1978).

(2) H. Igor Ansoff, The state of practice in planning systems, *Sloan Management Review*, **18**, 1–24, Winter (1977); and *Strategic Management*, Halsted Press, New York (1979).

(3) H. Igor Ansoff, *Strategic Management*, p. 128, 134.

(4) Dennis A. Rondinelli, Public planning and political strategy, *Long Range Planning*, **9**, 75–82, April (1976).

(5) Bernard Taylor, New dimensions in corporate planning, *Long Range Planning*, **9**, 80–106, December (1976).

(6) D. N. Michael, *On Learning to Plan and Planning to Learn*, Jossey-Boss, CA (1973).

(7) J. K. Friend, J. M. Power and C. J. L. Yewlett, *Public Planning: the Inter-corporate Dimension*, Tavistock, London (1974).

(8) For example, see John M. Bryson and Andre L. Delbecq, A contingent approach to strategy and tactics in project planning, *Journal of the American Planning Association*, **45**, 167–179, April (1979).

(9) See, for example, F. Beal and E. Hollander, City development plans, In *The Practice of Local Government Planning*, F. S. So, I. Stollman, F. Beal and D. S. Arnold (Eds.), International City Management Association, Washington, DC (1979); M. Meshenberg, *The Administration of Flexible Zoning Techniques*, American Society of Planning Officials, Chicago (1976); D. R. Mandelker, The role of the local comprehensive plan, *Michigan Law Review*, **74**, reprinted in *Management and Control of Growth*, Vol. IV, F. Schnidman, J. Silverman and R. Young Jr. (Eds.), Urban Land Institute, Washington, DC (1978); Di Mento, *The Consistency Doctrine and the Limits of Planning*, Delgeschlager, Gunn and Hain, Cambridge, MA (1980).

(10) R. C. Einsweiler, What the top people are saying about central city planning, *Planning*, **46**, 15–18, October (1980).

(11) J. K. Friend, J. M. Power and C. J. L. Yewlett, op. cit.; J. B. Quinn, op. cit.; and A. Wildavsky, *Speaking Truth to Power: the Art and Craft of Policy Making*, Little–Brown and Co., Boston (1979).

(12) C. E. Lindblom, Still muddling, not yet through, *Public Administration Review*, **39**, 517–526, November/December (1979).

(13) F. Beal and E. Hollander, op. cit., p. 165.

(14) Ibid., p. 166.

(15) M. L. Vasu, *Politics and Planning: a National Study of American Planners*, University of North Carolina Press, North Carolina (1979).

(16) For an interesting and relevant distinction between management and control see M. Landau and R. Stout, Jr., To manage is not to control, *Public Administration Review*, **39**, 148–156, March/April (1979).

(17) However, some cases studied by the authors seem to have prospects for improving the linkage between planning and budgeting. A generally favorable review was given to the preparation of an annual comprehensive plan by Altanta's new department of Planning and Budgeting. This plan appears to have some characteristics in common with the strategic plan discussed in this paper. See, American Planning Association, *Local Capital Improvements and Development Management*, U.S. Government Printing Office, Washington, DC (1980).

(18) A definition of strategy offered by Hofer and Schendel comes close to the meaning of the term as used in this paper. They define strategy as the 'fundamental pattern of present and planned resource deployments and environmental interactions that indicates how the organization will achieve its objectives'. See C. W. Hofer and D. Schendel, *Strategy Formulation: Analytical Concepts*, West Publishing Co., St. Paul, MI (1978).

(19) Functional areas, referred to here as activity centers primarily to avoid confusion with functional plans, is not a new concept for planners. Activities within these areas tend to have greater intra-area relationships than inter-area relationships. An activity center may consist of a mix of activities, as a high density commercial/residential center, or it may contain a single dominant activity, as a low density residential center. Further discussion on this point is found in Robert W. Rider, Decentralizing land use decisions, *Public Administration Review*, **40**, 594–602, November/December (1980). Also, areas defined for the application of performance zoning have some similarity to activity centers discussed in this paper. See Lane, Kendig, *Performance Zoning*, Planners Press, American Planners Association, Washington, DC (1980).

(20) It is possible that the city council may wish to include goals in the strategic plan, perhaps in response to pressure by citizens. This is, of course, possible to do and will probably cause no harm. However, it may detract from the primary thrust of the plan.

(21) See Clifford L. Weaver and Richard F. Babcock, *City Zoning: the Once and Future Frontier*, Planners Press, American Planning Association, Chicago (1979).

(22) Where there is conflict there will be a tendency for the city council to deemphasize uncertain but controversial long-range impacts and seek agreement on more immediate visible benefits. The planner may seek to offset this tendency by an analysis of longer-range futures which evaluates the implications of current trends. Lindblom, op. cit., suggests supplementing incremental analysis with analysis that involves speculative or utopian thinking about possible futures.

(23) American Planning Association, *Local Capital Improvements and Development management*, op. cit., p. 128.

(24) See, for example, R. A. Walker, *The Planning Function in Urban Government*, University of Chicago Press, Chicago (1950); and H. Fagin, Organizing and carrying out planning activities within urban government, *Journal of the American Institute of Planners*, **25**, 109–114, August (1959).

(25) Obviously the city council is also responding to the same set of complex problems as the chief executive. When it adopts a plan the council is generally responding to a number of conflicting pressures. The council may want a plan as a management tool. But there may also be legal requirements as well as citizen pressures for a formal plan. Citizens often view a plan as a control mechanism to provide stability.

(26) Kendig op. cit., would offset the 'pernicious trend' resulting from the exercise of discretion by 'introducing a large number of performance criteria against which every development must be evaluated'. The problem is that both the development and application of such standards requires heavy doses of judgment. Detailed rules do not eliminate discretion though they may alter who makes discretionary decisions.

(27) A number of CEs do utilize such a planning group though the activities of the group are likely to be limited and not necessarily viewed as a pivotal point in the planning process. The planning group may at times be headed by the planning chief. A potential danger here is that the agenda may be skewed toward issues which are important to planners but not to the CE. In this case the group will lose much of its potential impact.

(28) S. C. Wheelwright and R. L. Banks, Involving operating managers in planning process evolution, *Sloan Management Review*, **20**, 43–59, Summer (1979).

(29) G. L. Barkdoll, Making planning relevant to public agency management, *Long Range Planning*, **9**, 59–65, February (1976).

(30) L. L. Gremillion, J L. Mckenney and P. J. Pyburn, Program planning in the national forest system, *Public Administration Review*, **40**, 226–230, May/June (1980).

(31) Compiling a neighborhood plan need not involve extensive technical resources which are beyond the capability of neighborhood organizations to acquire. The plan primarily reflects the priorities, aspirations and problems perceived by residents.

(32) This may come about as performance measures are devised for activity centers, leaving specific land use decisions to the private sector. For further discussion of this point see Robert W. Rider, op. cit., and particularly Robert C. Ellickson, Alternatives to zoning: covenants, nuisance rules, and fines as land use controls, *The University of Chicago Law Review*, **40**, 681–781, Summer (1973).

Planning for Strategic Performance in Local Government

Ronald McGill

The transfer of business techniques into public administration, in order to make the latter more efficient and effective, is open to question. This article seeks to outline the difficulty of that transfer to local government. It goes on to develop an alternative framework for planning for strategic performance in local government. A strategic planning system is introduced. The development of appropriate performance criteria is also outlined. The overall argument is an attempt (1) to build a forward momentum into the strategic concerns of local government, (2) to develop a client-based orientation for that strategic concern and (3) to encourage a managerial approach to strategic planning in local government.

Introduction

The literature on policy planning in public administration is littered with accounts of the demise of a variety of strategic planning techniques. As part of this literature, an increasing concern for the output of various planning systems, as a necessary precursor to considering performance, is also evident. Planning, programming, budgeting (PPB); management by objectives (MBO); output budgeting (OB); zero-based budgeting (ZBO); policy analysis and review (PAR) are five management systems that made the attempt. In most cases they are now dead and buried. Either it is impossible to plan for strategic performance in local government or it is possible but a sufficiently robust system has yet to be established.

The current wave of theory and practice across British public administration is that of efficiency and effectiveness. The present British government places great emphasis on the enterprise culture and its concomitant benefits to public administration; the business (or efficiency and effectiveness) ethos.

The first question is whether the business analogy is the correct one for local government to model its

planning for strategic performance. The second question is what system *will* permit local government to plan for strategic performance. This paper seeks to answer both questions.

Debunking the Business Analogy

The over-worked comparison between public and business administration; the former's need to learn valuable lessons from the latter, is worth testing. It is necessary to confirm or refute the existence of such lessons. To start the test however, one must be absolutely clear about what is actually being compared.

Public administration is referred to here as the non-trading sector of government. The converse is the public trading sector. Public administration is therefore concerned with national departments of state—e.g. the Department of the Environment —and local government organizations—e.g. Kent County Council. Public administration is therefore not concerned with those organizations intended to be mainly or wholly trading concerns, deriving all or most of their resources from the sale of goods and services. Examples of these are British Leyland and British Coal.

The point is simple. The public trading sector measures the cost of goods and services produced against an income derived therefrom. The same is true of private business. The substantive difference is one of performance accountability; whether one is to break even (a public political decision) or make a profit (a private commercial necessity). Yet the measurement of that performance, through profit and loss accounting, will be the same for both sectors. Consequently, the public and private trading (or business) sectors have more in common by way of performance measurement than they have differences. This only heightens the dichotomy that exists between public administration and business administration. As Self states '[public administra-

Ronald McGill, formerly District Co-ordinator with Renfrew District Council in Scotland is now with the Taylor Woodrow group in London.

tion] agencies inhabit a political instead of a market environment . . .'.[1]

Rainey et al.[2] introduce a theoretical framework for comparing the two sectors. The analysis is undertaken under three heads: (1) environmental factors; (2) organization–environment transactions; and (3) internal structure and process. First, environmental factors are concerned with sources of revenue and resources. Whereas the market enforces its own discipline on business, the annual budget appropriation is a political decision in relation to public administration—whether a government department or a local authority. Secondly, the organization–environment transactions are concerned with organizational responsiveness. Whereas the business responds to market demand with its product or service, public administration has greater difficulty in making that immediate connection with its market. Finally, the internal structures and processes are concerned with how the organization actually works. In this respect there are more opportunities for similarity than difference. The operational details of an organization concern individual departmental objectives, line management responsibility and personnel issues. These can be classed as the traditional management concerns, common to both business and public administration. This three-tier principle is returned to later.

A simple method of comparing business with public administration is to draw from businessmen with direct government work experience. Such people are more common in the United States than the United Kingdom. The ex-chairman of the Bendix Corporation, a major multinational company, was for several years head of the U.S. Treasury Department. He has highlighted a central point:[3]

> One thing to realise is that the tests of efficiency and cost effectiveness, which are the basic standards of business, are in government not the only—and frequently not even the major—criteria . . . accepting inefficiency in one area to achieve certain goals in another, is foreign to a businessman.

That is the nub of the problem. A clear business goal based on business performance principles is distinct from the less easily defined political goal and the subsequent performance of its public administration.

The argument was presented earlier by Bower.[4] Nobody disputes the signal of profit as being the principal source of performance measurement in the business environment; the test of efficiency. 'But without a market to determine effectiveness, the process of measuring becomes diffuse and complex'. More ascerbicly, Bower quotes the late professor W. S. Sayer who suggested 'business and government administration are alike in all *unimportant* respects'. The difference between the two spheres is the political dimension. The issue is how to establish a concept of strategic performance in the political arena.

In Britain, there were two strands in a general approach to introduce strategic performance into public administration. The central government experience was captured in the Fulton Report—a 'managerialist manifesto'[5] and subsequent policy analysis techniques culminating in the recent demise of PAR. The local government experience was encapsulated in the underpinning of local government reform in 1974 (England and Wales) and 1975 (Scotland)—the systems management approach; PPBS supporting a rational and corporate decision-making process. It is no secret that the managerialist attempt to quantify and therefore measure the output of political organizations has largely failed. There is now 'considerable doubt [over] the relevance of transferring, wholesale, methods and working practices from public to private organizations. The civil servant cannot apply simple tests of efficiency in isolation from other [political] considerations.'[6] The local government experience is no less clear with the demise of PPBS and the elevation of corporate planning from concerns with technique to political debate about political priorities.

A successful business person was appointed as mayor of a large American city on the ticket of 'bringing business methods to government'. The mayor gradually learnt that efficient business solutions to problems were untenable. 'It would have aggravated racial problems or would have deprived certain neighbourhoods of amenities.'[7] The point is clear. The nature of the output of public administration differs markedly from the output of a business organization.

A Framework for Performance

By refuting the obvious comparison with business, public administration can start constructing a framework for strategic performance from within its own body of knowledge and experience. It does not have to import business-based management techniques which are proving unsuitable for transfer. Management therefore divests itself of its normally attributed neutral and technical qualities. In this sense, management can be redefined:

> . . . Management, like politics, consists to a large degree in the management of differences. Groups in organisations have different roles, different goals, different skills. So have individuals. The blending of these differences into one coherent whole is the overall task of management.[8]

In defining management in these terms, Handy is echoing the central theme of the celebrated article by Mintzberg.[9] Mintzberg refutes the technical rationality view of management and supports the political notion of the activity. The folklore is of management becoming a science and a profession. The reality is that management is still by flair.

The organization, then, is not a unitary technical

state. One is therefore rejecting the average public assumption of a public organization. If a member of the public talks to or is in written communication with a member of an organization (say, a local authority), the former assumes that his contact with one part of the organization is tantamount to contact with the whole organization. The general public assumes that the public organization is some sort of superperson:

> If we look at the organisation as a superperson, we exaggerate the parallel character of people acting in concert to achieve a collective outcome and omit the system. Policies are the outcome of organisational infighting, mutual concessions, and coalition formation.[10]

The political nature of the organization shines forth. Consequently it is unwise to look for organizational goals as a clear, consistent, and widely accepted set of collective objectives. Instead, organizations are characterized by a continuous bargaining–learning process that has irregular and even inconsistent outcomes.

The negotiated order (the political nature) of an organization, especially one concerned with public administration, must be a central feature of an evaluation of its performance. The nature of the political behaviour is bound to have a bearing on judgements concerning 'output and impact'. Analysis is above all a political activity, a fact too often forgotten, especially by those who seek to refine output measures or to establish undisputed price tags for options.[11]

Pedersen[12] uses the example of an anti-poverty programme to draw the distinction between output (by the organization) and outcome, or impact (on the people treated). In so doing, he distinguishes between managerial performance and social performance.

If Pedersen's analysis is to bear fruit, then three levels of performance analysis will be required. They are in descending order, at a social, managerial and operational level. The social level concerns the definition of multiple deprivation and why the statistics of the issue's key indicators change over time. The managerial level concerns the relevance of the particular programmes to the symptoms of the issue. The operational level concerns the implementation of the programme budgeted for the year in question. If one was forced to redefine these three levels of performance in more traditional terms one would suggest the following: for social performance, read 'economy'; for managerial performance, read 'effectiveness'; for operational performance, read 'efficiency'.

The performance indicators for each level of activity will differ. Their time horizons will also vary. Without going into a substantiation in this text, a policy evaluation of a major strategy is normally

associated with a 3–5 year time-scale. A managerial evaluation of the impact of specific programmes can run from the annual cycle and become a major contribution to the policy evaluation. An evaluation of specific operations budgeted for that year must be subject to a minimum of quarterly scans, culminating in an annual review of the operation itself.

The relationship between the levels of performance identified above concur with Rainey's original analysis in the early stages of this text. When comparing one set with the other the relationships shown in Table 1 emerge.

Table 1. The levels of performance

Level	Rainey	This text
1	Environmental factors	Impact or social performance
2	Organization–environmental transaction	Output or managerial performance
3	Internal structure and process	Operational performance

It is suggested that because the third or operational level is the one area common to business and public administration, it is the level of performance dominated by current evaluation (efficiency and effectiveness) studies. It is the easiest level at which to transfer management techniques from business to public administration. Consequently, the current wave of evaluation studies are dominated by a concern for organizational efficiency.

Authors[13] are correct in highlighting the operational inefficiencies that exist in central government departments; variance analysis is a useful tool for relating proposed budgets with actual expenditure incurred; specific value-for-money (VFM) studies add to the growing concern for operational efficiency. All three examples are likely to result in savings to the tax and rate payer. They are, however, concerned with the third level of organizational behaviour; that which is essentially common to the business and public sectors of administration; the traditional concerns of management.

Where business administration and public administration part company is at the first and second levels of organizational behaviour. The comparison for all three levels can be set out as shown in Table 2.

Whereas the business community has its automatic feedback of the market and subsequent profit and loss, public administration has no such feedback mechanism. It must therefore construct its own.

Planning for Strategic Performance

The only way local government can establish

Table 2. Comparing business and public administrative performance

Level	Business Sector Performance	Public Sector Performance
1 (3–5 years and longer)	Overall profitability and capital growth	Overall programme performance in relation to general social conditions (e.g. poverty)
2 (1–3 years)	Specific market success and consequent profitability	Specific programme success and citizen satisfaction (e.g. housing renovation)
3 ($\frac{1}{4}$–1 year)	Operational efficiency, budget control, personnel morale and production management	Operational efficiency, budget control, personnel morale and project management

feedback in relation to performance is to introduce a client-based planning system. Client-based planning would seek to identify strategic issues and match clients or client groups to these issues in order to mimic the need–response of the market-place.

Planning for explicit client groups is another form of public involvement in decision-making concerning projects and services that affect the public. However, the normal or uncontentious projects and services are not, by definition, strategic issues. They are operational; they are level 3 issues (see Table 2). What is required is a planning system that concerns itself with strategic performance on the one hand and its client groups on the other.

All local government is locked into the annual budget cycle. The process of budget setting is the opportunity for strategic issues to be identified and acted upon. This is the policy development process. Experienced officials know that expenditure is policy; policy is expenditure. They are so intermeshed that any either/or answer about causation is foolish.[14] The annual budget cycle is therefore the key to strategic influence. With a little imagination, that annual decision-making process can be extended not only to satisfy requirements for policy development generally but also to incorporate a community or public contribution to the process.

Pedersen uses the example of an anti-poverty programme to highlight the strategic concerns of meaningful planning and evaluation. He draws the distinction between policy and evaluation. The policy-makers will want to know why the added resources did not alleviate poverty (level 1). The agency will want to know whether the failure was due to some deficiency in the agency's programme (level 2). Evaluation must be based on production and outcome functions. Pedersen concludes his argument by drawing the necessary distinction

between institutional (or managerial) performance and social (or client-satisfying) performance.

The basic ingredients for success in planning for strategic performance are therefore that policy and evaluation:

☆ are linked to the annual budget cycle, and

☆ relate to explicit client groups.

The planning system should be designed to influence rationally the annual budget determination process. The policy recommendations carried by the system should carry justifications, including explicit client group support, for any recommendations that seek to influence resource allocations, whether through capital or revenue expenditure, in favour of the strategic issues the system has identified.

Renfrew District Council (RDC), through its community development subcommittee (of the policy and resources committee), is committed to developing policies and programmes to tackle multiple deprivation. In June 1983, RDC adopted a specific remit to prepare, review and evaluate annually a community development strategy for its designated areas (of multiple deprivation) and other disadvantaged groups.

That system is now into its fourth year of planning for strategic performance on behalf of areas of multiple deprivation. It is based on an annual cycle of review and evaluation (autumn) and preparation (spring) of the next round of the strategy (see Table 3).

The annual cycle shows that the strategy is reviewed and prepared in consultation with community (its client) groups. It also illustrates the important distinction between issue identification, as part of the review, and the development of specific proposals and policies arising from the issues. The annual round of the strategy is approved each year in the June/July committee cycle (a 6-week plan). The resource consequences of the annual round are then incorporated into revenue budgets and/or capital programmes as part of the autumn–spring budget process.

This approach to planning for strategic performance has met with some success.[15] Its limitation is that, though a corporate activity, it confines itself to a limited geographical sphere; its areas for priority treatment—the areas of multiple deprivation. Its advantage is that, as a test case in developing a new planning method, it is a sound basis for expanding into a total corporate, strategic planning system.

Criteria for Strategic Performance

Specific value-for-money (VFM) studies, using

Table 3. Strategic performance: the annual planning cycle

September–November	December–January	February–May	June–July	August
Review and evaluate the strategy, in consultation with: —community groups —RDC service departments —other agencies	*Review report,* through Committee cycle	*Prepare next round of the strategy* in consultation with: —community groups —RDC service departments —other agencies	*Strategy,* through Committee cycle	Start of Council's budget determination process for the next financial year
This stage includes the identification of issues to be developed in the next round of the strategy		This stage involves the refinement of issues to the point where specific proposals and policies can be prepared		

accepted performance critiera (comparable unit costs, personnel assessments, project management techniques) are legitimate concerns for level 3—efficiency. Put another way, they are concerned with the third level of organizational behaviour: that which is essentially common to the business and public sectors of administration. These involve the traditional concerns of management—hence the demand for the transfer of management techniques from business to public administration. However, such techniques should be restricted to this level. The question then is what is the criteria for strategic performance, say, in relation to an anti-poverty programme. In the first instance, performance criteria should be clearly related to the level and time-scale of the activity being considered.

RDC is developing such criteria now in relation to its anti-poverty programme. The criteria is governed by these principles. First, operational issues remain the concern of service departments. They only assume strategic significance where they raise issues of principle. Secondly, Pederson's important distinction between management (level 2) and social (level 1) performance is retained. Finally is the experience of the Manpower Services Commission for policy management; quick, crude but robust results from monitoring a few key indicators have been far more influential than detailed, refined and careful studies.[16]

RDC's (community development) strategy for tackling multiple deprivation is a corporate (and where possible inter-corporate) response to the issue. The strategy therefore covers five key programme areas. Performance criteria are being developed for levels 2 and 1—the strategic elements (see Table 4).

Level 3 (efficiency) remains a departmental concern. The strategic interest is in the effect of the co-ordinated programme (level 2) and the impact on a set of (where possible, quantified) variables or key indicators of performance (level 1).

Local government, like business, needs to be concerned with department (or operational) efficiency. This level 3 concern should be part and parcel of a general management philosophy. It can contribute to significant cost savings as the Audit Commission has proved since its creation in 1982. However, cost savings and efficiency generally are internal concerns for the organization. They do not, of themselves, identify and tackle issues in the market-place or with the necessary client groups.

Planning for strategic performance must therefore be elevated beyond operational matters. It must be elevated to notions of client satisfaction and the impact of strategic policy on the community. All local government should therefore be conscious of what its strategic concerns are. For many, these concerns will be familiar.

In RDC, there are seven identified areas of strategic concern. In each, a variety of specific issues are identified and pursued. The justification for claiming their strategic position is that each merits a working party! The areas, their working party and their policy documentation are set out in Table 5.

What must then be understood is the means–ends hierarchy of policy and implementation. Strategic issues become the context for lower-level policy development.

... the organisational structure [is] a layered, pyramidal means ends hierarchy with the ultimate goal at the top. In the next layer are means to the attainment of the goal, which in turn are goals for the layer directly below it ... the decision maker for one layer being the policy maker for the layer above.[17]

Most local authorities have generally accepted strategic issues confronting them. What they lack is a method of planning for strategic performance. The following two principles are therefore suggested:

☆ an annual planning cycle should be adopted,

Table 4. Strategic performance criteria for tackling poverty

Programme	Level of review		
	3:Efficiency ($\frac{1}{4}$–1 year). Operational efficiency, budget control, personnel, morale, project management	2: Effectiveness (1–3 years). Specific programme success, citizen satisfaction	1: Economy (3–5 years +). Overall programme performance in relation to general social conditions (e.g. census data on key indicators of deprivation)
Employment	(Departmental concern)	☆ How many new projects ☆ How many youngsters on to courses ☆ How much information is sought ☆ How many full-time jobs created	(%) (%) ☆ Unemployment APT 39, RDC 16 ☆ Households on low income APT 41, RDC 23 ☆ Households that lack access to a car APT 80, RDC 51
Housing	(Departmental concern)	☆ Client/tenant satisfaction in the houses/area ☆ Reduction in transfers 'out' ☆ Increase in numbers 'in' ☆ TRAPT 39, RDC 16 Reduction of voids ☆ Reduction in income poverty	☆ Overcrowding large households APT 23, RDC 11 APT 5, RDC 2 ☆ Vacant dwellings APT 6, RDC 3 ☆ Permanently sick APT 4, RDC 2 ☆ Single parents APT 14, RDC 15 ☆ Amenity deficiency APT 0, RDC 3
Community facilities	(Departmental concern)	☆ Develop community confidence ☆ Develop reading/constructive leisure habits ☆ Develop artistic potential	☆ Community development (Subjective)

Environment	(Departmental concern)	☆ Fewer derelict/unused sites
		☆ Develop self-help skills
		
		☆ Job creation
			☆ Derelict/unused land (acres) Derelict *X*
			    Planned *Y*
			    Used *Z*
			☆ Jobs created

Decentralization	(Departmental concern)	☆ Easier access to services ☆ Better co-ordination between departments ☆ Better response from clients/tenants to services provided ☆ Development of community expertise in helping to plan and monitor services	☆ Effect on services (see Housing) ☆ Community involvement (subjective)

Note: An external look of this kind involves some attempt to find out what difference a programme is making, what its distributive effects are, how popular or useful it seems to clients and how it overlaps with or frustrates other policy aims.
Percentages are averages for the areas for priority treatment (APT) and Renfrew District Council. APTs make up 10 per cent of RDC's 200,000 population.

relating the review of issues (autumn) to programme development (spring), and be linked to the annual budget cycle; and

☆ performance criteria should be concerned with strategic (levels 2 and 1) areas, external to the organization, preferably drafted in consultation with specific client groups and interested parties.

Planning for strategic performance in local government should therefore not be concerned with operational (level 3) matters such as VFM studies, except where savings or changes in operational matters become strategically significant.

Taking the RDC case again, a framework for determining strategic performance could be developed as shown in Table 6.

Conclusion

In the context of an organization as a whole, it is suggested that 10 per cent of time is devoted to preparing and reviewing the two-stage annual strategy. Ninety per cent of time is concerned with tactics, project development and committee/working party administration to see the strategy implemented. They key point is always to relate tactics, projects and committee work (almost subconsciously) to the strategic framework. That 10 per

Table 5. Strategic issues for Renfrew District Council

Strategic issues	Working party, etc.	Policy documentation
Housing	Housing plan working party	Approved housing plan
Poverty	Deprivation policy group	Approved community development strategy (per annum)
Decentralization	Decentralization working party	Various draft and approved policy statements
Employment	Economic development working party	Various draft and approved policy statements
Tourism	Tourism working party	*Ad hoc* papers
Leisure	Leisure plan working party	*Ad hoc* papers
Paisley Town Centre	Town centre working party	Draft local plan

cent of explicit strategic work then becomes virtually self-performing. The conditions have been created through implementation (widely defined) to encourage the reporting of progress on particular projects (annual), to reflect on general programme areas (1–3 years) and to undertake a major strategic review (3–5 years). It is suggested that this is a managerial approach to strategic planning; the manager must be his or her own planner.[18]

In the final analysis, the forward impetus in planning for strategic performance in local government is retained by a discipline which ensures that the annual policy development and review cycle is completed on schedule. It then forces supporting groups to produce work on time. In local government, without a self-imposed forward momentum, timings slip and the organization flounders.

It is arguable that there is no substitute for the discipline of the market-place when planning for strategic performance. Having dispelled the relevance of business techniques (except in terms of efficiency), it is suggested that the annual planning cycle, with relevant performance criteria, is a disciplined replacement for strategic performance in local government.

References

(1) P. Self, *Administrative Theories and Politics*, p. 262, Allen & Unwin, London (1979).

(2) H. Rainey, R. Backoff and C. Levine, Comparing public and private organisations, *Public Administration Review*, **36** (2), 233–244 (1976).

(3) W. Blumenthal, Candid reflections of a businessman in Washington, *Fortune*, p. 44, 29 January (1979).

(4) J. Bower, Effective public management—it is not the same as effective business management, *Harvard Business Review*, **55**, 131–140 (1977).

(5) D. Pitt and B. Smith, *Government Departments: An Organisational Perspective*, p. 105, Routledge & Kegan Paul, London (1981).

(6) Ibid.

(7) R. Buchelle, *The Management of Business and Public Organisations*, p. 294, McGraw-Hill, New York (1977).

(8) C. Handy, *Understanding Organisations*, Penguin, London (1981).

(9) H. Mintzberg, The manager's job: folklore and fact, *Harvard Business Review*, pp. 49–61, July/August (1975).

(10) D. Katz and R. Kahn, *The Social Psychology of Organisations*, p. 466, John Wiley, Chichester (1978).

(11) A. Gray and B. Jenkins, *Policy Analysis and Evaluation in British Government*, p. 73, Royal Institute of Public Administration, London (1983).

(12) K. Pedersen, A proposed model for evaluation studies, *Administrative Science Quarterly*, p. 307, June (1977).

Table 6. A framework for strategic performance in local government

Strategic issues	Level 3: Efficiency ($\frac{1}{4}$–1 year) (OUTPUT)	Level 2: Effectiveness (1–3 years) (IMPACT)	Level 1: Economy (3–5 years, plus)
Housing / Poverty	Service and project delivery issues	Specific programme success in the community	Changes to general social/economic physical conditions
Decentralization / Tourism	An operational and departmental concern	A programme of expert concern, e.g. on behalf of a corporate working party	A policy analysis concern, e.g. on behalf of a central policy unit
Leisure / Paisley town centre	The traditional but myopic concerns of management	Much subjective or gut-reaction work in partnership with client groups	Essentially quantifiable variables, e.g. from census data/floor areas, etc.

Note: The need is to gauge not only the *output* of the organization but also its *impact* on the community.

(13) See, for example, L. Chapman, *Your Disobedient Servant*, Penguin, London (1979); H. Bentham, The discipline of performance measurement, *Management in Government*, **36** (3), 155–161 (1981); K. Sharp, Evaluating value for money, *Management in Government*, **38**, 251–260 (1983); *LAMSAC, Value for money; studies in local government*, Local Authority Management and Computer Services, London (1980, 1982).

(14) H. Heclo and A. Widlavsky. *The Private Government of Public Money*, p. 345, Macmillan, London (1982).

(15) R. McGill, Continuous community planning, *Local Government Policy Making*, **13** (2), 17–25 (1986).

(16) I. Johnston, Framework for policy management, in *Policy Management and Policy Assessment*, p. 39, Royal Institute of Public Administration, London (1986).

(17) Op. cit., Pedersen, p. 311.

(18) P. Beck, Editorial: The Strategic Planning Society; the reason for the new name, *Long Range Planning*, **19** (1), (1986).

PART THREE

Strategic Planning in State Enterprises

Why Planning in State Enterprises Doesn't Work

Mansour Javidan and Ali Dastmalchian

In a study of chief executive officers at 65 provincially controlled corporations in Canada, it was discovered that most of the companies in the sample had set up formal planning systems but were not very satisfied with their outputs. This was shown to be due to the reasons for the establishment of such systems and the attitudes towards them. This article presents a set of recommendations on how to improve strategic planning at state-owned enterprises while taking into consideration their particular characteristics and constraints.

Although the exact number of provincially controlled corporations in Canada is difficult to determine due to the problem of definition, over 200 such companies have been identified. These corporations control approximately $62bn in assets, an amount which is equal to 10 per cent of total Canadian corporate assets, and is 23 per cent higher than the assets of the Canadian Federal Government. Most of these firms, more than 75 per cent, were created during the past decade by political parties with philosophies ranging from left of centre to right of centre.

In spite of their sheer aggregate size and their prevalance in the Canadian economy, there has been little research into managerial practices of such corporations. In order to help fill this gap, the present research was undertaken. The object of this research was to evaluate the strategic planning practices of provincially controlled corporations (PCCs) in Canada. The main research question was: As a unique group of corporations, how do provincially controlled corporations conduct long-range planning? Of particular concern were the process of long-range planning, the executives involved in the process, the content of corporate plans, and the extent of strategic control at these corporations.

The results reported here are based on extensive interviews, discussions in a specially designed workshop, and a large-scale questionnaire of 65 corporations. Table 1 shows the industry and size of the participating companies. The Appendix details the research methodology employed.

Research Findings

Types of Planning

Sixty-eight per cent of the participating companies reported having written long-range plans covering at least 3 years into the future. As illustrated in Table 2, the planning horizon at just over 80 per cent of these firms is less than 5 years with a great majority planning for 3–5 years into the future. In fact, more than 50 per cent reported having a planning horizon of 5 years.

During the interviews and discussions in Phases One and Three, when asked about the reasons for such plans, many executives suggested financial credibility. They pointed out that preparing such documents provided credibility to their requests for funds from the government. Others mentioned that their organizations had prepared such a document because their counterpart in another province had just produced a 'glossy document'. The participating executives felt that their organizations were becoming increasingly interested in long-range planning, but they were not clear as to the purposes and procedures in such endeavour.

In reference to planning horizons, the participants suggested that their long-range plans were mostly extrapolations of past figures. They also pointed out that their budgeting cycle was completed prior to the start of their planning cycle due to the prescribed timing for preparation of budgets. They suggested that such a constraint damaged the validity and

Mansour Javidan is an Associate Professor at the Department of Organizational Analysis, University of Alberta, Edmonton, and Ali Dastmalchian is an Associate Professor at the Department of Industrial Relations and Organizational Behaviour, University of Saskatchewan, Saskatoon, Canada.

Table 1. Size and industry of companies in the sample

Size (No. of people)	Insurance	Housing	Mining	Land development	Road development	Power supply	Finance and investment	Printing	Wood and lumber	Transport	Administration service	Machinery	Oil	Liquor	Telecommunications	Others	Total
1–100	2			4		3	8		1			1					21
101–200		2	1				3								1	1	8
201–500		3			1			1			1			1	1		9
501–1000	1		1		1	1				1			1	1	1	1	7
1001–5000	2			1	1	1			2	2				3	1—1	1	12
5001 and over						3				1					1		5
Unknown		1		1			1										3
Total	5	6	2	6	3	8	12	1	3	4	1	1	1	5	4	3	65

Table 2. Time horizon in corporate planning

No. of years	Present
Less than 3 years	7
3–5 years	76
6–10 years	13
Over 10 years	4

credibility of their planning process because of the importance of the budget. Most of the managers at these corporations saw the budgeting cycle as critical and the planning cycle as mostly 'window dressing'. In short, they considered their firms to be highly budget-oriented and not planning-oriented. Furthermore, they pointed out that their evaluation and reward systems were strongly tied to their budgets and only loosely, if at all, linked to their plans.

Lack of strategic orientation in long-range plans was further supported by the examination of the companies' major strategic decisions. When asked about such decisions, the participants identified them as:

(1) Development of new products or services.

(2) Offering of new products or services.

(3) Withdrawal of products or services.

(4) Modification of products or services.

(5) Pricing of products or services.

The above list is indeed very similar to strategic issues confronting business organizations, which are particularly concerned with topics related to portfolios of businesses, market segments, and product offerings. However, when asked during interviews and the workshop, whether their long-range plans actually contained such decisions, in all but one case, the answer was negative. They mentioned that their plans were generally biased towards status quo because usually there was no pressure or need to develop new products or services.

It was suggested that *state-owned organizations were generally reactive rather than proactive*. Innovation and entrepreneurship were not highly valued; in fact, the mechanisms and 'red tape' established acted as strong obstacles, frustrating any innovative attempt. Furthermore, these organizations have a very large threshold in the sense that they react very slowly. No change will take place unless they absolutely have to introduce one. For example, it was mentioned that in spite of slow economic conditions, most such corporations would not cut staff until they were absolutely forced to. Similarly, those companies operating in competitive environments would not consider any major changes in their products or services unless they felt they had no choice. In short, the general feeling was that there was very strong organizational inertia impeding any of the strategic decisions identified above.

The participants felt that another reason was a general lack of understanding of and commitment to strategic planning. They suggested that there was still confusion in their organizations over very basic strategic terminology which hampered their efforts towards any serious attempt. They pointed out that it was customary for executives to use the same terminology while meaning quite different things. In one company, they had concluded that the solution lied in an attempt to develop a corporate-wide dictionary for this terminology.

These difficulties existed despite the fact that, as shown in Table 3, most of the companies had several years of experience in corporate planning. More than 60 per cent had been preparing corporate plans for more than 3 years while 39 per cent had recently started this practice.

Types of Objectives
Table 4 shows the types of objectives formulated in long-range plans. As can be seen, financial objectives are the most important, developed by more than 90 per cent of the participating firms. Many companies also prepare marketing and human resource objectives.

The Organization of Planning
To understand the role of various executives in corporate planning, the participating presidents were asked about the existence of planning staffs and planning committees and their structures. Fifty-nine per cent reported having a planning department with its size ranging from 1 to more than 100. Eighty per cent of planning departments employed up to 10 people. Most of the participating companies, 70 per cent of them, also have planning committees. The number of executives on these committees ranges from 2 to 15 with almost 80 per cent having up to 10 members. The membership consisted of senior executives at 46 per cent of the firms, and senior and middle-level executives at

another 49 per cent. This extent of participation by middle-level managers is somewhat different from the practice at most business organizations, where planning committees consist almost exclusively of highest-level executives. This leads to greater status and importance for the function of corporate planning. It is generally difficult to make corporate strategic decisions at any lower echelon.

The participants in the interviews and the workshop discussed the criteria and procedures for appointing individuals to planning departments and committees. The consensus was that, in general, most of the executives in these positions were not very knowledgeable about planning and their appointment was based more on internal political considerations than on their qualifications. Several executives suggested that officials were assigned to planning units because that was where they can do the least harm.

The Role of the Board of Directors
In regard to the role of the board of directors, 27 companies (40 per cent) reported it to be final approval of corporate plans. In other companies, the boards tended mostly to act either as an advisory group providing consultation and suggestions, or simply producing general guidelines and directives without strong emphasis on review and approval. In general, the boards seem to play a minimal role in actual formulation of corporate plans at most companies. Their greatest involvement is at the final stage of planning in the form of review and approval. At some companies, the boards tend to act more as a political liaison between the company and the Government rather than focusing on the corporation's internal operations.

The participants were generally critical of the process of appointment of board members and the individuals chosen. The general feeling was that the boards were in some cases useful in facilitating the relationship with the sponsoring government agency but it seemed like the directors were in fact representing the interests of specific interest groups that interacted in some way with the corporation, rather than overseeing the company's operations on behalf of the government. Finally, there was concern over the qualifications of some of the directors.

Environmental and Resource Analysis
As shown in Table 5, environmental analysis seems to be an important part of long-range planning at most of these companies. Among the various sub-environments, economic factors seem to receive the greatest attention. All the participating companies conduct some form of economic analysis, with emphasis on employment, gross national and domestic product, and the general financial health of the provincial economy and government.

Social factors are the second sub-environment,

Table 3. Experience in corporate planning

No. of years	Per cent
Less than 3 years	39
3–5 years	34
6–10 years	25
Over 10 years	16

Table 4. Types of objectives in long-range planning

Objective	Per cent
Financial	91
Marketing	59
Human resources	53

Table 5. Environmental analysis in long-range planning

Factors examined	Per cent of companies
Economics	100
Social	50
Political	46
Demographic	44

Table 6. Expected benefits of long-range planning

(1) To help identify key elements in organizational activities
(2) To help adjust to political-economic changes
(3) To help keep up-to-date on industrial/technological changes
(4) To help develop and maintain a long-range frame of thinking
(5) To provide a more rational basis for decision-making
(6) To help keep our goals in perspective
(7) To help better control performance
(8) To help better evaluate strategic alternatives
(9) To help set direction and priorities
(10) To help build financial credibility

analysed by half of the companies in the sample. The political and demographic environments are examined by less than half of the firms. This relative lack of emphasis on the political conditions is somewhat surprising since being a state-owned enterprise would be expected to result in much greater emphasis on such factors.

As another step in long-range planning, 93 per cent reported conducting a corporate audit to examine their strengths and weaknesses. Among this group, 30 per cent did this infrequently, 28 per cent on a moderate basis, and 42 per cent on a very extensive and frequent basis. Of particular interest here were the company's financial resources and its pool of skilled staff.

The participants in the interviews described their environmental and internal analysis as rather rudimentary. They pointed out that historically they had collected very limited information in regard to their various environments. This was so because:

☆ Top management had grown accustomed to making decisions with very little information. They were used to making decisions in reaction to what was required and as fighting fires rather than making proactive plans developed based on relevant information.

☆ Many companies did not have the capability or the resources to collect the required information. Several instances were observed where managers felt they needed data, but they did not know what exactly they needed and how to get it. Furthermore, their management information systems were not equipped to provide the required information. Several comments were made to the effect that their strategic planning efforts were hindered due to lack of the needed information.

Value of Long-range Planning
When asked about their views on the benefits of long-range planning, there was general consensus among the participants in all three phases of the research that it is a very valuable exercise. They felt that a serious attempt at strategic planning would produce many beneficial consequences. Table 6 shows the participants' expected benefits from long-range planning. Such benefits are very similar to the findings of other surveys of executive views towards planning. The participants in interviews and the

workshop pointed out, however, that their own planning systems did not satisfy most of their expectations. The general feeling was that due to the problems described before, their planning systems had tended to become more bureaucratic than strategic.

Planning and Control
The final aspect to be examined was the link between long-rang planning and control. The participating executives were asked about the existence of a mechanism to detect differences between the plan and actual performance, procedures to correct such deviations, and preparation of budgets.

The findings show that 80 per cent of the companies did monitor their performance and compared it to their plans. This process was conducted in 6–9 month intervals at 53 per cent of these companies; it was done annually at another 45 per cent. Only 2 per cent did it for a period longer than 1 year. In spite of this close monitoring, however, there seemed to be a lack of emphasis on corrective action. Only 59 per cent reported having procedures for correcting deviations between the actual and planned performance, all taking corrective measures in a period of up to 1 year. Thus, at 40 per cent of the survey firms, even if deviations from the plan are detected, little is done to correct them.

During the discussions, this lack of emphasis on control was elaborated. Participants pointed out that it was due to lack of organizational commitment to planning. As described before, many firms prepared plans simply to have such documents and as such were not seriously interested in monitoring their actual performance. In two cases, one of which a $900m company, management realized that they were losing market share. They believed the reason was the competitors' lower prices and concluded that they should cut their prices. During several discussions they found out that the information on product line costs and profits was not available; the companies never evaluated their individual product lines.

The findings here raise some very important issues

in regard to commitment to implementation. Effective planning depends on the organization's ability to build a structure of interlocking commitments. Not only do the participants in the planning process exchange information and opinions, they also commit themselves to future plans of action. Such commitment is critical to effective implementation of plans and lack of it will result in promises that may not be kept and forecasts that may be of little use.

One of the most important tools in building commitment is a credible monitoring and control system. In the absence of such a system, and a mechanism to take corrective action, the goals and objectives formulated through the planning process are simply not rewarding or motivating.

The Reasons for 'Ceremonial' Planning

The evidence presented here raises questions about the validity and effectiveness of strategic planning at state-owned enterprises, or at least those companies participating in this study. It shows that most of these firms have adopted the mechanics of planning: they seem to be more concerned with establishing a 'fashionable' strategic planning process rather than setting-up a productive system that would promote strategic thinking. In fact, several executives suggested that due to bureaucratization, such systems have actually desensitized managers towards strategic planning since, rather than advocating real strategic orientation, they have converted it into a form-filling practice with little real impact. In other words, strategic planning has tended to become a ceremonial activity to legitimize financial demands.

It is important to examine the reasons behind such lack of commitment to long-range planning. A comprehensive review of the operations of state-owned enterprises and their differences with private corporations revealed the following reasons:

(1) *Vague organizational objectives.* Since many such firms are created by some higher body which consists of multiple and competing interests, the goals of state-owned enterprises tend to be formulated in the form of general and vague statements. Such vaguely worded goals enhance the process of coalition building and reduce resistance, but they also result in difficulties in the measurement and evaluation of organizational performance. Lack of measurable goals handicaps management in taking any meaningful corrective action.

(2) *Lack of market exposure.* With some exceptions, most state-owned enterprises are involved in non-competitive markets. Even those facing competition are generally assured of government support. In the absence of efficient market feedback, state-owned firms have little incentive to monitor their efficiency and effectiveness.

(3) *Limited top management authority.* Senior executives in government-owned firms tend to have more limited authority than their counterparts in the public sector. This is mainly due to their political nature; as political creatures, they are vulnerable to direct and indirect political influence. They also face constraints in their hiring effort and developing evaluation and reward systems.

All of the above characteristics result in top management reluctance or inability to take any major corrective action in spite of the fact that organizational objectives may not be accomplished.

What Should Top Management at State-owned Enterprises Do?

The evidence presented here shows that very little real strategic planning takes place at such enterprises. Some might argue that due to the constraints and limitations described above, this is the best one can expect. While there may be some truth to this argument, it is not satisfactory. These organizations are currently spending organizational resources on a practice with few tangible results. As explained before, most executives feel their planning systems are not producing the expected benefits.

Critics of government organizations may also argue that these corporations are simply no different from other government agencies with similar lack of commitment to strategic planning. The problem is that the expressed rationale for creating these firms has been to have organizations that are owned by the government, but *act as business enterprises.* The findings here show that this is clearly not the case.

To rectify the situation, top management need to take several steps:

(1) *Determine if there is a need for strategic planning.* Strategic planning is a time-consuming activity. It requires total organizational commitment; therefore, before engaging in such effort, management should determine if there is a real need for it. Yip[1] described the following as the purposes of strategic planning:

☆ To achieve a sustainable competitive advantage.

☆ To manage diversity.

☆ To manage turbulence.

☆ To achieve synergy.

☆ To create strategic change.

If an organization is facing any one or more of these issues, it can benefit from a concerted effort in strategic planning, but in the absence of these problems, there is little need for an elaborate process. It is top management's responsibility to make such a decision. If they decide to establish a comprehensive system, the following steps should be taken.

(2) *Communicate the rationale and the need for strategic planning.* One of the issues raised by the participants in this research was that most of the managers in these firms were not aware of the reasons the systems were set up and as such did not know what exactly was expected from them. To resolve this problem, top management needs to prepare a plan on how to educate the organization in terms of the reasons for greater emphasis on strategic planning.

(3) *Prepare line managers for strategic planning.* One of the biggest obstacles in strategic planning has always been poor preparation of line managers. It is almost universally agreed that long-range planning is a line management responsibility but there is generally very little done to prepare these executives for such an important task. Concerted effort should be put into providing teaching and coaching to line managers.

(4) *Move beyond 'motherhood' goals.* A critical challenge to top management in a state-owned firm is the need to formulate goals which would enhance implementation of strategies. As explained before, in such organizations there is strong motivation to develop vaguely stated objectives. If management does not go beyond this stage, it is signalling its lack of commitment. They need to not only formulate the strategic thrusts, but also more specific performance targets. One way of being specific without risking its consequences, is to use a mix of official and unofficial goals. They can use broadly stated goals for public consumption but communicate the more specific goals unofficially but vigorously. In this way, they will provide the detailed direction for their subordinates while avoiding inflexibility in public. It is important to point out that to be effective at this requires substantial top management effort and attention.

(5) *Emphasize the need for elaborate action plans.* Strategic planning without detailed action programmes is wishful thinking. There is substantial evidence that the biggest difficulty in strategic planning is to develop means for execution of plans. This will be particularly true for state-owned enterprises, which, as explained before are under more constraints than privately owned firms. To be effective, top management should use 'implementability' as a critical criterion in choosing strategic alternatives. Once a plan is deemed feasible, then top management should use input from middle and lower management to prepare more specific action plans.

(6) *Examine the fit between strategic thrusts and the organizational reward system.* As pointed out before, the reward systems in state-owned enterprises are rather rigid and inflexible. In preparing strategic plans, management should examine the consistency between their plans and the reward systems. Implementation will be very difficult, if not impossible, if there are inconsistencies between the two. In

such cases, management should either try to modify the reward system as much as possible, or should rethink their plans.

(7) *Examine the link between the planning and the budgeting system.* Traditionally, in state-owned enterprises, budgeting is the most important activity. Top management should examine the link between the two systems. The budget should be used as a support system to enhance implementation of long-range plans. In the absence of such a relationship, attention is automatically gravitated towards the budget.

(8) *Emphasize the need for monitoring and evaluation of accomplishments.* It was shown in this research that little attention is generally paid to monitoring of performance and taking corrective action. Such a vacuum will result in lack of organizational commitment to long-range planning. As much as possible, management should communicate the need for such monitoring and set up such a system. This will result in much greater emphasis on implementation and will reduce the possibility of wishful thinking.

To summarize, it has been argued here that state-owned enterprises should not set up strategic planning systems as an imitation of other firms in the private or public sector. They need to examine its benefits and costs. If such an analysis leads to the decision to put a system in place, the recommendations presented here will help improve these firms' efforts in strategic planning.

References

(1) George Yip, Who needs strategic planning?, *Journal of Business Strategy*, Fall (1985).

(2) James S. Ang and Jess H. Chua, Long range planning in large U.S. corporations—a survey, *Long Range Planning*, **12** (1979).

(3) Egbert F. Bhatty, Corporate planning in medium sized companies in the U.K., *Long Range Planning*, **14** (1981).

Appendix

In order to identify the exact number of PCCs, letters were sent out in the summer of 1983 to those firms with available addresses, requesting their annual reports. The annual reports received, along with an examination of provincial statutes, government reports and various Canadian Business Directories, produced a total sample of 113. These are corporations owned, wholly or partially, by the governments across Canada. The research methodology employed consisted of three phases:

In Phase One, case studies were conducted with three state-controlled corporations. At each company, in-depth interviews were conducted with several executives in regard to their planning and control practices. The participating executives described their planning systems, the types of strategic issues facing them, their problems in making strategic plans, and the linkages between the planning system and the control, reward, and information systems.

In Phase Two, based on the information collected during interviews, and the previous research on corporate planning,[2,3] comprehensive questionnaires were designed and mailed to the presidents of the 113 corporations identified. Sixty-five completed questionnaires were received (response rate of 58 per cent). As shown in Table 1, power supply, financing, housing and land development are the most represented industries while oil, machinery, and printing have the least number of companies in the sample. The table also shows the size distribution of the sample.

In Phase Three, a 1-day workshop was conducted with 12 executives from various provincially controlled corporations and government agencies interacting with them. The purpose of the workshop was to discuss some of the findings in the previous phases as well as the participants' views on strategic planning and control at state-owned enterprises and the nature of their relationship with their sponsoring government agencies.

Strategic Management of Public and Non-Market Corporations

Jean Ruffat, Manager of Strategies & Structures, Paris

The author has developed a strategic framework for the management of 'non-market corporations' which he thinks better meets their peculiarities and specific needs by framing them in a relatively tight and rigorous socio-economic system relating to their internal logic. He believes that the proposed approach should provide the basis for a more constructive relationship between such corporations and the community at large and for better levels of performance.

Because of their growth in scope and size throughout the world, 'non-market corporations' (i.e. most public corporations and state controlled industries, as well as monopolies, cartels or regulated utilities and industries) may become the predominant economic structures before the end of this century. Yet, in as much as they rarely satisfy simultaneously consumers, employers and tax-payers, they are often considered as poor performers.

As a matter of fact economic theory has not yet caught up with the challenge of managing non-market corporations, which do not fit in the traditional models of the firm that link most aspects of management to the maximization of financial yield.

In the course of consulting for public corporations (nationalized industries, transportation and communication systems etc.) in several countries, the author has developed a 'strategic framework' for the management of non-market corporations which, he thinks better meets their specific needs and peculiarities by framing them in a relatively tight and rigorous socio-economic system congruent with their internal logic. The article first deals with the challenge of managing non-market corporations, then presents the main elements of

Jean Ruffat, a former partner of McKinsey, is now manager of Strategies & Structures, a Management Consulting Firm, 91 rue du Faubourg St. Honoré, 75008 Paris, France.

the proposed 'strategic framework', and finally assesses its applicability.

Meeting the Challenge of Managing Non-Market Corporations

The main difficulties in managing non-market corporations stem from the absence of a proper management framework and the reluctance of the internal environment to any form of management pressure. The challenge is threefold: size, complexity and diversity; achievement and measurement of performances; accountability.

The Challenge of Size, Complexity and Diversity

The size of the non-market sector of the economy varies greatly from country to country depending on history, ideologies and political regimes. Yet leaving aside agriculture and traditional public agencies or services, but taking into account energy, transportation and communications, more than one-third of the world's gross product is already generated within 'non-market corporations'. Likewise, over half of all productive investments are made by such entities. Because of their size, coupled with the multiplicity and dispersion of plants and locations, they are in fact very heavy and complex organizations where responsibilities are very difficult to delegate and where tight control over such delegation is even more difficult to exert.

In most cases, they are very capital intensive with a need for substantial cashflows to feed very demanding balance sheets, in spite of frequent soft financing. Yet they rarely reach high levels of efficiency in their utilization of their capital assets, and cannot usually bear to pay a net positive cost for their capital. Largely because of such heavy investments direct employee productivity has not always kept pace with the rapid growth of equipment productivity, leading in many cases to significant and sometimes disruptive feather-bedding.

51

As a result of heavy investments coupled with high enrolment they suffer from tremendous inertia and are highly vulnerable to technological, sociological or economic evolutions which undercut the foundations of their monopolies and weaken their economic base. Therefore, they are hard to manage, reorient and 'redeploy', unless they are run with much foresight (strategic perspective) and a very tight hand.

The Challenge of Achieving and Measuring Performances
In a short-term perspective (regardless of long-term strategic outlook) private corporations which are healthy in potentially attractive markets generate substantial cash flows and manage to 'feed' their balance sheets, while, on the contrary, sick corporations do not produce sufficient cash flows and are bound to stifle, unless they recapture their ability to restore their financial health.

It is much more difficult and somewhat unrealistic to apply this logic to the performances of non-market/public corporations since they can move simultaneously along three interdependent axes. More explicitly, those that are or feel rich (or which act irresponsibly) try to meet the needs and fancies of all consumers/users by offering refined services at bargain prices (as long as taxpayers or inflation help balance the accounts); those that are socially oriented are mainly concerned with the well being and comfort of their employees; finally those which the unions call privatized primarily aim at generating a financial surplus for the community, not mentioning public corporations whose performances are simultaneously inadequate (or even totally unacceptable) along two or even three of the optimization axes.

As a matter of fact non-market/public corporations are generally caught in a web of conflicting pressures, with each group of stakeholders behaving as if it owned them and as if their main purpose was to cater to their own needs and wishes: users demand an optimum level of service for the lowest cost possible, if not for free; employees often try to maximize their earnings for as little work as possible; public trustees wish to best satisfy users/voters while minimizing the need for funds and subsidies (Figure 1). Yet, in most cases, they fail to satisfy all stakeholders simultaneously; services performed are generally perceived to be of insufficient quality for too high a price, work assignments as too long and too hard for too little pay; finally public corporations as too hungry for public subsidies of all sorts.

Performances of non-market corporations are too

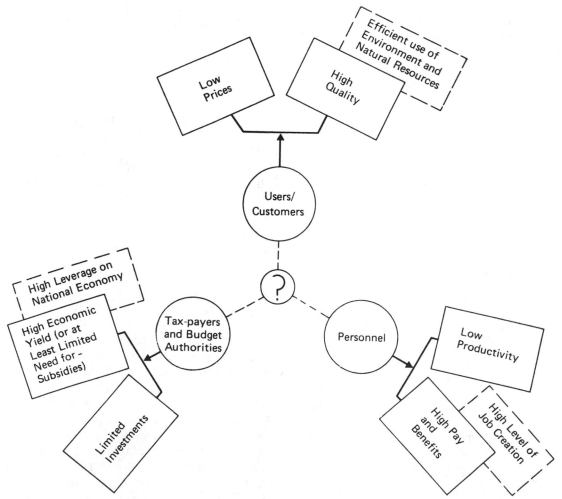

Figure 1. Non-market/public corporations are torn apart between the demands of their stakeholders

often evaluated solely from a financial and economic perspective. As long as they cover their operating costs they are considered as well managed and they can avoid scrutiny and pressures from their trustees. But whenever they start losing money the government rapidly seeks ways to reduce their deficit, either by debasing the service, or by increasing the price charged to users, but too often without really looking for improvements in their internal modes of operation, which generally remain a black box for their public trustees.

The complexity (should we say the impossibility?) of structuring the management of non-market corporations around the traditional return on investment logic makes them particularly hard to optimize. Socialist economies which are deprived of a market reference are especially weak in this area. They accept cost-efficiency trade-offs, but never express the full complexity of the trade-offs between the three optimization axes. Moreover, they are not really attempting to balance the system at the level of an individual corporation, but at the level of the whole socio-economic system, which weakens the pressure for tight management.

The Challenge of Accountability
Throughout the world, regardless of legal or political systems, accountability remains one of the best forcing devices to achieve high performances. But observation of many non-market enterprises under a broad assortment of political regimes shows that accountability is usually the weakest element in the public management chain. Accountability chains are usually very loose and thus 'self management' often becomes the rule at all levels in the operational structure.

Very frequently managers of non-market corporations pay only lip service to the principle of accountability. The more non-market corporations grow, the more they become intertwined in the socio-economic fabric of the country, the less transparent they become, the more they resist tight and comprehensive accountability, the more they reject the right of their technical and financial trustees to meddle in their internal operations and to ask for detailed information. Even, in some cases, public managers go as far as having their own hostages among political circles through campaign contributions and many other favours.

When non-market/public corporations manage to avoid controls to the point of practising 'self management', fairly serious problems occur. First it raises a political issue because of a direct challenge to the authority of the State and it generates a management crisis because it loosens or even dissolves the hierarchical structure. Then internal pressures tend to prevail and to dictate the future course of the enterprise.

In the case of traditional market corporations the market under its various forms (market for goods and services, labour market, financial market) acts as the regulating agent for each of the three optimization axes. Therefore, the economic dimension becomes the main concern of both shareholders and managers of the traditional organization who must concentrate their efforts on reaching the highest economic surplus possible, by dealing simultaneously with all the components of the return on investment tree, so as to maximize profits for the owners. In this context, delegation of responsibilities is relatively simple: whoever is in charge of revenues must maximize income, whoever is in charge of costs must minimize expenses, in line with the 'yield tree' of the company.

It is much more difficult to delegate simple, coherent and motivating objectives in non market/public corporations and even more difficult to hold operational units accountable for their performances. The less the logic of the return of investment tree applies because of weaker controls by the various sorts of markets, the more the organization lives in an artificial world and the more difficult it becomes to exert management pressure because it is not constrained in a tight and rigid framework.

In fact very large public corporations tend to intimidate their managers and even more so their public trustees. In as much as tight management of public corporations does not really pay, it is usually very daring to challenge directly all the constraints and factors of inertia that limit the performances of public corporations. As a result, the authority of many public managers often lies on make believe.

At the same time, under the pressure of lobbies and politicians, sophisticated regulation (based on in-depth economic analyses, objective criteria and the search for an optimum from the public interest point of view) is in serious decline in the United States which were its pioneers and champions, mainly because it had fallen into the trap of bureaucracy.

Overall we seem to have entered a phase of active deregulation and of relative passivity of politicians toward the operating conditions and performances of public and regulated corporations. Beyond the political reasons that explain this evolution, there are technical constraints tied to the lack of a sound optimization and accountability system built around the internal dynamics of non-market corporations.

Developing a Strategic Framework Tailored to the Specificity of Non-Market Corporations

In as much as they are bound by an income

statement and a balance sheet, non-market corporations are supposed to fit in the same economic logic as that of private corporations, which forces them to balance their accounts through the generation of revenues sufficient to cover all their operating and annualized investment expenses. Deficiencies must be compensated through loans or subsidies. Taking into account the need to go beyond the simple logic of the return on investment tree the approach suggested here to improve the management processes and the operating results of non-market corporations aims at linking all management efforts and processes to their basic objective structure, so as to make sure that all elements of the optimization process are taken into account in a coherent and consistent manner. The idea is to start from the basic goals of the corporation, from its key missions, and to carry this logic all the way down the hierarchy to the basic building blocks in the organization and then to account for actual performances by going up along the same structure.

Developing Yield Trees for Each Stakeholder Group
As we have seen, non-market corporations must meet three types of complementary yet conflicting obligations: a service obligation, a social obligation and an economic obligation. Therefore, there is a definite need for an optimization and ac-countability system built around the internal dynamics of the non-market corporation. It should underline the obligation to optimize simultan-eously around the three axes and spell out the internal contradictions, the main trade-offs and the key management decisions required to run a tight ship.

As evidenced in Figure 2 'yield trees' can be built for each of the three optimization axes in order to simultaneously: maximize quality of service for users, income for employees and return for public investors, but also minimize price for users, personnel costs per unit of output, investment and operating costs of available capacity. In all non-market corporations each category of stakeholders first seeks to optimize its part of the equation, to get the highest yield, the highest surplus for its involvement in the actual operations of the system. However, the system is of little value to the community unless each of the stakeholders makes a significant and balanced contribution to the income statement of the corporation: the user by paying a reasonable price, the personnel by being produc-tive, the State by financing the investments (and possible operating deficits).

Managers of public corporations must avoid sub-optimization on just one or two of the axes; they should rather seek to optimize the system in a comprehensive manner by making simultaneous trade-offs between the three optimization axes. The proposed strategic framework enables managers to focus their attention on the critical components of the income statement, by pinpointing what each stakeholder receives for his contribution to the overall optimization of the system. Moving from a market to a non-market environment (for example through nationalization of all participants in an industry) is a great challenge, in as much as it leads to a direct shift from self-control over a single optimization axis (financial and economic) to self-control and regulation over the three axes. In a way it would be like trying to switch from driving a car, to flying a plane (or even a helicopter) without special training and instruments.

Actually, the overall yield of non-market corpor-ations can be assessed at two levels: the '*direct yield*', which we have just described and which is built into the economics of the corporation and directly related to specific components of the income statement; and the '*indirect yield*' for the community at large as described in Figure 3, that is: efficiency in utilization of the environment and natural resources on the service axis, ability to create jobs for the general workforce on the social axis, and leverage effect on the national economy on the economic axis. It represents a different and more abstract level of optimization which relates to external stake-holder groups and to the external dynamics of the corporation and thus it reflects its overall contribution to the general socio-economic equili-brium of the nation.

This area of 'indirect yields' is very important (especially in LDCs where non-market corpor-ations are supposed to be one of the prime moving forces in their social and economic development plans), but it is far more difficult to manage and to measure because it is much more elusive. Therefore, this paper acknowledges the great importance and relevance of these indirect yields, but it does not attempt to deal with them from a methodological and strategic point of view. The logic would be the same as that presented here for managing the direct yields, but on a more complex and far reaching scale.

Controlling the Evolution of Stakeholder's Yield
Non-market/public corporations are submitted to very strong pressures from their stakeholders. Their relative weight and position can vary tremendously and, over the years, the overall system can take many different configurations as each category of stakeholder seeks to maximize its benefits for the smallest contribution possible. Beyond their efforts to limit the demands on the system (Figure 3) and to avoid its breakdown, public managers must maintain a balance between the relevant stakehol-ders, since, depending on situations, some stakehol-ders are much better positioned than others to get a bigger share of the pie and to turn the system to their advantage. As a result public managers are under high pressure to suboptimize on each of the optimization axes and to run a relatively loose system.

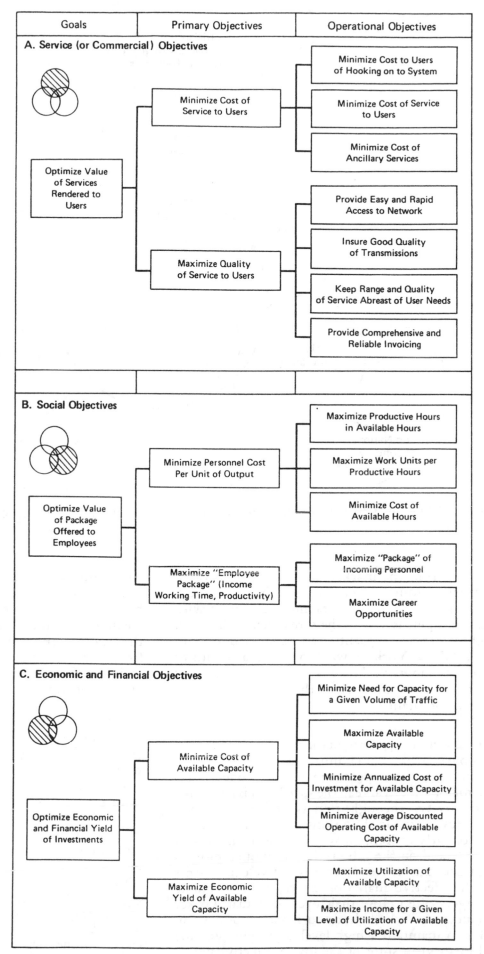

Figure 2. 'Yield trees' can be built on each of the three optimization axes of non-market corporations

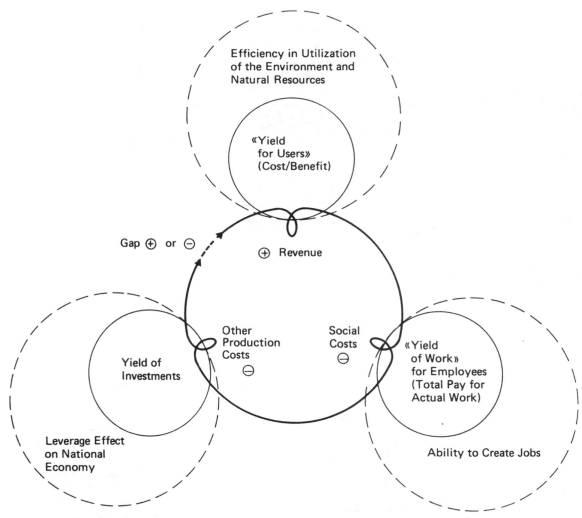

Figure 3. The need to balance the accounts ties the interests of the stakeholders and limits their flexibility

Pressure from the market and from users is often relatively limited because of the monopoly situation and generally users must be content with what they get, as long as they are given a minimum level of service. Quality can range from 'bum service' (New York subway) to 'gold plated' utility (Moscow subway). There is usually much greater resistance to rising prices than to slow down-grading of quality.

Here, as in any private/market corporation, most employees seek to maximize their income while minimizing time spent and actual productivity. The major safety valve in the social area is personnel productivity, through tireless and very strong pressures for reduced working time and workload, and for early retirement without cut in salary. Yet attitude and on the job productivity of employees condition the efficiency of productive equipments and the effective quality of service, therefore public managers often close their eyes on actual worker productivity, which leads to inflation of staff in order to maintain a high level of output (volume and quality) in spite of the low productivity.

In the economic and financial area, non-market

corporations are generally fairly sensitive to the level of their operating expenses, because their budgets and price levels must be approved; but they are much less interested in efficient management of their capital investments: high demands are made for heavy investments, high levels of enrolment are maintained, yet overall productivity stays low and quality remains insufficient. In today's inflationary world there is usually too little pressure to worry about the optimal use of equipment financed with what amounts to a negative cost of capital (because of soft financing). Yet, especially in LDCs, whenever capital is used inefficiently the accumulation process breaks down and the country suffers from slow growth or inflation, or from both.

In as much as the pressure exerted by personnel is often much higher than that applied on the other two optimization axes (Figure 4) there is frequently a 'negative surplus' both on the service axis (poor quality for too high a price, compared to potential or objectives) and on the economic axis (obligation for the State to pay for the operations and often the service of the debt of corporations already heavily subsidized for their investments and therefore supposed to be much more productive and financially self-sufficient).

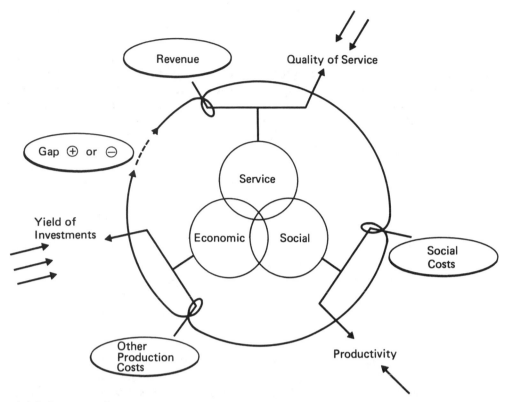

Figure 4. The yield for specific stakeholder groups acts as a safety valve on each of the optimization axes

Keeping a Balance Between the Optimization Axes
Unlike private corporations, which often die from excessive skimming of their balance sheets, non-market corporations often drown in excess fat, unless strong pressure is exerted to develop and renew the tension to maximize the surplus/yield on each of the optimization axes. Many different performance patterns exist, some of which are very unbalanced and costly for the nation.

Aside from the 'ideal' non-market corporation with strong and balanced tension on each of the optimization axes, as many as seven different scenarios can be observed (Figure 5). Often (scenario 1) the tension slackens first on the economic axis which is the most vulnerable performance parameter of non-market corporations and the income statement deteriorates until it can no longer feed an over inflated balance sheet. Only direct subsidies from the national budget can keep these corporations from going bankrupt, like the Paris subway which covers only 40 per cent of its costs through sales of tickets, or the brilliant railroads of Europe whose revenue cover only a fraction of their expenses: 77 per cent in Great Britain in 1977, 61 per cent in Germany, 55 per cent in France, 32 per cent in Italy (as compared to 39 per cent in 1979 for Amtrak in the U.S.A.).

Sometimes (scenario 2) the service/market axis slackens first. In such cases providing a service to users, which had justified the creation of the enterprise, loses its priority to social and/or economic considerations when it is possible to

shortchange customers/users for economic or political reasons like with the national television in France or with products or services for export in monopoly situations (OPEC oil producers).

In other cases (scenario 3), the social axis is sacrificed to the economic and the service axes. This happens in LDCs when public corporations attempt to generate a surplus for the country by selling products (textiles, handcrafts, minerals, etc.) or

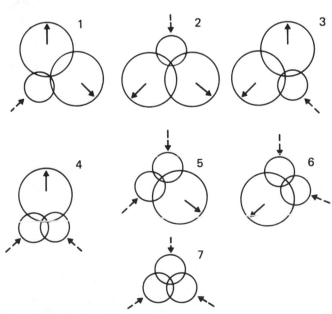

Figure 5. Performances of non-market corporations can evolve in very different and contradictory manners

providing services (tourism) based on very cheap labor (sometimes child labor) on highly competitive international markets.

Then pressure can slacken on two of the axes which leads to still more fragile and unstable configurations. When prestige is paramount (scenario 4), both the social and economic axes are sacrificed to the service axis. This could be the case of the Concorde, of Egyptian pyramids, or of Gothic cathedrals.

When the corporation wants to be social at any cost, it is led to give priority to employee needs and demands regardless of the economic and market/service position of the corporation (scenario 5). This is the case of the New York subway and frequently that of many nationalized corporations in many 'petro-socialist' countries where newborn industries are mainly a vehicle for the redistribution of oil revenue.

Then (scenario 6) some non-market corporations are real money making machines (mining for example) with the service and social axes sacrificed to the economic axis. But they are rapidly 'privatized', either by the executive team

(Pertamina in Indonesia), or by the employees, who are never at a loss to find uses for excess funds.

Finally (scenario 7), the tension ends up disappearing on all three axes, which reflects the inability of the State to regulate public corporations. Many public corporations in LDCs often fall in this category of systems with no tension, no ambition which are not really trying to achieve anything beyond bureaucratic survival. In the northern hemisphere many U.S. railroads or municipal services belong to this category, along maybe with the Italian Post Office, where mail bags sometimes end up in paper mills.

Managing the Strategic Configuration
It is possible to position the actual performances of non-market corporations in the 'stakeholder accountability framework' presented in Figure 6. It seeks to reflect the relative performances and management tension on each of the optimization axes, and it is a very useful device to compare the performances of non-market corporations with similar types of activities throughout the world. Based on this framework, the main operational objectives of public managers should be to push the lines that characterize the performances on each

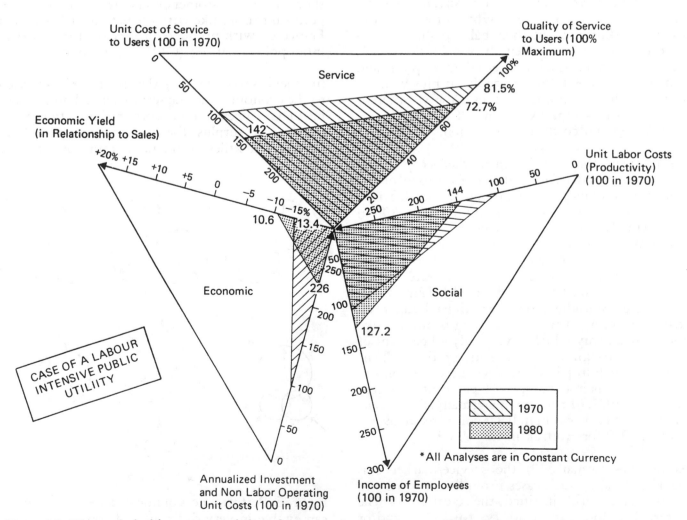

Figure 6. The stakeholder accountability framework sets the game-board for strategic management

optimization axis as far out as possible, by strengthening the tension on each of the axes.

The example presented in Figure 6 refers to a large European public service. The stakeholder accountability framework shows a very serious decline in its performances between 1970 and 1980. As a matter of fact, the system has loosened up quite a bit during that period. From the analysis of the diagram it is clear that labour is getting a much better deal than it was in 1970, since its net income has moved up from 100 to 127·2 after discounting for inflation, even though there was a serious drop in productivity (with unit labour costs moving from 100 to 144, also after discounting for inflation). The community as a whole is also slightly better off, in as much as the direct deficit has decreased from 13·4 per cent of sales to 10·6 per cent of sales, even though total annualized non labour costs were skyrocketing from 100 to 226 (not counting inflation).

The only stakeholders that are really worse off are the customers since the price they are paying has gone up from 100 to 142 (discounted for inflation) for a lower level of service (72·7 per cent of standard, versus 81·5 per cent 10 years ago). Overall there has been a clear transfer of value from customers/users to personnel, as is often the case nowadays with a number of non-market corporations which cannot always benefit from heavy investments in automated equipment.

The example shown in Figure 6 refers to the traditional public utility with very little input (aside from a little electricity). Whenever the inputs are significant, the framework as presented here applies only to the value added by the corporation. The measures on the diagram must be tailored to the specific nature of the industry, but they should reflect the notion of yield (input and output) for each of the three key stakeholders.

Since non-market corporations are usually in a monopoly or quasi-monopoly position on their specific market niches, strategic management is somewhat different from that of market corporations, which must redeploy their activities and their assets regularly to keep abreast of market shifts, technical progress and changing economic prospects in specific market segments. In their case, strategic management consists mainly in managing their long term position on the 'stakeholder accountability framework' by influencing and coordinating the evolution of key ratios: 'cost-benefit' for customers or users, 'income/productivity' ratio for personnel and 'financial yield' of investments made by the community. The dialogue with public trustees and with the community at large should mainly address the trends in the relative position of the corporation in the 'stakeholder accountability framework' versus that of comparable organizations in other countries and the desired configuration for the future.

Seeking Transparency Throughout The Organization
Delegation of operational objectives from top to bottom of large entities is a fairly complex task which is not really possible unless the same language is spoken and understood all the way down to the basic building blocks in the organization. In traditional private (market) corporations delegation hinges around the responsibility to optimize specific elements of the return on investment tree (production volume, unit costs, etc.). But in order to be really effective, public managers should be able to delegate the three pronged objective structure as far down as possible in the hierarchical structure and to control separately the achievement of sub-objectives on all three optimization axes (Figure 7).

Therefore, the organization itself should be 'finalized', that is, geared to give full responsibility for finalized (integrated) objectives to specific managers high up in the system and from then on as far down in the organization as possible. This sort of finalized or integrated organization is very favourable to a decentralized mode of management in as much as it is built around the same logic as industry divisionalization, which aims at decentralizing profit responsibility as far down as possible, and it contrasts sharply with the heavy functional organizations that often prevail in public enterprises throughout the world (because there appeared to be no way to build real profit or at least accountability centres down in the organization). One of the key benefits of finalized organizations is that they allow for aligning the concerns and motivations of elementary building block managers with those of top management. Moreover they foster tight delegation and accountability chains, which prevent the dilution and distortion of responsibilities and priorities. It is clear that demanding objectives require fairly elaborate management systems and information flows focused around weak spots and high leverage areas.

Reshaping the Strategic Configuration
Over the long term, the economic and social needs of the country are met only through high quality service delivered at reasonable prices, and with employee living and working conditions in line with those of their contemporaries, provided subsidies are kept to a minimum. Therefore managing a non-market/public corporation means taking the long perspective, looking for continuous and consistent improvements in the overall performances of the corporation on its three optimization axes and preparing it to face up to future changes and new requirements from the environment (Figure 8).

Over 20–30 years non-market corporations generally show a great deal of plasticity and manage to

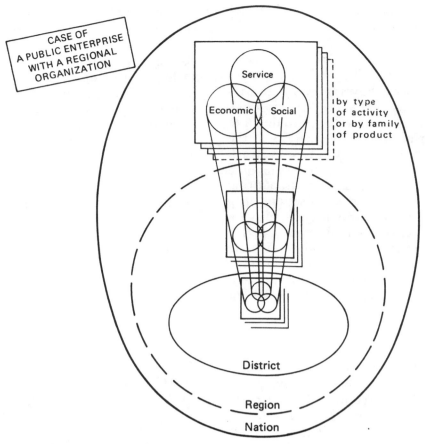

Figure 7. Objectives assigned to operating units and control mechanisms of non-market corporations must reflect priorities set for each of the optimization axes at the top

adapt to changing times, needs and pressures, because of permanent prodding and erosion from all stakeholders. Within such a time framework public managers have a good deal of freedom to reshape the configuration of the non-market corporation and to improve its contribution and usefulness to the nation. However, trying to reshape the configuration of the performances of the corporation makes sense only if its managers and trustees have a project, if they have sound and coherent improvement objectives on each of the optimization axes. But they often have only partial projects leading to sub-optimization of overall performances. At worst they accept to be

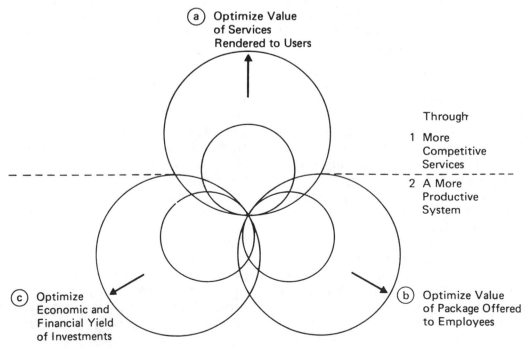

Figure 8. Managers of non-market corporations must exert firm management pressure simultaneously on all three optimization axes

manipulated by internal and external pressures, while avoiding comprehensive accountability at all cost.

When there is a definite will to improve and optimize performances, each 'yield tree' or optimization axis must be considered as a 'mine' for management purposes. But these three mines for management are uneven in potential and, like oil wells, they have both positive and negative interactions. Some modes of exploitation increase the recoverable capacity of the wells, while others reduce this capacity by killing the wells, as oilmen say. In any case, in the absence of management pressure from their trustees, many public corporations must generate their own internal pressure for results. As a consequence, the upgrading of their management systems is of little use unless the executive team really wants to improve overall results.

For the long term and from a strategic point of view, regulating management pressure on each of the optimization axes is not sufficient. As a matter of fact, effective strategic management requires that the whole socio-economic equation of the corporation be reviewed and reassessed on the basis of redefined user needs (cost-quality ratio, availability of service, etc.) every 10 or 15 years. Then new and more productive combinations of human resources and equipment should be sought. This is the planning process that led to superhighways, high speed trains or nuclear power plants.

Coping with Resistance to Implementation

The proposed strategic framework is fairly easy to understand as a concept, but it is much more difficult to implement, since in most cases public managers are quite reluctant to being locked into a rather transparent and restrictive accountability framework, unless it is imposed on them by the community through their trustees. But in as much as self-control rarely leads to effective optimization versus the public interest, the need to improve the performances of non-market corporations forces the government to seek the integration of their objectives in a framework similar to that proposed here.

Managers May Resist the Implementation of a Comprehensive Strategic Framework
Public managers that have been confronted with the framework are intrigued by the concept, but many of them dislike the fact that it changes the rules of the game and leads to transparency of performances on all three optimization axes and to positioning with respect to the public interest. Yet the framework is not deterministic and does not impose a specific value system or specific targets for results. It is merely a technical tool aimed at sorting out and specifying the key constraints that bear on the system and at clarifying the interactions that condition its overall effectiveness. It can be looked at as a sort of generalized strategic framework allowing for a possible and gradual shift towards a more balanced distribution of power between all three types of stakeholders, whether in public or even private corporations.

But the Sheer Weight of Non-Market Corporations Calls for Tighter Objectives and Management Processes
Trying to solve the development problems of a country or to maintain its overall level of economic activity and employment through the development of non-market/public corporations makes sense only if the community seriously intends to exert its control rights over the long haul. Ultimately, the main challenge in the management of non-market corporations is the challenge of accountability in a meaningful and comprehensive framework. The difficulty stems from the fact that many public trustees are not really serious about their responsibilities, either because they do not care, because they do not have the necessary information, or because they are more receptive to pressure groups that represent specific vested interests, than to forces that are supposed to defend the public interest.

Given the current performance imperative, will non-market/public corporations continue to escape the general drive for greater transparency and accountability and for greater efficiency which is affecting all structures and institutions? We doubt it, at least in democratic countries. This is why we think that the proposed strategic framework provides a technical answer to this need for clarity, rigour and ambition; assuming that the community at large really intends to exert a strong pressure for results on its non-market/public corporations.

PART FOUR

Strategic Management of Projects

Planning Development Projects: Lessons from Developing Countries

*Dennis A. Rondinelli**

Projects of varying kinds are, and will remain, a dominant feature of organizing investment in developing countries. However, the path from selecting optimal projects to achieve development goals to the planning, management, and execution of such projects too often leads to disaster. This paper examines some of the major reasons for problems and failures and draws on the past quarter century of experience of development project management to indicate some important lessons for more effective and efficient management.

The financing and implementation of development activities through physical, economic and social investment projects has been an integral part of public planning and management in developing countries for more than a quarter of a century. National ministries, international lending institutions and private corporations have used project management as a means of planning and executing billions of dollars of investments to stimulate economic growth in developing countries since World War II. Indeed, projects have become one of the most important instruments of public and private management in the Third World and a primary means of activating national and sectoral development plans.

But the record of project management in the Third World has been mixed. The obstacles and difficulties that inhibit overall economic growth and efficient public administration also constrain effective project planning, organization and execution. Many developing countries have become highly dependent on foreign experts and international assistance for many aspects of project planning and management. Yet most projects still regularly meet unanticipated difficulties, and many simply fail. Some that succeed produce only temporary or narrowly distributed benefits; others do not generate the rate of return or the flow of goods and services anticipated in their conception and design. The problems of planning and managing projects in developing countries are varied and sometimes intractable, running the gamut from difficulties of translating national and sectoral plans into feasible investment proposals, the inability to formulate and prepare internationally acceptable prospectuses, overambitious or technically deficient designs, inappropriate or ineffective appraisal, and political interference in project analysis and selection, to the difficulties of activating and organizing project management units, faulty planning, programming and scheduling of tasks, weaknesses of supervision, monitoring and control, the failure to transfer project resources and technologies to operating institutions upon completion, and the laxity in evaluating project results and assessing opportunities for further investment.[1]

The problems can be attributed to a myriad of causes. Low levels of administrative capacity, scarcities of skilled planners and managers, and lack of adequate physical, economic or social preconditions make development projects risky from the outset. The scarcity of local resources for supporting or maintaining projects and the problems of budgeting and allocating funds frequently cause problems even for internationally assisted projects. Inappropriate and overly sophisticated planning and management techniques sometimes imposed by international lending agencies or the foisting of unwanted or exploitative projects on governments by aid agencies or multinational corporations, together with the use of culturally incompatible management methods by foreign consultants also reduce the effectiveness of projects in many parts of the Third World.[2]

Despite the problems and failures, however, projects will remain the dominant means of organizing investment in the foreseeable future. They offer important advantages to all participants in development—government agencies, lenders, private firms and beneficiaries—because by definition they are, or should be, manageable units of activity. A properly designed project should be a related set of tasks co-ordinated to achieve a specific objective or output at a given location within a limited budget and period of time. Inherent in the development

*Dennis A. Rondinelli is director of the Graduate Planning Program at the Maxwell School of Citizenship and Public Affairs at Syracuse University, 721 Ostrom Avenue, Syracuse, New York 13210, U.S.A., and has served as a consultant on project planning and management, development administration and urban and regional planning to international agencies and public and private organizations in Asia, Latin America and the United States.

project, as Hirschman notes, is 'the introduction of something qualitatively new, and the expectation that a sequence of further development moves will be set in motion'.[3] Projects are especially appropriate ways of organizing highly innovative, experimental or risky ventures or those with high priority in development policy. As the United Nations points out, 'the kernel of the project concept lies in its application to other than routine activities of an organization or government agency, for purposes of special emphasis and action'.[4] Finally, the aim of development projects is to concentrate resources and attention on activities that will produce change—to stimulate economic growth, for example or to promote employment, introduce more productive technology, increase the effectiveness of service delivery or extend services, facilities, infrastructure and productive activities to new groups of consumers or geographic areas. Thus, projects are temporary activities intended to generate permanent, and replicable, economic, social or physical change.[5]

Because projects are often the most appropriate means of organizing innovative or untried activities, they are especially difficult to plan and manage even in advanced industrial nations, but particularly so in less developed countries. Yet the past quarter century's experience with development project management is beginning to yield some important lessons about how to plan and implement them more effectively.

Lessons from Experience in Developing Countries

A review of experience with development projects offers some clear insights into causes of failure and attributes of success. If project planning and implementation are to be improved substantially, it seems essential that those responsible for development management begin to: (1) perceive of projects as complex administrative activities requiring an integrated management framework; (2) recognize and stimulate informal as well as formal sources of project identification; (3) link project design more realistically to objectives, needs and conditions in developing countries; (4) simplify appraisal, selection and approval processes; (5) extend the concept of project organization to a wider variety of institutional forms and managerial arrangements; and (6) redefine project management skills from narrow programming and co-ordination functions to broader leadership capabilities.

1. *Perceiving of Projects as Complex Administrative Activities —the Need for an Integrated Management Framework*
Development projects are extremely complex activities. Even small-scale projects of short duration involve a myriad of administrative, technical and co-ordinative tasks that must be carefully scheduled and integrated. The complexity is compounded in most developing countries by the fact that many of the tasks are not performed by or under the control of the sponsoring organ-

ization or project management unit. The idea for a public project may be identified by a national planning agency or by a high level political authority, assigned to a staff committee or operating agency for definition and preparation, contracted to private consultants for detailed design or feasibility analysis, and appraised by a private bank or international funding institution. If judged feasible, the project may then be assigned to another ministry or organization for implementation. The implementing unit may be a semi-autonomous agency, private firm or special management organization established specifically to execute the project. In any case, the project manager and technical staff are usually not hired until after the project has been formulated, designed, appraised and approved, and may not have had any participation in those activities. The project is usually supervised, monitored and evaluated by higher levels of political and administrative authority and by the lending institutions. Often projects depend for their success on resources, supplies and support from a variety of other organizations over which their managers have little, if any, control and with which they may be in competition for limited amounts of money and manpower.

Yet, project management is often perceived of quite narrowly. Each organization tends to emphasize that aspect with which it is most directly concerned—planning agencies with formulation, sponsoring organizations with preparation and funding, operating units with design, programming and scheduling, lending institutions with appraisal and selection procedures, and beneficiary groups with output and distribution. But in reality, project management involves a series of related activities, which should form an integrated planning and implementation cycle. Experience suggests that nearly all types of projects go through similar life cycles, perhaps not explicitly in all cases, or in the same way, or sequentially as a cyclical framework may imply, but most projects evolve through stages depicted in Figure 1.

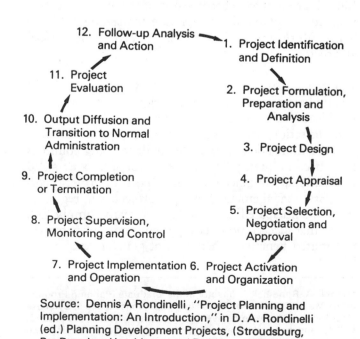

Source: Dennis A Rondinelli, "Project Planning and Implementation: An Introduction," in D. A. Rondinelli (ed.) Planning Development Projects, (Stroudsburg, Pa: Dowden, Hutchinson and Ross Inc., 1977), p. 5.

Figure 1. Project planning and implementation cycle

Moreover, evaluations of internationally funded development projects reveal that many of the most serious problems arise in managing the relationships among stages in the cycle, rather than in the performance of tasks within any one stage. The types of problems noted repeatedly in evaluation reports include those such as inadequate communications among organizations setting investment policies and those responsible for identifying and funding individual projects, lack of interaction between project designers and ultimate users, clients or beneficiaries, misconceptions and misunderstandings between sponsors and funding institutions of the nature, purposes or goals of projects. Post-evaluations also regularly uncover the failure to redesign projects upon discovery of unanticipated obstacles during execution and operation, failures of one government agency to train personnel or provide inputs needed for projects undertaken by another government department, and the failure to plan for and manage transfer of project personnel, technology, excess equipment and outputs to permanent production or service delivery organizations at the project's completion.[6]

For these reasons, the United Nations considers it essential 'to visualize the phases in the life-cycle of a project in terms of links in a chain and to think of project administration as an instrument for making those links of equal strengths. Unless this is done, the weakest link will affect the performance of the whole project.'[7] This suggests that government agencies and private organizations should plan and implement projects within an integrated management framework tailored specifically to the decision making procedures of the country in which the project is undertaken. Moreover, it implies several levels of project management—not only the scheduling and programming of construction and production tasks, but also the management and co-ordination of complementary activities within other organizations which are crucial to the success of the project at each stage of the cycle. In addition, if the performance gaps between stages of projects are to be reduced, responsibility and authority must be assigned to an appropriate organization or individual for administering and co-ordinating the *entire management cycle*; that is, the overall *process* through the project evolves—from initial identification through completion and follow-up analysis—must be carefully planned, managed and monitored. This is a function that is often beyond the capability or authority of the project construction or operations manager or of those providing inputs from other organizations. Unfortunately, in most developing countries management of the entire project cycle is either ignored or delegated to a planning agency as a routine supervision task. But this function is crucial to the success of projects and requires a new, distinct and active project management role at a high level of authority within developing country governments.

2. Recognizing and Stimulating Informal as well as Formal Sources of Project Identification

The literature of project management and the policies of national governments and international lending institutions have placed strong emphasis on establishing highly formalized and centralized procedures of project identification. Indeed, most funding agencies, such as the World Bank, have usually insisted that developing nations establish central planning agencies and national plans to explicate investment strategies and identify development projects. Yet, national planning has been a disappointing source of development projects—in many countries national plans have either been loosely defined strategies with vague and amorphous goals that do not specify investment implications or 'laundry lists' of projects generated independently by ministries and agencies without reference to the national plan. Few national plans identify private sector investment needs or opportunities.[8] Where they have affected allocative decision making, national plans often biased the identification of projects toward capital-intensive, large-scale, export-oriented industrial and physical infrastructure projects that have had limited spread effects, and that have tended to reinforce the already inequitable distribution of income and wealth.

More frequently, however, the projects included in the investment programs of developing countries were identified outside of formal, centralized planning procedures. And, indeed, it seems essential to recognize and stimulate informal as well as formal processes of project identification if the number of potentially feasible projects is to be increased and their quality improved. Figure 2 outlines the types and characteristics of major sources of project identification in developing countries.

Although international lending institutions, national governments and private organizations use formal, deliberative, centralized and active methods, such as country programming, preinvestment studies, reconnaisance surveys, national and sectoral planning, annual investment programming and budgeting to generate investment proposals, many are conceived of through informal, decentralized, spontaneous and reactive means. Many projects are simply replications, imitations, follow-ons or linkage investments. Some result from the discovery of crucial shortages of resources or development bottlenecks, the discovery of excess or new resources, or from the R & D discoveries of private organizations and foundations, and are less susceptible to formal, deliberative planning. Others result from government incentives to private firms or individual entrepreneurs to invest in high priority development activities. And many emerge entirely from informal interaction among government officials, lending agency personnel and private entrepreneurs with novel ideas, from political demands and payoffs to supporting coalitions, by crises and emergencies or as responses to external political and economic pressures.[9]

In any case, little evidence supports the contention that centralized planning generates inherently better projects than those emanating from more informal decentralized and spontaneous sources. Indeed, a strong argument can be made that reliance on centrally planned investment analysis has often resulted in a shortage of projects, and that if more rapid and pervasive development is to occur, deliberate efforts must be made to stimulate project identification more widely and to diffuse administrative

Characteristics / Sources	Formal ——————————— Informal / Deliberative ——————————— Spontaneous / Centralized ——————————— Decentralized / Active ——————————— Reactive			
International Aid or Lending Agencies	Assistance Policy Analyses, Country Programming, Preinvestment Studies, Sector Analysis, Reconnaisance Surveys	Expansion or Replication of Existing Projects, Piggyback or follow-on Projects	Informal Identification by Program or Loan Offices, Personal Interaction Among Lenders and Government Officials	
Developing Country Governments	National Planning, Sectoral Planning, Annual Programming and Budgeting, Project Identification Missions, Linkage Investments	Government Incentives for Private Investment, New Experiments from Previous Project Failures, Replication of Successful Projects, Discovery of Shortages or Development "Bottlenecks", Discovery of Excess or New Resources	Imitation of Foreign Projects, Political Demands for Services or Facilities, Political Payoff of Porkbarrel Projects, Ideological Commitment Projects	Pressures from Crises or Emergencies, Response to External Threats
Private Organizations	Direct Foreign Investment, Joint Venture Proposals	Innovations from Organizational Research and Development	Licensing Agreements, Voluntary or Charitable Agency Projects	Entrepreneurship

Figure 2. Sources and characteristics of development project identification

capacity for mobilizing and investing resources in developing societies.

3. Linking Project Design more Realistically to Objectives, Needs and Conditions in Developing Countries

Design is a crucial stage of project planning, and although it is given the greatest attention just prior to detailed feasibility analysis and appraisal, it should be an integral part of all stages of project management. Yet, evaluation reports recurrently cite problems of poor design—inclusion of components that are inappropriate to local conditions or needs, underestimation of resource needs and availability, inadequate or inappropriate specifications, lack of financial contingency planning, failure to assess realistically the potential for support and co-operation by other organizations, underestimation of the ability of government to recruit and retain managerial and technical staff, and improper location.

Design problems are caused in part by the failure of planners to involve clients or ultimate beneficiaries in the formulation and preparation of projects, by the use of foreign consultants unfamiliar with local conditions to draw specifications, by overambitious and unrealistic assessments of administrative capacity and by the lack of an effective design framework. Moreover, project management literature often emphasizes the technical aspects of design, especially in construction or production projects, without concern for broader social, political, economic and cultural factors in developing countries.

Even rather 'routine' replications, however, can meet unanticipated problems in the Third World. If projects involve new technology, attempt to introduce new ideas or aim at generating substantial social or economic changes, they should be designed as experimental projects and evolve incrementally through a series of stages. A four-category framework that includes experimental, pilot, demonstration and replication or full-scale production stages, may be useful in improving project design.[10] (See Figure 3.)

(a) Experimental projects are needed when little is known about the problems to be solved or the most effective means of reaching objectives. They are often used for agricultural, scientific, health and some types of social services projects, but can be applied to a whole range of ill-defined development problems. Because the problems are not well-defined, little is known about alternative solutions, the most appropriate or effective methods and technologies for ameliorating adverse conditions, the types, magnitudes or combinations of inputs, the timing of activities, or the best production and delivery systems. The project is designed to explore these and other questions and to test alternatives under highly controlled conditions. These projects should be small in scale. They require highly trained and technically skilled staff, must remain flexible in design, have access to specialized inputs and resources, and be located in areas where conditions are appropriate for solving the problem under consideration. Moreover, they must be organized in such a way as

	Project Type or Stage			
	Experimental	Pilot	Demonstration	Replication or Production
Unknowns or Design Problems	Problem or Objective			
	Possible Alternative Solutions			
	Methods of Analysis or Implementation	Methods of Analysis or Implementation		
	Appropriate Technology	Appropriate Technology		
	Required Inputs or Resources			
	Adaptability to Local Conditions	Adaptability		
	Transferability or Replicability	Transferability	Replicability	
	Acceptability by Local Populations	Acceptability	Acceptability	
	Dissemination or Delivery Systems	Dissemination or Delivery Systems	Dissemination or Delivery Systems	Dissemination or Delivery Systems
				Large Scale Production Technology

Characteristics (High ... Low):
Uncertainty and Risk
Political Vulnerability
Innovativeness
Addition to Existing Knowledge
Need for Creative Management
Need for Flexibility of Organizational Structure
Rare or Specialized Technical Skills

Figure 3. A development project design framework

to protect their autonomy, minimize their responsibility for performance of routine duties, and allow administrative flexibility. Finally, they should be protected from the political adversities of early failure as well as from political pressures to expand or replicate their methods too quickly in cases of early success.

(b) *Pilot projects* are useful to test the results of experimental projects under less controlled or a greater variety of conditions and to adapt or modify methods, technologies or organizational arrangements tested and proven successful in other countries to local conditions and needs. Pilot projects are appropriate when the problem or objective is relatively well-defined and something is known about alternatives for problem solving. Pilot projects are designed primarily to test methods and technology, determine their relevance, transferability and

acceptability and to explore alternative dissemination or delivery systems. Careful attention must be given to choosing appropriate locations, structuring components to fit local needs and cultural constraints, collecting baseline data, and especially, formulating an evaluation system that will clearly indicate the conditions of success or failure, the preconditions necessary for replication, and the resources necessary to adapt them in other locations. Again, pilot projects must be designed to protect their managers from undue political interference or pressures to show quick results, since implementation is still primarily by trial and error, requiring creative and flexible management.

(c) *Demonstration projects* are designed primarily to exhibit the effectiveness of solutions and to increase the acceptability of new methods and techniques on a broader scale.

Although they are less risky and uncertain than experimental and pilot projects, innovative and creative management is still required in gaining acceptance. Experience with agricultural, rural development and small-scale industrial projects in Africa and Latin America clearly indicate that successful demonstrations must be profitable to the participants, novel and innovative yet related to the experience of beneficiaries. They should include all components required to support successful adaptations, be relatively simple to understand and apply with a minimum level of skill on the part of the client, be relatively inexpensive and make use of accessible materials or tools. Moreover, they must have highly visible results which are easily communicable and can be reliably replicated with a minimum of supervision and training.[11]

A major problem with demonstration projects is not necessarily to protect them from political criticism, but often to moderate political enthusiasm for their widespread replication until applicability under a variety of conditions is adequately tested. Weiss, Waterston and Wilson point out that design must be adjusted to larger scale. 'The scale of operations is significant for such demonstration projects,' they note, '. . . because many problems do not become fully apparent until a large-scale operation has been reached. In effect, more of the system is tested in demonstration projects because logistics and support mechanisms, a full range of personnel, and other needs must be met to integrate all of the organizational and physical inputs . . .'[12] Again, an effective evaluation procedure should be an integral part of design.

(d) *Full production or replication projects* are the final stage of evolution in an experimental series of projects or a type that can be used when all of the uncertainties and problems inherent in other types have already been solved. The primary design problems in these projects are to test full-scale production technology and to develop delivery and distribution systems for project outputs. Scheduling, programming, co-ordination, production and distribution activities must be carefully adapted to local conditions to ensure efficient and economical operations. 'In the production stage and even in some of the larger demonstration projects,' development analysts note, 'an additional need has been the quality of entrepreneurship, of working with and exhorting and co-ordinating the multiple organizations to achieve production-oriented goals.'[13]

Finally, it should be noted that all development projects are somewhat experimental and that even seemingly routine replications often meet unanticipated difficulties when transferred from one cultural setting to another. Experience in developing countries suggests some important general criteria that should be met in the design of all projects. Shaefer-Kehnert has concisely summarized them as: simplicity and clarity of objectives, availability of an economically attractive technology to promote the product; integration of basic production processes and services; access to necessary specialists and provision of training for needed personnel; ability to recognize potential constraints and to design contingency plans to

overcome them; and compatibility with existing administrative structures.[14] Projects in developing countries must be designed to fit existing practices and cultural constraints while generating sufficient innovation to overcome problems and promote change.

4. *Simplifying Appraisal and Selection Procedures*
The tendency over the past quarter century among international lending agencies, such as the World Bank, has been to insist on increasingly complex appraisal and selection analysis, using sophisticated cost-benefit, rate-of-return and ranking or comparison techniques. But developing nations have had great difficulty in applying complicated analytical methods. In countries where data are scarce, statistics unreliable and costs and benefits only vaguely calculable, appraisal is at best an art, falling far short of scientific or systematic analysis. Vast amounts of money and time have been invested in overly detailed feasibility and appraisal reports, delaying the processing and approval of proposals. The complexities of the methods often require expatriate experts or foreign consulting firms to apply them in a way acceptable to international funding agencies. Economic and financial criteria are usually overemphasized to the neglect of less easily identifiable or quantifiable administrative, social, political and cultural factors that may have as much bearing on the potential success and impact of the project as financial factors. In many cases the complexity of appraisal and selection methods results in subtle game playing between borrowers and lenders. 'Projects requiring foreign aid must, therefore, be "packaged" with a view to finding a "buyer",' Ahmad has noted, 'This takes the form of "window dressing". It is the general feeling in most developing countries that the more technical and complex the presentation, the more the use of shadow prices, tradeoffs, engineering coefficients, convincing evaluation of investment criteria, the better the chances of finding a bilateral or multilateral donor.'[15]

But more often these practices have far more serious consequences for developing nations. Chambers argues that in Africa, for instance, complex appraisal procedures and the foreign experts who are usually needed to apply them are biased toward large, capital- and import-intensive projects that are easy to monitor and inspect and that are most conducive to rapid construction using foreign technology and expertise. Indeed, consideration of proposals is often limited to those that can be appraised by social cost–benefit analysis. But such projects tend to be inappropriate in predominantly rural countries where more widespread and direct benefits to rural people come from small, long-term administrative- and labor-intensive projects using local technology and manpower.[16] Chambers suggests displacing sophisticated cost–benefit appraisal techniques with simple decision matrices, using simple ranking systems focusing on the effects of alternative projects on intended beneficiary groups, checklists of desired socio-economic characteristics, approximate cost listings instead of complex ratios, and indexes of unit costs and benefits—all calculable by simple mathematics and priority rankings. Projects would be selected on the basis of the knowledge and judgment of developing country planners and managers about the needs and constraints in their own country, which ultimately, is how the decisions are really taken even when laborious attempts are made at complex quantification. Sinha has noted that in much of the developing world 'subjective judgment plays such an important role in measuring prospective gains and losses that it is pretentious to attach any real significance to *precise* numerical results. A "phony" precision is probably as dangerous as no quantification at all.'[17]

5. *Extending the Concept of Project Organization*
Much of the project management literature derived from American and British corporate experience prescribes a matrix arrangement—in which a distinct project unit within an organization carries out substantive work with support by functionally specialized divisions—as the ideal form of project management. But in developing countries creation of a matrix organization may be neither possible nor desirable. Little attention has been given to alternative arrangements; and indeed, little attempt has been made even to describe systematically alternative organizational forms, let alone analyze their advantages and disadvantages under differing conditions. Although it is beyond the scope of this essay to explore the latter issues, it is essential to recognize that a wide variety of organizational arrangements are being used in developing nations and to begin systematic analysis of their characteristics.[18] Among the organizational alternatives currently in use are assignment of the project to:

(a) An *existing operating department* or ministry in which the project is implemented as part of an on-going program without creating a distinct project management unit. Sometimes an administrator is assigned primary responsibility for co-ordinating project-related activities and maintaining separate financial accounts; in other cases, the project is subcontracted in whole or part to other organizations, and an administrator in the sponsoring agency is responsible for monitoring progress, providing support, and evaluating results.

(b) A *distinct project management unit* within an existing government ministry, either with all of the resources needed to implement the project or with functional support from specialized departments in a matrix arrangement.

(c) An *autonomous implementation unit* outside of the regular government organizational structure, with sufficient resources and authority to implement the project. In most cases the autonomous unit has independent sources of revenue; recruiting, hiring and training authority; the ability to pay higher salaries and provide greater amenities than regular civil service agencies; and usually depends on expatriate or foreign experts for consultation or to fill high level managerial positions. The units, such as marketing boards, power commissions and highway authorities are sometimes created to undertake special functions or may be organized geographically as regional development authorities and areawide development commissions.

(d) A *decentralized field unit* reporting to a central government agency, usually created to undertake func-

tionally specialized or regional development projects that cannot be implemented directly by a central government ministry.

(e) An *interagency co-ordinating committee*, which attempts to integrate the inputs of a variety of ministries, subordinate units of government, and private organizations or groups, with staff seconded from one or more of the ministries for temporary duty.

(f) A *private contractor or production firm* which undertakes construction and operation of the project under government supervision or on a 'turnkey' basis, whereby a private firm constructs the project and then turns over facilities to a government ministry for operation.

(g) A lower level of government through *devolution of project management functions* to provincial, state or local units, with or without central government supervision or monitoring.

(h) *Joint venture organizations* in which government and private firms share responsibility for the construction and operation of the project, with duties, powers and responsibilities of each clearly delineated.

The proper form of organization depends, of course, on the type of project to be undertaken, the existing administrative structure, technological requirements, current administrative capacity, availability of skilled managers and technicians, and locational considerations. Some governments and international aid agencies prefer to assign projects to existing organizations and to integrate them closely with ongoing programs to build administrative capacity within operating ministries. Others insist on creating autonomous implementation units for each project because of the weaknesses of public administration in much of the developing world, as a means of hedging against risk by ensuring that a single organization has sufficient resources to carry out the project and as a way of sheltering the project staff from performance of routine administrative duties.

6. *Redefining Project Management Skills—Leadership vs Programming*
Finally, if project planning and implementation are to be improved in developing nations, it seems essential to redefine the skills and capabilities required of project managers. In the past, project management has often been narrowly defined as the scheduling, programming and co-ordination of work activities and great emphasis has been placed on technical, engineering and programming skills. Indeed, project management positions are often defined specifically to recruit technical analysts rather than those with general management capabilities. But it seems evident from experience in developing countries that not only must project managers have diverse technical and managerial skills, but must also provide strong leadership, especially in resource mobilization, political interaction, motivating staff, clients, sponsors and potential beneficiaries, building a network of organizational support, and creatively solving problems. Moreover, they must be able persistently to overcome the inevitable political, technical and bureaucratic obstacles that face nearly all development projects. A recent series of studies

of the problems of implementing development projects in Asia concludes that the crucial factor in explaining differences between successful ventures and failures was strong and persistent political leadership on the part of project managers and higher level authorities. Agricultural production projects in Nepal were ineffectual during the 1960s because they were administered bureaucratically, whereas similar projects in the Philippines became highly successful after being assigned to energetic, determined and persuasive leaders with the political motivation and authority to take decisive action. Land development and colonization projects in Sri Lanka became bogged down in delays and red tape, eventually failing completely for the lack of responsive leadership, while similar types of projects in nearby Malaysia were strongly guided and directed towards successful completion by men who were widely regarded by their staff, clients and higher level authorities as honest, intelligent and strongly committed to pursuing development goals.[19]

Moreover, evaluations suggest that political commitment and leadership from authorities at levels higher than the project organization are also crucial. The lackluster experience with large-scale public housing projects in Hong Kong has been attributed to their routine style of administration whereas Singapore's attempts at similar projects have achieved international recognition. Success in Singapore has been attributed primarily to the 'highly effective leadership of a young prime minister, Lee Kuan Yew, for whom no detail was too small to be considered'.[20] In Malaysia, rural development projects were efficiently administered through extensive programming, co-ordinating and scheduling procedures —known as the red book and operations room—vigorously promoted by Prime Minister Tun Abdul Razak. For several years during the 1960s, one analyst notes, 'Tun Razak made this system work by exhaustive pressure—surprise visits to state and district operations rooms and dramatic intervention on the spot. He exhorted officers to greater effort, to speed up performance, to work together, to concentrate on development activities, and he achieved results in speeding up action and demonstrating to rural Malays the government's concern for their welfare.' But when active political leadership decreased, the once-effective programming and scheduling techniques become frozen in bureaucratic procedures; the impact of the projects was dissipated and progress ground slowly to a halt.[21] Without broader administrative ability and strong leadership, managers with only technical programming skills are largely ineffective in implementing development projects.

Project Planning as a Development Function

Ultimately, projects are more effective instruments of development when they are related to broader development policies that have been translated into well-defined plans, programs and investment proposals. Projects in developing countries have two types of goals: immediate and longer-range, both of which are crucial for economic growth and social progress. Immediate goals are concerned with developing the methods, technology and output of the project itself; longer range objectives with the impact, 'spread effects' and socio-economic changes resulting from those outputs. Planning that focuses on one at the expense of the other will either lead to poor project results or constrained development impacts.

Experience in developing countries clearly indicates that project planning requires new and broader perspectives. Development projects must be implemented within an integrated planning and management framework, but project management must come to be viewed as an instrument of development policy-making and planning. As such, projects are crucial aspects of public administration in developing nations. Thus project management methods and techniques cannot simply be transferred from Western industrial societies without careful testing, adaptation and modification. Indeed, the record of project management in the developing world is not likely to improve until developing nations can create innovative, indigenous, planning and implementation procedures.

References

(1) For a more extensive list of problems see Dennis A. Rondinelli, Why Development Projects Fail: Problems of Project Management in Developing Countries, *Project Management Quarterly* **7**, 10–15 (1976).

(2) See Dennis A. Rondinelli, International Assistance Policy and Development Project Administration: The Impact of Imperious Rationality, *International Organization* **30**, 573–605 (1976) and Dennis A. Rondinelli, International Requirements for Project Preparation: Aids or Obstacles to Development Planning? *J. Am. Inst. Planners* **42**, 314–326 (1976).

(3) Albert O. Hirschman, *Development Projects Observed*, Brookings Institution, Washington, D.C. (1967).

(4) United Nations, Department of Economic and Social Affairs, *Administration of Development Programmes and Projects: Some Major Issues*, Document No. ST/TAO, M/55, United Nations (1971).

(5) E. K. Hawkins, *The Principles of Development Aid*, Penguin Books, Baltimore, MD (1970).

(6) Rondinelli, *Why Development Projects Fail*, pp. 11–12.

(7) See the article by the United Nations Public Administration Division, Developing Planning as a Framework for Project Administration, in *Planning Development Projects*, Dennis A. Rondinelli (Ed.), Dowden, Hutchinson and Ross Inc., Stroudsburg, PA (1977).

(8) See Naomi Caiden and Aaron Wildavsky, *Planning and Budgeting in Poor Countries*, Wiley Interscience, New York (1974); and Dennis A. Rondinelli, National Investment Planning and Equity Policy in Developing Countries: The Challenge of Decentralized Administration, *Policy Sciences*, **10**, 45–74 (1978).

(9) A detailed discussion can be found in Dennis A. Rondinelli, Project Identification in Economic Development, *J. Wld Trade Law* **10**, 215–251 (1976).

(10) See Wayne Weiss, Albert Waterston and John Wilson, The Design of Agricultural and Rural Development Projects, in *Planning Development Projects*, Rondinelli (Ed.), pp. 95–139, for a discussion of these categories based on a model initially developed by Raymond Radosevich and Dennis Rondinelli, *An Integrated Approach to Development Project Management*, mimeographed, Office of Development Administration, U.S. Agency for International Development, Washington, D.C. (1974).

(11) See David Hapgood, *Policies for Promoting Agricultural Development,* MIT Center for International Studies, Cambridge, Mass. (1965); Uma Lele, *The Design of Rural Development: Lessons from Africa,* Johns Hopkins University Press, Baltimore, MD (1975); and Development Alternatives Inc., *Strategies for Small Farmer Development: An Empirical Study of Rural Development Projects,* U.S. Agency for International Development, Washington, D.C. (1975).

(12) Wayne Weiss, Albert Waterston and John Wilson, The Design of Agricultural and Rural Development Projects, in *Planning Development Projects,* Rondinelli (Ed.), pp. 95–139.

(13) *Ibid.,* p. 101.

(14) Walter Shaefer-Kehnert, Approaches to the Design of Agricultural Projects, A PASITAM Design Study translated by Arlene S. Hall, *Program of Advanced Studies in Institution Building and Technical Assistance Methodology,* Indiana University, Bloomington, IN (1977).

(15) See Yusuf J. Ahmad, Project Identification, Analysis and Preparation in Developing Countries: A Discursive Commentary, in *Planning Development Projects,* Rondinelli (Ed.), pp. 161–165.

(16) Robert Chambers, Project Selection for Poverty-Focused Rural Development: Simple is Optimal, *World Development* **6,** 209–219 (1978).

(17) R. P. Sinha, Project Evaluation: Measuring the Immeasurable, in *Planning Development Projects,* Rondinelli (Ed.), pp. 156–160.

(18) Aspects of some forms of project organization have been discussed in Dennis A. Rondinelli and Kenneth Ruddle, Local Organization for Integrated Rural Development: Implementing Equity Policy in Developing Countries, *International Review of Administrative Sciences,* **63,** 20–30 (1977), Weiss, Waterston and Wilson, *op. cit.,* pp. 121–127; and Lele, *op. cit.,* Chapters 8–10.

(19) See Ram K. Vepa, Implementation: the Problem of Achieving Results, in *Planning Development Projects,* Rondinelli (ed.), pp. 169–190.

(20) *Ibid.,* p. 171.

(21) Milton Esman, Monitoring the Progress of Projects: The Redbook and Operations Room in Malaysia, in *Planning Development Projects,* Rondinelli (ed.), pp. 225–229.

How NASA moved from R & D to Operations

John L. Hunsucker, Shaukat A. Brah and Daryl L. Santos

This paper investigates the initial planning process for the transition of an organization from a R & D environment to an Operations environment. Using a developed transition life cycle model, the paper demonstrates a four step analysis of the management of the transition. Further, the paper suggests the utilization of existing methods for achieving a smooth transformation under various levels of technical, political, cultural, managerial, and economic uncertainties. Finally, the paper lists possible courses of action and considerations for the transition once the initial planning stage is completed. The concepts herein were used to begin planning the change, from R & D to Operations, of the Space Shuttle Program at NASA.

Introduction

Any organization wishing to undergo a major transition, such as moving from a R & D environment to an Operations environment, should organize the process by which it changes. Human nature's tendency to cause people to resist change forms a foundation on which this need is established. Although the disturbance caused by change in the present system may be necessary, it is not desirable to see the disturbance grow to a size which may consequently disrupt the steadiness of the organization. Although the magnitude of the change process can be and possibly is different for different organizations, one thing such changes have in common is that they follow a life cycle process. As with any project, there is a beginning, a growth, a decay, and an end. The management of transition follows the same life cycle.[4]

Quinn and Cameron did an extensive literature search on the models addressing organizational life cycles.[21] They integrated nine different life cycle models and described four basic stages—Entrepreneurial, Collectivity, Formalization and Control, and Elaboration of Structure—on which the organization was presumably based. The one major short-coming of this organizational life cycle as applied to transition, is the absence of a termination stage. This stage may not be necessary nor desirable in the organizational life cycle, but termination is extremely important in the life cycle of transition management. Unlike the case of an organization, where it may be irrelevant to think of phasing out, one expects the transition to end.

The authors have developed a four phase Transition Life Cycle Model.[4] The four phases are the Creativity Phase, the Control Phase, the Integration Phase, and the Stabilization Phase. Table 1 lists the different considerations and actions to be taken during each of the different phases. Incidentally, the phases of the transition life cycle are also in phase with the three states of the familiar Kurt Lewin's conception prevailing in the literature: Unfreezing, Change, and Refreezing of the planned transformation. In summary of the four phases of the model, Figure 1 gives an overlay of the stages on the change curve for the management system. The creativity phase is the birth and planning period. The control and integration phases are the periods of the most activity since nearly all of the employees will be involved in these two phases. The stabilization phase is the death period of the transition in which the transition structure is disposed. The shape of the curve, not necessarily symmetric, reflects the magnitude of the changes in each of the stages.

Using NASA's Space Shuttle program as an example, this paper outlines strategic considerations in planning the transition from an R & D environment to an Operations environment. Further, the paper suggests possible courses of action upon completion of the initial planning stage.

Background Problems

The research on this subject matter was inspired, and in fact sponsored, by the National Space Transportation System (NSTS) of the National Aeronautics

The authors are members of the Department of Industrial Engineering at the University of Houston, Texas.

Table 1. The four phases of transition management

I. Creativity Phase

Things to consider:
- ☆ Technical/Political/Cultural/Managerial/Economic aspects of an organization as a resistance to change.
- ☆ Environmental analysis before endeavouring the change process helps in understanding the organizational situation.
- ☆ Management flexibility leads to organizational success.
- ☆ Systematic approach is the best method of changing a high technology organization.

Things to be done:
- ☆ Form/Implement a planning group.
- ☆ Determine the organization's change targets and strategy.
- ☆ Design specific events needed to point towards the need (or awareness) to change.
- ☆ Develop the organizational structure after the change.
- ☆ Formulate the timetable for change.
- ☆ Institutionalize the expectation of change.
- ☆ Formulate the goals for the organization state assessment.
- ☆ Emphasize experimenting before making final commitment to the change or process.

II. Control Phase

Things to consider:
- ☆ A guiding executive articulates the vision of the new organization and its transition goals.
- ☆ Top management must be involved in monitoring and control of change process.
- ☆ An effective leader helps people understand how their work contributes to objectives of the total organization.
- ☆ There is an increased need for a two-way communication in all spheres of change.
- ☆ Culture of organization must evolve in order to implement a new mission.

Things to be done:
- ☆ Implementation of the strategy for change.
- ☆ Emphasize on pattern breaking.
  Some of the tools available for management:
  - ☆ Training, or re-training, is a useful tool for change.
  - ☆ Recruitment can be used as a tool for change.
  - ☆ Retreats or gatherings are other tools for change.
  - ☆ A task force is a useful approach for the change process.
  - ☆ Change agents act to facilitate the change.

III. Integration Phase

Things to consider:
- ☆ The employee involvement in the problem solving and in the making of a new organization aids in a higher probability of success.
- ☆ Organizational change requires the commitment and support of the individuals and groups.

Things to be done:
- ☆ Decentralization of the change program strategy.
- ☆ Some people must be held accountable for the change process.
- ☆ Use rewards, intrinsic and extrinsic, as a change agent.

IV. Stabilization Phase

Things to consider:
- ☆ Is the job really done?
- ☆ What tools and experience from transition can be used in the steady state?

Things to be done:
- ☆ Study the state of the organization and see if the change has been made in a feasible direction.
- ☆ Disband the working group involved in transition, if a feasible change has been made.
- ☆ Establish the proper needs of the evolved organization in terms of human and non-human resources.
- ☆ Effectively utilize the prized people who have been instrumental in accomplishing this goal of transition.

---

and Space Administration (NASA). The thoughts presented in this paper were used as a basis to begin the planning of a major transition at NASA. Along with other concepts presented by the research team, see Hunsucker, Law and Sitton[16] for example, these concepts serve to provide structure and organization to a large complex problem, that of moving the Shuttle Program to an operational era. Operations is used here in the context of sustained routine timely space flight over a long duration of time with an increased flight rate of the shuttle. While NASA has always been concerned with flying often and flying safely in space, the shuttle program is the first

NASA program with such a long duration that it has no foreseeable end. Actually this transition is quite unique for essentially few organizations have made a change equivalent to the proposed movement of NSTS. The complicating factors in this movement include the size and complexity of the organization along with its complete public exposure. The situation has been further complicated by the space shuttle Challenger's accident in January 1986. In addition the product under consideration, the service of flying routinely in space, is one for which there is no previous experience base. Furthermore, in a rather exhaustive literature search, no

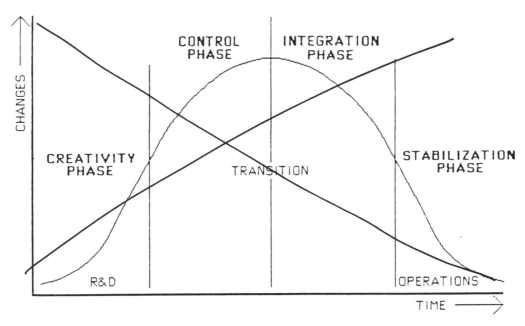

Figure 1. Transition curve with overlay of life cycle phases

specific reference was found which dealt with the transition of an organization from R & D to Operations.

Using over 170 articles related to the task at hand as a beginning to the research, interviews were conducted with 19 major organizations which underwent significant transitions. These interviews were conducted over the period from January 1985–1989.[12,13,14,15] The interview process was, in turn, supplemented with a questionaire on transition that was sent to 277 Fortune 500 companies.[13] The concepts presented in this paper and the beginning of the planning for the resolution of problems of NSTS are based on this research.

Planning the Change

Strategy Development

In developing a strategy for transition, we contend that the planners must understand the considerations and actions for each of the four phases of the transition life cycle. The Creativity Phase is essentially the time period where the transition strategy is created. In order to facilitate the creation of the strategy a four step analysis of the transition has been developed by the authors (Table 2). As an implementation consideration, the Four Step Analysis was utilized in numerous industrial interviews and with NSTS at NASA. Furthermore, the analysis can be used as a guideline to help in determining courses of action as the life cycle matures.

Most of our experience, including that with NASA and with the industrial interviews, lies within the Creativity Phase. As this phase is that which determines the transition strategy, this paper concentrates on this phase of the transition life cycle and the Four Step Analysis. Furthermore, the analysis

should be used in each of the remaining phases. The analysis will be beneficial due to the fact that it, by design, can be used as a monitoring tool. Additionally, each of the questions should be answered in a rigorous manner. In order to address the problem of transition management for any organization, this analysis forms a foundation on which the planning of the change can occur.

Creativity Phase

The information presented in the following sections describes, in general terms, the R & D and Operations environments. The information is, in essence, an application of our strategy to the R & D to Operations transition. It serves, therefore, as an example of the problem solving structure. In addition, it helps to illustrate the depth required in the analysis. While not necessarily complete, the information presented is intended to paint a picture of the two environments. Although specific organizations may differ from the descriptions presented, the general sense of the descriptions is still applicable to help define the boundaries of the transition problem. In essence, a good path for the transition can be created by an initial understanding of where the organization is and where the organization wants to be.

Step 1: Where are We Now?

The trivial answer to 'Where are we now?' is 'We are a Research and Development organization.' However, there must be an in-depth understanding of the R & D system. This section intends to develop this 'in-depth' understanding through the analysis of the environment, function, and means of controlling the organization.

Table 2. Four step analysis of the transition management

The following are the questions to be addressed and some of the issues to consider and gain understanding of at each step of the transition management.

(1) Where are we now?

(2) Where do we want to be?

Both Question 1 and Question 2 should be addressed in terms of:
☆ The internal position of the organization with respect to the technical, political, cultural, managerial and financial situations.
☆ The external position of the organization with respect to its competitors, other organizations and market conditions.
☆ Performing systematic environmental analysis of the internal and external position of the organization.
☆ The organization's long and short term goals, targets and strategies.
☆ Establishing the expectations of and from the organization by the employees, stockholders, community and others.

(3) How do we get there?

The answer to this question necessitates:
☆ Developing a complete definition and understanding of the change.
☆ Considering all options of the desired change strategy.
☆ Definition of the level of involvement and degree of commitment of all human and non-human resources.
☆ Establishing the expected level of change in the technical, political, cultural, managerial and financial aspects of the organization.

(4) How badly do we want to get there?

The answer to this question is a function of:
☆ The uncertainty in the technical, political, cultural, managerial and financial aspects of the organization.
☆ The time frame available for the change.
☆ The level of perceived need for the change at different levels of the organization.
☆ The availability of human and non-human resources for the change.
☆ The level of commitment to the change at different levels of the organization.

Environment

The key to a successful R & D organization is the very presence of the atmosphere of creativity.[3] The approaches taken and followed by the management have a tremendous potential to increase the morale and productivity of the organization. One of the more important approaches in effective R & D management is the judicious balancing of the behavioural and technoeconomic considerations. The approach calls for a collaborative, not a competitive, work environment and flexibility in the operating procedures. The management job, while maintaining the economic viability of the organization, is to provide the following features for establishing a creative climate:[17]

☆ Autonomy and challenge to the individuals and groups;

☆ Responsiveness to individual ideas;

☆ Ability to foster curiosity and wonderment;

☆ Tolerance of differences of ideas; and

☆ Inter and intra organizational communication.

The extent to which these features are to be made available to a research group depends upon the type of the work involved. For example, the creativity of an undirected research group following an offensive/defensive strategy should itself be 'undirected', since ideally its desired output is a continued but unspecified flow of novel inventive ideas.[17,22] Much of the work in this category involves theoretical investigation and conceptualization.[5] This intellec-tually demanding activity performed mostly by highly mature scientists demands low bureaucratic activity and a more supportive work environment. On the other hand, the success of the company following an applications engineering strategy is dependent upon the continued ability of its development engineers to provide creative solutions to particular user problems in a timely manner.[22] The two examples in a way are two extremes in an R & D environment. In most situations, it is generally a mixture of complete autonomy on some subjects and considerable control on the others. Whatever the situation, it is important to realize that the very survival of an R & D organization is dependent upon its ability to be creative and innovative, and this objective may not be sacrificed for any short term goals.

Function

The function of an effective R & D management is not only that of usual short term planning of uncertainties and daily routines, but is also that of planning for the future growth and direction of the organization.[18] A representative research and development organization may have one or more of the following primary objectives along with some secondary objectives as well:[6,22]

☆ Discovering and furthering knowledge;

☆ Developing new products;

☆ Improving the existing products;

☆ Finding new uses for the existing products;

☆ Improving production processes;

☆ Finding potential uses for by-products or waste products generated by the present production system;

☆ Providing technical services to the functional departments;

☆ Analysing and studying competitors.

How some of these functions and objectives are realized is the responsibility of the R & D management. Quite often it is possible that some objectives may have conflicting requirements. Under such circumstances, it is again the responsibility of the management to find a compromise formula which does not sacrifice the organizational interests. The important aspect while making such decisions is to keep in mind that the very survival of the R & D organization is dependent upon the ability of its members to foster innovation. Any organizational policy which curbs the innovative environment will eventually result in substandard performance. The organizational attributes do not produce creativity, but are aimed at motivating the individuals to be creative.[24]

Besides the proper environment, the organization requires the right kind of people to do the job.[11] It demands people who can work independently and develop innovative ideas in an often undirected research oriented organization. However, if the research activity is of a directed nature, then the pressure caused by the demand warrants hiring people who have the capability of working under pressure. In simple terms, the R & D organization requires hiring people who can perform the work expected of them. Furthermore, there is a requirement of creating a forum such that all of the top researchers in the organization can effectively communicate with each other and with the management of the organization. The proper interface will help in a better utilization of the resources and a close conformation to the corporate management strategy.[11]

The next issue is that of behavioural and technoeconomic considerations for highly motivated researchers. Inherently the R & D people require a collaborative environment in which the decision making process is shared. The day-to-day decision making is also mostly delegated, and operating procedures are flexible to support and encourage the ingenuity of the researchers. The interaction between superiors and subordinates, being informal, is usually low-keyed. One of the watchdogs for the R & D people, however, is their inherent nature of being perfectionists. At times the cost of perfection goes beyond the limits of the control system. In such situations a compromise which does not discourage the researchers is necessary.

Implementation and Control
A major difficulty in R & D management arises on the economic side of the picture. An environment which fosters innovation seems mandatory for a research and development organization. Unfortunately, there is a high cost—mainly arising from salaries—associated with obtaining this environment. Given a perfect arrangement an organization is in a good position to flourish in the long run. However, every organization requires economic viability. Moreover, the lack of historical data to evaluate the alternatives makes the problem of economic analysis more difficult. Any activity directed toward control could actually be curbing innovation and should therefore be cautiously planned and monitored. Thus, the solution to this delicate situation remains. The one-phrase answer for the solution is, 'Balancing of behavioural and technoeconomic considerations.'[22] R & D management needs to perform that balancing act without hindering the creativity.

Application to NASA
In order to help NASA answer the first question, our research team conducted a thorough demographic study.[12,13,14,15] It was found that NASA's

☆ average technical employee is 43 years old;

☆ employees are mostly engineers;

☆ work force has 27 per cent of the employees with a master's degree or higher;

☆ average employee service length is 16·4 years;

☆ average employee starting age is in the late 1920s;

☆ workforce is experienced with most experience in R & D programs;

☆ workforce has had significant decreases in manpower; and

☆ workforce reduction is due to hiring freezes, transfers to other programs, and employee pursuit of higher wages.

In addition to the demographic study it was found that each Shuttle flight is unique thus requiring unique preparations. In this respect, NSTS is essentially working as an R & D organization with each of the flights acting as different projects.

Step 2: Where Do We Want to Be?

Given the foregoing examination of the R & D environment, the next question, 'Where do we want to be?' deserves attention. This section examines the answer to this question in a form similar to that used in the discussion of the R & D management section.

Environment
The important factor in the smooth functioning of Operations management is the presence of a well structured organization. The leadership of the organization is instrumental in providing this

function. Leadership is also responsible for creating the operational objectives and ensuring smooth work flow. The principal function of the leadership of Operations management is its responsibility to maintain the future direction for the economic growth of the organization. In other words, leadership is responsible for what the organization must do to remain economically viable. In the process of maintaining economic viability, a participative environment should exist in order to gain the support and commitment of the employees. In addition, effective Operations management requires:

☆ A healthy and competitive work environment;

☆ A judicious reward and incentive system;

☆ Independence in decision making in congruence with the organizational guidelines;

☆ Formality in the procedures;

☆ Flexibility towards change.

Function
The function of Operations management is to provide goods and services to fulfill an anticipated demand on a routine and timely basis. Due to the quantitative nature of the function, the performance of the Operations management can be evaluated on the basis of physical and economic considerations.[8,19] The criteria of physical performances are those related to the quantity and the quality of the work produced. Whereas those related to the economic considerations are the measures of how effectively the resources were utilized to achieve the overall objectives of the organization. The economic considerations include timing and location of the production, along with the equipment, material, energy and labour utilization. All of these considerations must be converted to common economic terms in order to evaluate the contribution of the resources toward the organization's objectives.

The objectives of the Operations are well defined and, for the most part, are quantifiable, which simplifies the evaluation. Similarly, the performance is also measurable in terms of how well the management handles the conversion process that transforms the inputs into the desired outputs. This implies that the working model and performance criteria of the Operations management are well established. Moreover, because the structure which forms the basis of management control is well established, implementation of the working philosophy of Operations management is facilitated.

Characteristics of Operations Management
The evaluation of Operations management is much easier compared to that of R & D management. Most of the variables in Operations management are quantitative and therefore can be readily measured and appraised. The leadership function of planning, as in any other management situation, is very

important in the operational environment. Unlike R & D, where most of the future direction of the organization is prescribed by the scientists and researchers working within the corporate philosophy, Operations management has the primary responsibility for this function. However, the planning function of 'What has to be done', performed by the top management may not be interpreted to imply non-participation by the employees. The employees participation is very important in 'How it could be done', primarily because they have the proper expertise and definite interests in the area. The absence of participation in the latter situation can very likely result in low morale, lack of commitment to the work, and eventually lower productivity. The other requirement in the smooth functioning of Operations management is the presence of well defined functional boundaries. Within the boundaries there is tremendous room for employee participation which will enhance the smooth working of the operating unit. Further, there is need for the cooperation and participation between the operating units. Such linkages are important from macro perspective and they eventually reduce the need for a strict control system, thereby improving productivity. The organizational structure must provide for such defined channels by which such cooperation can be achieved.

Table 3 provides a pair wise comparison of 13 elements between the two management systems—R & D and Operations. The comparison of these elements will create a strong understanding of the organization before and after the change beneficial in making a smooth transition.

Application to NASA
NSTS needs to determine its goals and objectives and to have them accepted and understood throughout its workforce. Without goals and objectives, the organization is in danger of becoming a directionless program. In addition, some effort must be expended to get the people to sign on to the program. Goals and objectives provide purpose. Without purpose there is nothing for the members of the organization to sign on to, commit to, or to work for.

As of now, it is not apparent that a thorough set of goals and objectives exist at the NSTS. Related to this question is the question of what is hoped to be gained by the utilization of the shuttle resource. Whatever the overall strategy, goals, and objectives may be, they should be well defined if the program does not wish to lose direction.

Further, in order to become operational, NASA must realize that some of their hiring and training practices must change. As pointed out by the demographic study, NASA has had a recent workforce reduction. Also, the employees in the workforce are mainly practiced in R & D methods. In addition, the people who do R & D and the

Table 3. Characteristics chart of R & D vs operational management

Elements of organization	R & D management	Operational management
(1) Objectives and targets	☆ Discovering and furthering knowledge under corporate planning. ☆ Provide technical services to functional departments. ☆ Objectives are generally defined as opposed to means. ☆ Looking for significant breakthroughs.	☆ Fullfilment of well defined purpose which are reason for its creation and existance. ☆ Achievement of the economic balance between demand and resources. ☆ Looking for minor changes in incremental fashion. ☆ Concerned about stability of the system.
(2) Organizational structure	☆ Fragmented: Divisional, Functional, and Flexible. ☆ Allows easy transfer of information and personnel.[10]	☆ Hierarchical. ☆ Specialized, and clearly defined tasks.
(3) System hierarchies	☆ Authority is based upon the technical expertise.[7] ☆ Commitment to the task is negotiated.	☆ Authority is based upon the organizational position.[7] ☆ Responsibilities are mostly accepted.
(4) Leadership behaviour	☆ Responsible to provide input to the strategic planning on a proactive basis, and not solely reactively.[6] ☆ Provide proper career development programs for scientists and researchers. ☆ Provide behavioural and technical support at all levels.	☆ Provide motivation and the targets. for achievement. ☆ Unity of command. ☆ Provide technical guidance on how and what is to be performed.
(5) System management	☆ Easy access to resources. ☆ No short term work pressures. ☆ Corporate strategy must be driven without long formal process. ☆ Self directed and mostly responsible for own work. ☆ Open discussions. ☆ Friendly competition. ☆ Decentralized power base.	☆ Defined/restricted access to resources. ☆ Institutional organizational channels. ☆ R & D and ventures must be tied-in with other growth oriented activities. ☆ Worker is a part of the whole; guidelines are therefore necessary for coordinating activities. ☆ More focused power base.
(6) Performance criteria	☆ Long-term, risk/reward oriented on new businesses. ☆ Encourages the strategic innovation.	☆ Short-term, result oriented on existing businesses. ☆ Short-term evaluation programs are used where external factors are easily predictable.
(7) Reward system	☆ Recognition, status, and more complex assignments.[10]	☆ Financial and hierarchical progression.[10]
(8) Communication system	☆ Across the major operating units.[10] ☆ Mostly informal networks of communication. ☆ Communication at low level.	☆ Within major operating unit. ☆ Lateral communication is too specialized and at the high levels. ☆ Formal communication network.
(9) Information system	☆ Forward and outward oriented towards future needs. ☆ Large amounts of the data received and processed.	☆ Highly structured towards the need of existing businesses.[10] ☆ Minimum amount of information is handled.
(10) Flexibility	☆ Long-term commitment to the projects. ☆ Flexible control of people. ☆ Mostly undirected activity. ☆ Room for creativity.	☆ Short-term schedule of the changes. ☆ Structured job description. ☆ Limited undirected activity. ☆ Flexibility to allow room for productivity.
(11) Work environment	☆ Friendly, with respect for peers. ☆ Working with, instead of working for. ☆ Intellectual freedom. ☆ Flexibility to some extent in organizational rules.	☆ Competitive and target oriented. ☆ Structured work schedules. ☆ Conformance to organizational rules. ☆ Formal work environment.
(12) Cultural climate	☆ Motivation by peer recognition and job satisfaction.[23] ☆ Internalized standards, as a result of extensive training. ☆ Collegial approval sought; often based upon long run quality.[7]	☆ Competitive and financially oriented. ☆ Motivated by rewards, job satisfaction, recognition of work and authority. ☆ Established norms for the overall organizational rationality; often based on short term efficiency. ☆ High work pressure.
(13) Political climate	☆ Loyal to profession and organization; seek collegial approval and external recognition; identify with goals, values and incentives of profession.[9] ☆ Referent, information and expertise is the source of power for people with high maturity.	☆ Loyal to organization; seek super-ordinate approval and recognition; identify with goals, values and incentives of organization. ☆ Organizational participants are in contest for resources and their control.

people who do operations are two different sets of people. The people who do well in managing transition programs may well be a different set yet. The usual programs for employee control and change such as attrition, turnover, and rehires will be of some use here. However, the bulk of the employees will have to be trained in the new ways. This training is going to be perhaps the major component of the transition program.

Step 3: How Do We Get There?

When applied to the Creativity Phase, the answer to 'How Do We Get There?' is reached by a consummate understanding of the Four Step Analysis, the transition life cycle, and the transition curve. Further, the answer to this question is in fact the essence of this paper.

The basic strategy of the concepts we have been presenting herein is to overlay or integrate the four step analysis on the transition life cycle which has, in turn, been integrated into the transition curve. See Figure 2. While the fit between these three pieces may not always be exact, at the very least, a more complete picture of a transition strategy is determined. Further, it is the transition managers, along with all people involved in the change process, that are the missing pieces. Therefore, some changes must be made to ensure that all necessary people get committed to facilitate a smooth transition program.

When applied to later phases in the life cycle of the transition, the answer to this question would be found, again, after considering the present state (where the organization is in the transition), the future state (including new, or changed, objectives and goals), and the activities and objectives of the different phases of the transition life cycle until the Stabilization Phase is completed.

Step 4: How Badly Do We Want to Get There?

Before a model is chosen for the transition, the organization should answer the final question of the Four Step Analysis. The answer to this question decides the amount of resources to be expended and the amount of disturbance in the organization caused by the transition. The answer will also help to uncover various uncertainties in the technical, political, cultural, managerial, and economic facets of the organization. Noel M. Tichy states that whenever a change is made in the organization, the technical, political and cultural aspects of the organization should be considered.[25] However, he does not provide a guiding strategy for consideration of these aspects.

We have found that a large degree of uncertainty in any one of these facets would suggest a conservative change for transition.[13] Conversely, no facet having a particular large uncertainty degree would suggest a quicker, more radical change.

There have been many models developed which consider different types of transition management strategies. In a previous manuscript,[16] Hunsucker, Law and Sitton have described several of these strategies—for a more thorough description of these models we strongly refer the reader to this manuscript. Two areas of concern in the development of a transition program are the Size of the Transition Increment and the Shape of the Transition Management Structure.

The Size of the Transition Increment reflects the magnitude of the changes the organization undergoes as the transition moves through its life cycle. The Dissipative Change Model (DCM) and the Logical Increment Model (LI) are two extremes in the size of the transition increment. DCM can be

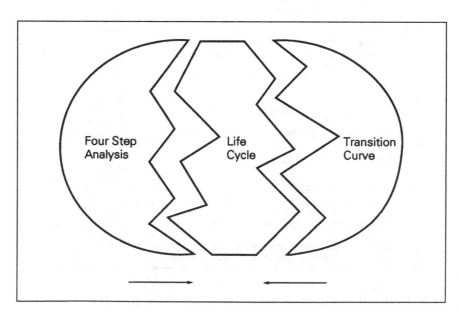

Figure 2. Transition management concept

used when a seemingly instantaneous change, i.e. radical change, is necessary.[2] On the other hand, LI provides an evolutionary process for making changes and proposes that such changes be made in small increments.[20] The selection of the Transition Increment is mainly a reflection on the technical/ political/cultural uncertainties.[13]

The Shape of the Transition Management Structure makes provisions for the management of the change program. Three different ways of managing the transition have been researched. One method of managing transition consists of utilizing the current management to manage the change—Managerial Dual Role. Two methods involve the creation of a transition committee to control the transition—Parallel Track Method and Hand Over Team. The selection of the Transition Management Structure is mainly a reflection of the managerial/economic uncertainties.[13]

Application to NASA
Most of the managers for NSTS are engineers. As a general rule, engineers are relatively comfortable with the technical aspects of a project. However, for a transition to occur, the cultural and political aspects must be considered as well. To this end, it is not clear that NASA understands the significant cultural difference between R & D and operations. As an example of this difference, the motivation for doing 'good' work is extremely different in these two environments.

So for NASA, the cultural and political aspects of a major transition perhaps provide the most difficulty. The managers will simply be uncomfortable with dealing with these two and may therefore tend to ignore them. This could of course prove to be a major stumbling block to a successful transition. Consequently, precautions should be made at all times to consider and handle these factors.

Because there is a high level of political and cultural uncertainty, the planned change should be a conservative one. Consequently, the size of the transition increment NSTS should use for its proposed change is the Logical Incremental Model.

Further, NSTS will have to decide what structure it wishes to use to manage the transition. One thing is reasonably clear: the people who manage the transition should have a major stake in the organization after the transition. This concept is related to the idea that if a proposal team is successful in their bid for a contract, then they should have significant responsibility in the management of the contract. More than likely, a transition team would have to have representation from all the major centres and program elements. In addition, the leadership would have to come from the NASA headquarters.

Considerations for the Life Cycle Maturation

Upon determining the method by which the transition is to occur, that portion of the Creativity Phase—dealing with the creation of a mechanism for making the change—is completed. Similarly, the Four Step Analysis as it is applied to the Creativity Phase is completed from the determining of the method of change.

However, as this is just the planning stage, we offer a warning. As we have suggested, there are three additional stages in the transition life cycle. Therefore, the transition management team must be fully aware of the objectives and actions to be taken during these phases. Further, the transition program itself goes through changes. Due to the variation in the dynamics of the two environments, the organization is susceptible to continual transformation until the desired environment is reached. Thus, where one concentrates on the proposed transition method, conceivably it becomes apparent that the study of change is an ongoing one. Therefore, by consideration of the life cycle of transition, management has a way of monitoring the change and can thus determine proper actions to take as the life cycle matures.

Conclusion

When an organization wishes to move from an R & D environment to one of Operations, a shift of this magnitude warrants the development of a strategy to manage this transition. The consideration of the Four Step Analysis as it applies to the four phases of the transition life cycle provides a structure in the development of this strategy.

In the R & D to Operations shift, the diversity of the two systems is so remarkable that a consummate understanding of the two congregates is necessary before planning the transformation. This consummate understanding is reached by answering the first two questions of the Four Step Analysis and presenting, if you will, a side by side comparison of the two systems. Once the organization understands the current and future states it can concentrate on the planning of the movement. This planning process is facilitated through the answering of the remaining two questions of the Four Step Analysis.

Finally, there are several change models available in the literature. The strategy chosen for making the transition is selected, upon consideration of the final questions of the analysis, as a function of the uncertainty in the technical, political, and cultural (T/P/C) dimensions of the organization; i.e. the model is situation unique. The strategy is also selected according to the level of managerial and economic uncertainty. As the transition moves though the remaining three phases, the analysis must be repeated.

The concepts presented in this paper are certainly not a complete description of the change process, neither are they a 'blueprint' which, if followed, will guarantee success. They are, as they claim to be, a theoretical process useful in formalizing the initial planning stages of a transition. As such, they have been of value in assisting NASA in the initial strategic considerations of moving the shuttle program to a more operational nature.

Acknowledgement—This research was partially supported by the National Aeronautics and Space Administration (NASA) through Grant No. 9–BC4–19–6–1P.

References

(1) Linda S. Ackerman, Transition management: an in-depth look at managing complex change, Organizational Dynamics (1982).

(2) Gloria Barczak, Charles Smith and David Wilemon, Managing change in high technology organizations, Unpublished Paper Presented at TIMS/ORSA Joint National Meeting, Dallas, Texas, 26–28 November (1984).

(3) Stewart P. Blake, *Managing for Responsive Research and Development,* W.H. Freeman and Company, San Fransisco (1980).

(4) Shaukat A. Brah, John L. Hunsucker and Japhet S. Law, R & D to operations—a path for transition, Working Paper, University of Houston, Houston, Texas (1986).

(5) Joseph L. C. Cheng, Organizational staffing and productivity in basic and applied research: a comparative study, *IEEE Transactions on Engineering Management,* **EM31** (1), (1984).

(6) K. Colmen, M. Percel and J. Piniella, Managing growth strategies work: the changing role of R & D and new ventures, *Research Management,* **27** (4), (1984).

(7) Patrick E. Conner, Professionals in organizations: some research suggestions, *IEEE Transactions on Engineering Management,* **EM31** (1), (1984).

(8) Kostas N. Dervitsiotis, *Operations Management,* McGraw-Hill Book Company, New York (1981).

(9) David D. Dill and Alan W. Pearson, The effectiveness of project managers: implications of a political model of influence, *IEEE Transactions on Engineering Management,* **EM31** (3), (1984).

(10) Gian F. Frontini and Peter R. Richardson, Design and demonstration: the key to industrial innovation, *Sloan Management Review,* **25** (4), Summer (1984).

(11) Vincent L. Gregory, Managing research to improve efficiency and productivity, *Research Management,* **27** (2), (1984).

(12) John L. Hunsucker and Japhet S. Law, An investigation of transitional management problems for the NSTS at NASA, NASA Contract No. 9-BC4-19-6-1P, Unpublished Annual Report, University of Houston, Houston, Texas, January (1986).

(13) John L. Hunsucker and Japhet S. Law, An investigation of transitional management problems for the NSTS at NASA, NASA Contract No. 9-BC4-19-6-1P, Unpublished Annual Report, University of Houston, Houston, Texas, January (1987).

(14) John L. Hunsucker, An investigation of transitional management problems for the NSTS at NASA, NASA Contract No. 9-BC4-19-6-1P, Unpublished Annual Report, University of Houston, Houston, Texas, January (1988).

(15) John L. Hunsucker, An investigation of transitional management problems for the NSTS at NASA, NASA Contract No. 9-BC4-19-6-1P, Unpublished Annual Report, University of Houston, Houston, Texas, January (1989).

(16) John L. Hunsucker, Japhet S. Law and Randall W. Sitton, Transition management—a structured perspective, *IEEE Transactions on Engineering Management,* **EM35** (3), (1988).

(17) Michael J. C. Martin, *Managing Technological Innovation and Entrepreneurship,* Reston Publishing Company, Reston, Virginia (1984).

(18) Martin R. Moser, Managerial planning in R & D settings, *Managerial Planning,* **33** (3), (1984).

(19) William H. Newman, Charles E. Summer and E. Kirby Warren, *The Process of Management,* Prentice-Hall, Inc., Englewood Cliffs, New Jersey (1972).

(20) James Brian Quinn, *Strategies for Change,* Richard D. Irwin, Inc., Homewood, Illinois (1980).

(21) Robert E. Quinn and Kim Cameron, Organizational life cycles and shifting criteria of effectiveness: some preliminary evidence, *Management Science,* **29** (1), (1983).

(22) Daniel D. Roman, *Research and Development Management: The Economics and Administration of Technology,* Meredith Corporation, New York (1968).

(23) Wickham Skinner, Blind spot in strategic planning?, *Management Review,* **73** (10), (1984).

(24) Wyne Smeltz and Barrington Cross, Towards a profile of the creative R & D professional, *IEEE Transactions on Engineering Management,* **EM31** (1), (1984).

(25) Noel M. Tichy, *Managing Strategic Change,* John Wiley & Sons, Inc., New York (1983).

PART FIVE

Strategic Planning in Non-Profit and Voluntary Organizations

Strategic Planning for the World Wildlife Fund

G. J. Medley

WWF United Kingdom introduced strategic planning in 1978. In the next 9 years, as a result of planned actions, cohesive team work and clear objectives, the organization increased net funds by a factor of 5 and productivity by a factor of 6. Careful analysis, on an annual basis, of the organization's strengths and weaknesses and the opportunities available in the marketplace, led to the development of major strategies. Action plans designed to achieve and implement these strategies concluded the process which is described in detail.

Introduction

The National Organization of the World Wildlife Fund operating in the United Kingdom (WWF U.K.), is a 'not for profit' organization registered as a charity. It was founded in 1961 with the object of promoting education and research on the conservation of world fauna and flora, water, soils and other natural resources. In its early years, it developed like the majority of 'not for profit' organizations using relatively low-paid staff who had a concern for the charity's objectives. By 1973 gross income had risen to around £750,000 per annum and it stayed in this region for the next 5 years.

In 1977 a new Chairman of Trustees, Sir Arthur Norman, was appointed who was, himself, chairman of a major British Corporation. He identified the necessity of bringing in sound business management to develop the charity and when the previous Chief Executive Officer (CEO) left in April 1977, he searched for a Senior Executive who had already demonstrated a sound and successful business career. The author took up appointment as CEO of WWF U.K. on 1 January 1978, arriving to a relatively demoralized staff who had been without direct leadership for 9 months.

G. J. Medley is Director of the World Wildlife Fund United Kingdom.

Preparing for Change

The first task was to identify, from the existing staff of 70, those who would fit in with a sound business approach compared to those who were working because of their interest and dedication to conservation. Whilst there was a need for good conservationists in the project departments, those in the fundraising areas needed to be capable of taking a wholly professional and sound business approach to their work. A structural reorganization took place in September 1978 and coincided with the introduction of strategic planning based on a 'management by objectives' (MBO) process developed by the author in his previous assignment as CEO of the subsidiary of a large multi-national. This was the first time that WWF U.K. had taken a hard look at its operations and it turned out to be a most revealing exercise.

The management team consisting of the Heads of each of the organization's departments of Promotions, Membership, Regional, Information, Education, Finance and Administration under the Chairmanship of the Director, met for the strategic planning exercises for two days at the end of September 1978.

To help with these exercises we were very fortunate to have the late Ron Felstead, a member of the Urwick Orr Partnership, who had been a considerable assistance to the author in introducing MBO in his previous assignment. Ron's quiet, clear, concise and informative control of the discussions played a very substantial part in converting a somewhat sceptical management team to a realization that strategic planning was not only an essential to success but also a major annual therapy and a forum at which matters could be brought out into the open which, for the rest of the year, were difficult to address.

87

Photo by courtesy of WWF and Behram Kapadia

Plate 1. Project 'Tiger'. WWF's first major conservation success. At the turn of the century there were 80,000 tigers in India which had declined to only 2000 by 1972. Today there are estimated to be over 4000 tigers in 11 nature reserves in India

Deciding on the Purpose

The first essential was deciding the purpose of WWF U.K. The purpose is the reference point which makes possible the formulation of clear and realistic objectives. Prior to the strategic planning exercise the general view was that WWF U.K. was a conservation organization. After some considerable discussion however, it was recognized that in fact WWF U.K. was a fundraising business but that it also had as its purpose the proper spending of the funds raised. In 1978 the team decided that the purpose was 'to raise the maximum funds possible from U.K. sources and to ensure that the funds are used wisely for the benefit of conservation of the natural environment and renewable natural resources with emphasis on endangered species and habitats'.

Key Areas

Having decided the purpose, attention was then turned to the result-influencing areas of the organization, specific areas in which success would contribute significantly to improve results or areas in which failure would have an adverse impact on results. The team were asked to give free range to their thinking and a list of some 60 possible areas emerged on the blackboard. Further analysis of these showed that many of them were in fact overlapping or similar and a final list of nine was chosen.

It is interesting to see that these nine can be matched to the more usual designations found when this process is followed in industry. 'Marketing' is the

Photo by courtesy of WWF and Woodward

Plate 2. The Arabian oryx. The Arabian oryx was hunted to extinction in the wild but fortunately a few animals were in captivity in San Diego, California. Selected individuals from this captive herd were re-introduced in Oman and in Jordan and are now thriving back in their natural habitat under the watchful eye of local tribesmen

same word. 'Public Awareness' and 'Fund Status' relate to customer and shareholder perceptions of a business. 'Innovation' is the same concept as research and development and, most importantly, 'Net Funds' is the same as profitability. The full list is shown in Figure 1.

```
1. Marketing
2. Public Awareness
3. Fund Status
4. Quality of Application
5. Use of Personal Resources
6. Use of Financial and Physical Resources
7. Administrative Control
8. Innovation
9. Net Funds
```

Figure 1. WWF U.K. key areas 1978

Each key area was then taken in turn and subjected to a strengths, weaknesses, opportunities and threats exercise. This systematic review identified the internal strengths and weaknesses of the organization and examined the external environment to identify the opportunities that might be available and the threats that might exist.

Photo by courtesy of WWF and Vollmar

Plate 3. Pére David's deer. A similar situation to that of the Arabian oryx affected Pére David's Deer which were re-introduced to their natural habitat in China in 1987

The marketing strengths of WWF U.K. in 1978 were seen largely to be its emotive and visually appealing message, its 'Panda' logo and the uniqueness of its work. It was weak in its lack of a large donor base, its poor record on innovation and its lack of marketing penetration.

The rising awareness of the need to conserve the earth's natural resources, the size of the market-place and the general increase in disposable income, all presented opportunities to be tapped. On the other hand, competitive charities were also growing and some legislation proposals threatened certain freedoms to fundraising in specific areas, notably national lotteries.

In the key area of fund status, WWF U.K.'s international connections and scientific authority were seen as strengths offset by the weakness that the organization was not itself active in conservation work nor was it campaigning.

A major effort to devise and publicize a strategy for world conservation was to be carried out in the near future by WWF's international scientific sister organization, The International Union for the Conservation of Nature and Natural Resources (IUCN) with the financial backing of WWF and the United Nations Environmental Programme (UNEP) and this was seen as a major opportunity to improve further the public perception of WWF U.K. A concomitant threat was the Government's disinterest in the environment and its reluctance to enhance existing legislation in this field.

The full lists of strengths, weaknesses, opportunities and threats in the areas of marketing and fund status are shown in Figures 2 and 3.

Agreeing Strategies

At this point in the exercise, comprehensive answers to questions such as: (a) Where are we now? (b) What do we think will happen in the future? and (c) Where do we want to go? had been determined.

It was now necessary to devise guidelines—termed strategies—which would be developed for all future actions—a strategy is a guide for action. Clearly the marketing strategies concentrated on improving those areas of fundraising that were perceived to be weaknesses. Thus the first strategy was to increase membership and the second to increase the number and yield effectiveness of WWF's volunteer supporter groups around the country. Business would be concentrated on through effective commercial promotions and licensing the 'panda' trade mark and increased efforts would be made to raise income from business and charitable trusts. As the donor list had been identified as a major weakness, significant efforts would be made to build these lists. At that time, the cleaned list yielded 12,000 members

Photo by courtesy of RAF Kinloss

Plate 4. Sea eagles. Sea eagles used to breed in Scotland but no breeding pairs had been sighted for many years until WWF collaborated with the Nature Conservancy Council to re-introduce them to the Island of Rhum. The RAF assisted in this project by flying a pair of eagles from Norway for the re-introduction programme

STRENGTHS	WEAKNESSES
Image	Image
Logo	Small Membership
Charity	Poor Lists
Emotive Appeal	Communications
Visual Appeal	Inadequate Intermediaries
Achievements	Transience of Fashion
Communications	Reference to Cost: Income Ratio
Schools Lecture Service	Conservatism
Flexible	Inadequacy of Follow Through
Technical Support	Lack of Innovation
Diverse	Lack of Physical Resources
In Fashion	Scientific Inflexibility
Cost: Income Ratio	Inadequate Market Penetration
Recognition of Need	No Active Conservation
Awareness of Market Research	No Audio-visual Equipment
Unique	Photographic Resources
Caravan	
OPPORTUNITIES	**THREATS**
£700m Given to Charity in 1977	Competition
Schools	Legislation
Legislation	Economic Climate
Better Positioning	
Current Events	
Economic Clinate	
Untapped Sources	
Growing Awareness of Conservation Importance	

Figure 2. WWF U.K. SWOT analysis: key area—marketing

STRENGTHS	WEAKNESSES
Achievements	Non-controversial
Clear Aims and Programmes	Snob Charity
Non-political	No Active Conservation
Practical	Lush Literature
Affiliate of Largest Most Effective Conservation Organization	Trading Company
Scientific Authority	
1001	
Elitism	
Good Financial Standing	
Management	
OPPORTUNITIES	THREATS
World Conservation Strategy	Possible Defeat by Government on Major Conservation Issue
Lack of Conservation Legislation	Adverse Publicity
Confused Conservation Ethics	
Global 2000	

Figure 3. WWF U.K. SWOT analysis: key area—fund status

together with a further 25,000 trading customers. The full strategies in the key area of marketing are shown in Figure 4.

This exercise covering all the nine key areas took 2 days, at the end of which WWF U.K. had a document setting out its clear objectives for the immediate and medium-term future.

The last key area—'net funds'—equates to a corporation's profitability. The achievement of the net funds objectives would show the progress of the organization. Net fund objectives were therefore

agreed by the management team for the coming 3 years.

Action Plans

The next part of the process was to devise the actions needed to achieve the strategies. Each department was asked to take each of the strategies and write down the actions they proposed in the coming year to fulfil the strategy. Clearly a number of strategies were not applicable to all departments whereas others had impact across all departments. The final

1. We Will Increase Our Membership and Improve Services to Members
2. We Will Increase the Number and Yield Effectiveness of Supporters' Groups
3. We Will Undertake a Research Programme to Asertain the Best Marketing Opportunities in Schools and Will Then Increase Fundraising in This Sector
4. We Will Increase the Yield Effectiveness of Commercial Promotions and Licensing
5. We Will Liaise Closely With WWF International to Improve the Yield Effectiveness in the United Kingdom of International Promotions
6. We Will Make a Concerted Effort to Increase Substantially Our Income from Business and Charitable Trusts
7. We Will Improve the Profitability of Our Trading Operations and Will Search for New Wayes of Increasing Income from Trading Opportunities
8. We Will Ensure That We are Able to Take Advantage of Special Opportunities for Raising Funds
9. We Will Build Our Lists in Order to Maximize Fundraising
10. We Will Seek to Further Improve and Widen Our Market Image
11. We Will Build up Active Key Contacts in Show Business, Commerce, and Conservation and Programme Them Centrally
12. We Will Ensure That We Have Adequate and Effective Audio-visual Equipment
13. We Will Ensure That We Use the Caravan to the Greatest Advantage
14. We Will Ensure That WWF Photographic Material is Made More Readily Available for Fundraising Purposes
15. We Will Encourage Donations in Covenant Form
16. We Will Increase Our Share of the Legacy Market

Figure 4. WWF U.K. strategies: key area—marketing

Photo by courtesy of WWF and Dr C. F. Tydeman

Plate 5. Grey seals. The United Kingdom is home to more than a quarter of the world's population of grey seals. These seals were being hunted for their pelts and were threatened with a severe decline in population. Harnessing public opinion, legislation and Parliament, WWF were able to ensure a ban on the hunting of these seals until population levels were restored

action plans from each department were amalgamated into a single document and this became the working forward plans for WWF U.K.

Budgeting to Meet Objectives

At the end of this strategic planning exercise, written documentation existed to show what WWF U.K. was hoping to achieve in all the key areas and how each department was going to take action to

fulfil these strategies. At this stage however, there were no financial figures determined. The second part of the planning process involved the compilation of departmental budgets designed to achieve the strategies. Each department produced both income and expenditure budgets for the coming year and forecasts for the next 2 years. The departmental budgets were then consolidated to produce the budget for WWF U.K. It was a surprise to most members of the management team that

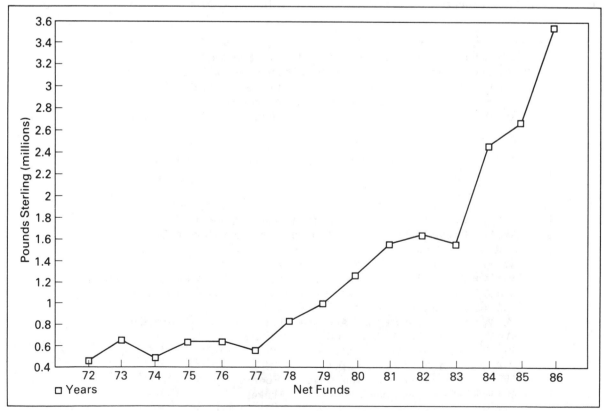

Figure 5. WWF U.K. net funds

Photo by courtesy of WWF and Paul Schauenberg

Plate 6. Tropical rainforests. Tropical rainforests are being destroyed at the rate of 100 acres every minute. Not only are the forests part of the world's natural heritage but they contain over 50 per cent of all known plant species, many of which have not yet been described to science. Destruction of the forest could therefore be destroying plants that might have the potential for considerable benefit to mankind. Forty per cent of prescription drugs come from plant origins and most of the world's major food crops rely on wild relatives for cross-breeding.
WWF has campaigned internationally to bring the plight of the tropical forests to the attention of Governments, industry and the general public with the result that a number of large areas of forest have been set aside as reserves, a more responsible attitude to forest products is emerging and the International Timber Trade Organization has recognized the necessity of using forest products only on a sustainable basis. The Korup Forest in the Cameroon is a project taken over and managed by WWF U.K. in 1987

when the departmental budgets were amalgamated the overall net fund projected for the budget year was extremely close to the objective net fund set in September as the final stage in the strategic planning exercise. This came as no surprise to the author because in his experience in the subsidiary of a major multi-national, the management team setting itself objectives with considerable 'stretch' produced budgets which met those objectives, and more importantly produced results which came within a

very few percentage points of achieving the budgets.

The setting of objectives in a strategic planning process and the compiling of budgets to achieve those objectives, are of no use without adequate factual information to show progress and achievement. WWF U.K.'s financial management was strengthened and systems set up to provide quarterly reporting by department against budget. At the end of each quarter departmental performance was assessed and where necessary corrective action was taken although the disciplines of budget and assessment of performance against budget led very rapidly to excellent control of expenditure.

The strategic planning exercises have been carried out each year in WWF U.K. and it is interesting to see how the process has evolved. The basic structure has remained unchanged but over the years, a number of key areas have been identified and a number dropped. For example, regional activities became important but when the problems within the regional area were resolved, that area no longer merited the microscopic examination of the planning process. It is also interesting to look at three measures of success and to see how the planning process has helped in the achievement of these successes.

Measures of Success

Net funds is the best measure of success. Net funds remained static between 1972 and 1977 at £400,000–£600,000. After the introduction of strategic planning in 1978, net funds grew steadily although there was a slight decline in 1983 due to an unexpected and unexplainable drop of significant proportions in income from legacies that year. The upward trend was resumed in 1984 and the last 2 years have been exceptional. Figure 5 shows the growth of net funds from 1972 to 1986.

Productivity in WWF U.K. is measured in terms of both gross and net income per employee. Staff numbers at 70 remained fairly constant from 1972 through to 1980 but since then marginal increases have occurred giving staff numbers at the end of 1986 of 85. With the growth in net funds by a factor of some eight times, it is clear that productivity will have increased substantially, as is shown in Figure 6.

At each annual strategic planning meeting net funds are projected forwards for the next budget year and the two following forecast years. Plotting each year's projections produces a matrix and adding to that matrix the actual achieved for each year gives an interesting diagram showing the fluctuations in objectives year on year set by the management team compared to actual achievement.

In the first 3 years, 1978–1980, actuals were remark-

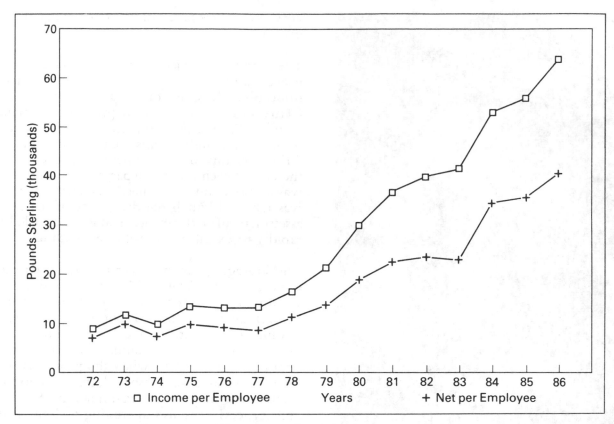

Figure 6. WWF U.K. income per employee–productivity

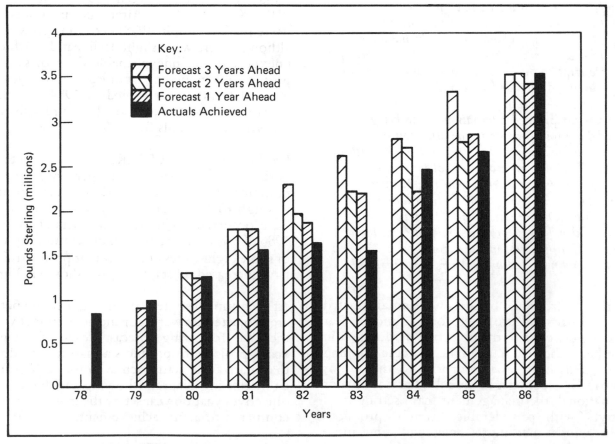

Figure 7. WWF U.K. forecast net funds vs actuals

1978
'To Raise the Maximum Funds Possible from U.K. Sources and to Ensure that the Funds are Used Wisely for the Benefit of Conservation of Renewable Natural Resources, with Emphasis on Endangered Species and Habitats.'

1986
'To Raise the Maximum Net Funds Possible from U.K. Sources and to Ensure that these Funds are Used Wisely for the Benefit of Conservation of Renewable Natural Resources, in Accordance with the Principles of the World Conservation Strategy.'

Figure 8. Statements of purpose compared

1. Marketing	1. Fund-raising
2. Public awareness	2. Reputation
3. Fund Status	3. Implementation of
4. Quality of Application	World Conservation
5. Use of Personnel	Strategy
Resources	4. Use of Personnel and
6. Use of Financial and	Physical Resources
Physical Resources	5. Communications
7. Administrative Control	6. Education
8. Innovation	7. Management
9. Net Funds	8. Lists
	9. Leverage
	10. Net Funds

Figure 9. A comparison of key areas

ably close to projections but in the following period, there were considerable shortfalls against projections which have been corrected in the last 2 years. Actuals now appear to be running ahead of projections which perhaps indicates that inadequate 'stretch' is being placed in the objectives, even though growth in the last 2 years has been considerable. This is clearly seen in Figure 7.

One other measure of success is the growth in the size of the donor list. At the end of 1986, WWF U.K. had 110,000 members and a donor list of 450,000 names. This compares with the 12,000 and 25,000 in 1978.

The purpose of the organization has changed but little and for comparison Figure 8 shows the 1978 purpose and underneath the 1986 purpose. Figure 9 shows the 1978 key areas alongside the 1986 key areas.

Conclusion

When strategic planning was first suggested for WWF U.K. there was a considerable degree of scepticism coupled with a willingness to try a new business method which might bring good results for the organization. After the first year it became clear to the whole management team that the exercise was invaluable, giving an opportunity for the whole team to participate in the forward planning resulting in a feeling of commitment by the whole team to the objectives that had been agreed after full and open discussion. This commitment seemed to transfer itself to other staff members giving the whole organization a sense of purpose and of drive which, coupled with team work, produced the outstanding results that the organization has achieved. It is now inconceivable to think of WWF U.K. working without an annual strategic planning exercise, developing clear strategies in key areas with action plans to achieve those strategies. The success of this method of management by objectives must be seen in the light of WWF U.K.'s performance in the last few years.

Reference
World Conservation Strategy, IUCN, Gland, Switzerland (1980).

PART SIX

Managing Participation

Participative Planning for a Public Service

Timothy Grewe, James Marshall and Daniel E. O'Toole

This article aims to provide managers in public administration with information about strategic planning as a tool for promoting adaptation in a changing environment. The authors' collective experience with strategic planning in the public sector includes facilitating creation of strategic plans for state and local government and non-profit agencies, and their experience has provided the data on which the conclusions drawn are based. They believe in the participative approach to planning and that this approach has benefits for the participants which are as important as the contents of the plan.

In public administration, strategic planning continues to receive increasing attention.[1] A number of factors contribute to this growing interest. Strategic planning focuses on long-recognized crucial management concerns—the need to understand the organization's environment, examine the future, and adapt the agency accordingly. Many public managers realize that if they do not accommodate their agency to a changing environment, organizational change will be based on someone else's plan. The widespread use of strategic planning in the private sector confirms that it is both a feasible and valuable tool for promoting adaptation.

For many public organizations there is an urgent need to adapt. They face continuing fiscal stringency accompanied by unabated if not expanding service demands. Figure 1 depicts the impact of this condition on a public agency. The organization's inability to maintain its revenue base creates greater pressure for increased productivity and reinforces the need to reconsider agency goal(s) and to discern how to accommodate it to this environment. Strategic planning promotes examination of both the fit between agency goals and the environment and potential improvements. In addition, the tool can be used to foster a participative consideration of these areas. The Japanese experience demonstrates

The authors are members of the Graduate Programme in Public Administration at Portland State University.

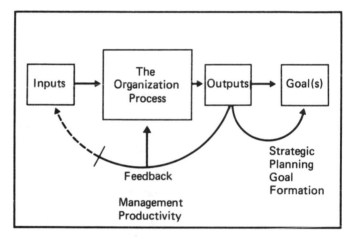

Figure 1. The impact of fiscal stringency on a public agency

the efficacy of a participative management approach, particularly in a resource scarce environment.

Public managers who look to public administration literature for information about this tool find that it does not yet include an in-depth consideration of how to *manage* a strategic planning process, particularly one that involves the participation of more than just the top managers. Only the steps in developing a strategic plan receive attention. How to accomplish the steps is not discussed.[2] Yet this concern is vital to the success of a strategic planning project. A belief in the value of participative strategic planning is not enough. It must be reflected in careful attention to the preparation, design and facilitation of the process.

This article seeks to fill this gap in the literature. The authors' collective experience with strategic planning in the public sector includes facilitating creation of strategic plans for state and local government and non-profit agencies in the Pacific Northwest as well as training managers of several state agencies in how to do strategic planning. One of these projects involved 35 participants in developing the strategic plan. This collective experience has provided us with data about managing and facilitating a strategic planning process. We believe much of this data is pertinent to managing other group process endeavours.

Preparation

Strategic planning entails the creation of a strategic plan—a long-term, co-ordinated plan for meeting goals based on explicit assumptions as well as an investigation of past, present and future conditions. The plan ranges anywhere from 3 to 10 years in length and focuses on the organization's target population, its service area, and potential technological advancements and service modifications necessary to meet the changing needs of its service clientele.

Figure 2 is an example of a strategic plan outline. It indicates the general directions the Portland (Oregon) Fire Bureau will pursue in order to attain its strategic goals by 1990 (the end of the time frame) and the year work begins on each direction. This outline is the Bureau's action agenda (in general, conceptual terms) for the future. Top management can use this outline to oversee the planning and managing of a more specific set of action plans (i.e. tactical actions) that will implement the directions.

A fully developed strategic plan contains both the strategic directions and the tactical actions. It pinpoints specific objectives and action steps to attain the organization's goals through a specified date. It identifies what is to be done, by whom, and in what order, to adjust the agency to its probable future environment(s) and attain its goals by the end of the plan's time frame. This plan can lead to the assignment of responsibilities and completion dates and to monitoring progress. Careful consideration of a number of factors prior to the start of the strategic planning process can help achieve such a plan.

PORTLAND FIRE BUREAU

1984–1985   1985–1988   1986–1987   1987–1988   1988–1989   1989–1990

1. **More** Emphasis on Emergency Medical Services _____

2. **More** Emphasis on Hazardous Materials _____

3. **More** Emphasis on Training _____

4. **More** Emphasis on Resource Management _____

5.   **More** Emphasis on Prevention _____

6. **More** Emphasis on Interagency Coordination of Emergency Service Delivery Systems _____

7. **More** Emphasis on Alternative Financing _____

8.   **More** Emphasis on Public Relations _____

9.   **More** Emphasis on Minority Recruitment _____

10. **More** Emphasis on Strategic and Other Planning _____

11.   **More** Emphasis on Public Education _____

12.   **More** Emphasis on Legal Affairs _____

13.   **More** Emphasis on Productivity _____

14.   **More** Emphasis on Technological Advances _____

15. **Same** Emphasis on Fire Suppression _____

16. **Same** Emphasis on Planning for Annexation and/or Consolidation _____

17. **Same** Emphasis on Public Services: Non-emergency _____

18. **Same** Emphasis on Labour–Management Relations _____

19. **Same** Emphasis on Bureau Re-organization _____

20. **Same** Emphasis on Decision-making _____

21. **New** Activity: Leadership Role in Regional Disaster Planning and Emergency Services _____

22.   **New** Activity: Exercise of Political Influence _____

23. **New** Activity: Establish Critical Staffing Levels _____

Figure 2. Strategic plan for 1990

The Facilitator's Role

We have found that the complexity of participative strategic planning warrants the involvement of a facilitator who is knowledgeable about strategic planning and skilful in fostering group processes. Establishment and clarification of the facilitator's role is an important initial step. While we consider the various facets of this role throughout this article, some comments about its general features are pertinent here.

The facilitator plays a key part in preparing for as well as managing the strategic planning process. In the preparation phase this role includes ensuring that top management understands strategic planning and the implications of its use and helping devise a design for the process of developing the strategic plan. During the strategic planning process the facilitator's responsibility centres on implementing the design and managing the process participants to go through to create *their* plan. The facilitator does not participate in specifying the plan's contents and must resist the impulse to do so and sometimes, the pressure from participants to 'give us the plan'. This approach and participant perception of the facilitator as a 'neutral' concerning the project, i.e. viewed as not having an agenda regarding the outcome, promote their involvement in the process and focus on the task and their ownership of the final product.

Top Management Risk

Top management needs to be aware at the beginning that strategic planning is a risk for the organization and its management. The participants in the process and others in the organization assume that its final product will lead to action. This action involves top management pursuit of the directions indicated by the strategic planning process. Hence, this tool's viability depends upon top management's willingness and ability to risk acting on the basis of the plan. Strategic planning should not be undertaken without top management's recognition and acceptance of this risk.

Another initial issue top management faces concerns the potential threat strategic planning poses for participants' jobs. Participants may be less open and honest about sensing the environment and identifying appropriate organizational adaptations if they feel the results may jeopardize their jobs. Any steps top management can take at the beginning to enhance participant job security can help avoid the tendency to 'play safe'.

The Procedures Followed

Careful preparation includes creating an appropriate design of the process for developing the strategic plan. The major purpose of the design is to have the plan emerge logically and consistently from the process. Creation of the design involves both the facilitators and top management. The facilitators present a model of the process. The final design is the result of the modifications and fine tuning made by both parties to adapt the facilitators' model to the needs of the particular situation.

A number of model designs for developing a strategic plan are available.[3] Figure 3 depicts an overview of the model we have found useful. The specific steps the participants follow in order to move through the process are:

(1) Setting the time frame for the strategic plan (e.g. 1984–1990).
(2) Identification of the organization's *existing* mission, goals and organizational structure.
(3) Specifying the values that underlie the agency's operation (e.g. loyalty to the public and fiscal responsibility).
(4) Conducting the 'futures research' necessary to identify and consider key levers/elements in the agency's future environment (e.g. an expenditure or tax limitation).

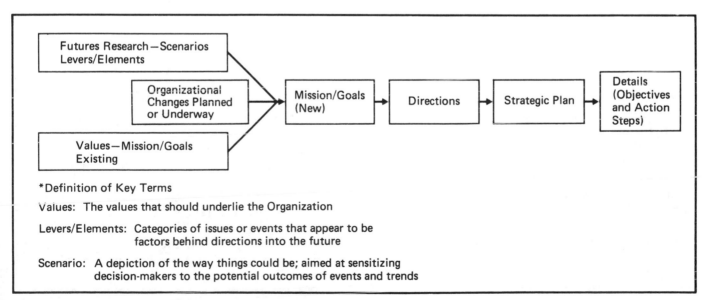

Figure 3. An overview of the strategic planning process

(5) Formulating the scenarios the agency will face at the end of the time frame.

(6) Identifying new or substantially modified goals derived from the scenarios and/or stated values.

(7) Identifying general activities/directions (current and new) needed to adjust the organization to the scenario(s) (e.g. what we need more/the same/less of).

(8) Identifying opportunities in the scenario(s) the agency can use to achieve its mission and goals.

(9) Identifying problems in the scenarios the agency must manage, avoid, and/or solve.

(10) Noting any proposed efforts to change elements in the scenarios.

(11) Listing specific actions derived from this analysis. Decide on the basis of steps 7–10 the organization's specific future activities.

(12) Sequence the proposed activities during the time frame of the strategic plan.

The Time Span

Completion of the strategic planning process requires approximately 4 to 6 full-day sessions. The variance in the number of sessions needed is due to the nature of the group developing the plan (size and cohesiveness) and the amount of detail desired in the final product. The actual time span can vary considerably. Among the possible arrangements for these sessions are:

☆ A short period—completion of the plan within 1–2 weeks.

☆ A medium period—plan completion within 1–2 months. Sessions are about 1 week apart.

☆ A long period—completion of the plan requires at least 4 months. Sessions are approximately 1 month apart.

We prefer the medium period. It allows enough time to obtain additional data for futures research; affords participants time to digest what is going on and share their experience with and receive input from other organization members; and still avoids problems that may arise with a long period (participants forgetting and losing interest). Also the plan is ready in a reasonable amount of time.

Selection and Preparation of Participants

Participant selection is a key element of preparing for the strategic planning process. It gives top management an opportunity to develop a participative approach toward environmental sensing and organizational adaptation. Use of such an approach enhances the acceptability of both the tool and its final product in the organization. If only top management participates, then others may view strategic planning as a control device.

One participation issue concerns the role of the top manager. The most appropriate role for the top manager may not always include active involve-

ment in developing the plan. In one strategic planning process the top manager did not directly participate because he believed it would impede others from freely participating. However, he did play an essential role throughout the process—a strong advocate and active supporter of strategic planning.

We try to prepare participants so that they are ready to work when the first session begins. This preparation entails providing them with the following prior to the first session:

☆ A communication from the top manager that notes their selection as a participant and the significance of the strategic planning process and its final product;

☆ A project schedule that contains session dates and activities;

☆ A brief description and overview of the strategic planning process, including definitions of key terms and a flow chart of the steps involved; and

☆ An article that describes the process.[4]

However, undue burdens or disincentives on participants should be avoided. Participants may feel punished if too much preparation is required outside the sessions.

Location and Materials

Two prominent features of our strategic planning processes are participant interaction in various types and sizes of groups and the use of graphics to depict information pertaining to the process and to record and illustrate the participants' tentative and final products. The group processes we use receive attention in a later section of this article. The use of graphics helps in communication and results in a faster decision-making process.[5] Other studies of the use of graphics support our findings.[6]

Both features influence the type of physical setting that is appropriate for a strategic planning process. Moveable chairs and tables permit various group configurations. Blank wall space allows the posting of charts. The graphics approach also requires chart paper, 5×8 in. cards, marking pens, and masking tape. The importance of the physical setting and materials and supplies is more evident when they are not suitable.

Data Base for 'Futures Research'

During the preparation phase the facilitators must develop a set of relevant information participants will use early in the strategic planning process as a basis for doing 'futures research'. This data base is an important ingredient. The scenarios and the eventual plan emerge from the data. It is essential for testing participants' assumptions and possible predetermined scenarios.

The creation of an appropriate data base can be

difficult. At this point all the data needs may not be evident. One virtue of doing strategic planning is that the process will indicate the kinds of information the organization should collect and analyse. Part of the plan's final product is an identification of key data needs. Even if facilitators know what information is necessary, it may not be available.

The participative approach helps with these problems. The inclusion of the 'experts' in the process means that the participants already possess some of the relevant data. Hence, there is less call for voluminous information. The facilitators can be more selective in developing the data base. The participants can also help determine data needs. During the 'futures research' step they may want additional data. The facilitators and planning specialists in the organization can try to obtain information for the participants if there is sufficient time between sessions.

The First Session

The first session sets the tone for the entire strategic planning process. Hence, a principal goal for this session is to start the process well. This involves taking a few initial steps that will launch the process in the right direction and help keep it on track until its completion.

An introduction by the top manager is the first step. The top manager's stated support for strategic planning, and commitment to use the final product reinforces the earlier letter sent to the participants and emphasizes the project's importance. The facilitators follow with an overview of the strategic planning process and a discussion of the project's goals. This procedure enables the participants to check and clarify the impressions of strategic planning and the task they obtained from the preparatory material.

The final initial step consists of setting ground rules for participant behaviour during the strategic planning process. These rules are intended as a preemptive strike to limit potential disruption. They help manage behaviour by establishing at the beginning what is appropriate and inappropriate. They also strengthen the desire of the majority of the group to get the job done.

A collaborative process involving the facilitators and the participants produces the rules. The participants reach a consensus on a final set after considering the facilitators' suggested rules. Figure 4 contains the rules adopted for a recent strategic planning project. Among other considerations are attendance, interruptions and smoking. The collaborative approach to setting the rules expedites their use during the process. Participants pick them up. For instance, during one project they posted a sign on the door leading out of our meeting room that read,

- Be Serious About the Task—Emphasize "Task" and "Maintenance" (process) behaviour and avoid "Self-oriented" behaviour.

- Avoid Competition for "Air Time"—Speaking for the sake of being noticed.

- Avoid Other Agendas—Such as setting your social calendar.

- Maintain a Low-risk Climate or Environment

- Play Appropriate Roles

Figure 4. Session rules for a strategic planning project

'Now leaving low-risk environment'. Participants engage in self-policing behaviour by telling members when they are violating a rule. This behaviour indicates that facilitators and participants share responsibility for rule enforcement.

Development of the Plan

Management of the strategic planning process to maximize the effective use of participants' time is a key aspect of a successful project. It helps participant involvement and interest in the process and reduces the time and cost needed for project completion. Both factors promote a positive attitude toward the tool and its continued use.

Some features of the process design and preparation discussed earlier facilitate the plan's creation. For instance, the presence of the overview of the strategic planning process (Figure 3) and the accompanying steps on a wall give participants a general sense of direction (an overall framework) and the discrete and more manageable segments of this large, complex task. This enhances the perceived feasibility of the project by providing a clear agenda and desired outcome for each segment of the process.

This example also suggests the value of graphics for managing the process. Charts and movable cards play an important role in the application of a number of tools.[7] In strategic planning we use charts to depict information pertaining to the process and charts and movable cards to record and illustrate the participants' tentative and final products. The flexibility of the movable cards expedites the identification of levers and elements (one element per card) and the selection of the most important ones. They are also useful for developing relationships between components of the plan over time (i.e. constructing a time line that displays scheduled activities). The cards and charts focus participants' attention on the task at hand and how it fits into the overall process. They also help document the process and confirm what participants have already accomplished. The plan is the sum of the products created during the process.

The contribution of the overall process design and graphics to managing the strategic planning process is substantial but insufficient by itself to secure an optimal final product. Accomplishment of each step in the process requires the facilitators' constant attention. They must be prepared to deal with attitudes and behaviours that inhibit development of a strategic plan. The rules mentioned earlier help. Nevertheless, a participant may still attempt to disrupt the process, particularly at the end (e.g. 'Why are we doing this?'). Other pitfalls that may appear include consideration of only the status quo, avoidance of tough issues, unfounded assumptions, predetermined scenarios and hidden agendas. Anticipation of these problems and dealing with them quickly and firmly, often by referring to the overall process design and the accompanying instructions and rules, usually removes them. We have found that peer pressure in favour of the process usually nips such problems in the bud.

The facilitators must continuously attend to the process for developing the strategic plan, for it is always idiosyncratic and evolutionary in nature. Each application is unique. A process 'formula' does not work equally well for all situations. This is due, at least in part, to the nature of the group working on the plan. For instance, large groups (at least 20 participants) require a more complex process to achieve participatory decisions on each segment of the plan. Groups often differ in their members' experience and effectiveness in group problem-solving. Less experienced groups generally need more help and structure. The facilitators must also respond to particular concerns of the group. For example, during one recent project some participants became worried that the final product could end up in the 'wrong hands' and be used against their organization. The facilitators took care in working on this concern with the participants. The group's adoption of the facilitators' suggestion to stamp 'DRAFT—NOT FOR CITATION' on each page of the final product alleviated their apprehension. The participants viewed the stamp as reinforcing the idea that their plan is for the agency's internal use and is dynamic.

These factors suggest that the group process for each step emerges as the process continues. While planning for the process before it begins is important, facilitators must also be prepared to adjust and change their initial plan as their knowledge about the task, the situation and the participants increases (e.g. the number of scenarios required?). Especially with large groups, the facilitators create some of the processes as the project unfolds. These aspects of implementing the plan also indicate why having two facilitators for the process is helpful. The use of two facilitators increases the attention paid to diagnosing the situation. Development of the

process as it unfolds benefits from their shared diagnosis and resulting collaboration on an appropriate design for completing each part of the plan.

The importance of diagnosing the situation and integrating the findings into the structure of the process as it unfolds is a key to effectively managing the idiosyncratic and evolutionary nature of developing a strategic plan. The facilitators' task here is to devise and implement an optimal group arrangement that fosters completion of each step in the overall process. Two considerations guide these decisions: The nature of the step and the desire for an effective participatory process. The group arrangement must promote accomplishment of the task *through* participation. This approach reflects a belief that participation is a 'good' in itself as well as leading to better decisions and outcomes. It requires the facilitators to find ways to foster, structure and manage effective participation. They must continuously structure and channel participation to avoid boredom, meaningless tasks, cliques and the continuation of unproductive small groups; promote the exchange of ideas and perspectives; and stay on target. Consequently, the facilitators are constantly reconstituting groups during the strategic planning process.

Group Processes
The frequent reformulation of groups involves the use of various group process arrangements and configurations. Two examples of these arrangements and their specific applications to steps in developing a strategic plan are below:

Example 1: The intramural exercise. Figure 5 depicts the structure of an exercise we have found useful for formulating a group composite view of the values that underlie their agency's operation. The facilitators provide an example of a 'Values' list (one produced by a different organization) and instruct the participants to individually prepare their own lists. The process consists of developing a single list of 'Values' in successively larger groups. For the project that contained 35 participants the procedure moved from individual lists to a list for each group of three then to one for each group of eight or nine

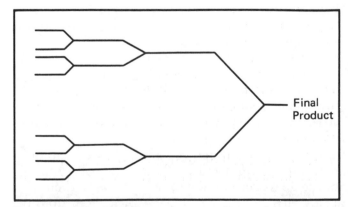

Figure 5. Formulating a group view of values in successively larger groups

and finally to a composite list composed by a task force of representatives from each of the four larger groups. The task force presented the list to the entire group for their adoption.

Example 2: Futures research. Categories of issues or events (levers) provide the structure for performing 'futures research'. Participants receive a list of these levers (social, technological, environmental, political, economic and agency resources) and examples of the issues and events (elements) each one contains.[8] Each lever becomes the focus of one small group, whose membership is determined on the basis of interest and expertise. Each small group identifies elements of the lever that pertain to the agency's environment and selects and further details each *key* element on a 5 × 8 in. card (i.e. whether and how the element will change and its impact on the agency). A chart for each lever that contains the finished cards for the selected elements in that category is posted on the wall. An ensuing plenary session that includes a report by each small group of its findings and a review of the list by other participants for questions and possible changes or additions to it, completes the 'futures research' step.

The participative approach can alter the roles of the facilitators and the participants during the strategic planning process. Participants may at some point begin to take interest in process concerns (i.e. how various tasks should be accomplished). This development often occurs when the process 'jells' and becomes more 'theirs'. Facilitators must be prepared for this possibility and encourage it by moving to a more collaborative approach with participants regarding the process. This feature of the participative approach reflects the facilitators' interest in promoting growth in group problem-solving capabilities as well as task completion.

The Final Product

The approach discussed in this article produces a strategic plan by the end of the final session. There is little 'lag' time between the final session and when the plan is available. The charts that display the final products of the participants' work constitute the plan. Figure 2 is an example. The transfer of the plan from the charts to a publishable form and its subsequent dissemination to the participants and others requires only a short time.

The strategic plan's value is not limited to helping the organization adapt to a changing environment. Among other potential benefits a strategic plan offers are:

☆ A plan to head off someone else's plan that may be imposed on the organization from the outside;

☆ Assistance for overcoming some problems that often accompany management turnover; and

☆ A guide for restructuring the agency, making budget decisions, choosing personnel, deploying capital improvements, etc.

However, the availability of a plan does not mean it will be used.

Others have noted the difficulty of implementing strategic plans.[9] Among the problems that often impede effective execution of a plan are limited integration of it into other agency decision processes, lack of staff commitment, an ineffective monitoring system, and a tendency to view the plan as an immutable strategy. We have found the following helpful in overcoming these problems and facilitating implementation:

☆ Disseminate the final product to the participants and others as soon as possible. This step is an important part of the participative approach. It fosters participant advocacy for the plan and its execution, thus increasing the impetus for implementing the plan.

☆ A statement by the agency's top person shortly after completion of the process that acknowledges creation of the plan, details how its implementation will occur, and assigns responsibility for its implementation to a co-ordinator. This statement should confirm top management's commitment to the plan and its implementation.

☆ Present the plan to the agency's governing body. This step should increase commitment to its implementation.

☆ Integrate the strategic plan into the organization's annual budget preparation process. It increases the likelihood that the plan is a major part of the 'data' upon which decisions are made.

☆ Design the final product to be the basis for monitoring progress on achieving the objectives of the plan.

☆ Have the agency institute an annual review and update of its strategic plan. This procedure insures the plan's continued utility and emphasizes that it is always subject to change if the assumptions underlying it change significantly.

Strategic Thinking

Our experience with strategic planning in public organizations has yielded a number of insights. First, strategic planning underscores the importance of the conceptual skill area for managers. This skill area focuses on a manager's, 'ability to understand the complexities of the overall organization and where one's own operation fits into the organization'.[10] The need to think conceptually; to see things from different perspectives; and the ability to consider beyond the status quo (i.e. what the organization currently does and the way it is done) are components of this area. They are essential for adapting the organization to a dynamic environment. Everyday management concerns and problems can drive out conceptual thinking. Strategic planning provides a forum for it and helps to cultivate 'strategic thinking' in the organization's line managers.

We have found that some characteristics of public organizations present particular concerns or issues for the application of strategic planning. For instance, their 'publicness' raises the consideration of who should participate in developing the plan (e.g. the role of the public?). This characteristic also affects the final product. Issuing the plan probably makes it public information. This factor can benefit strategic planning efforts by promoting public input to the plan and accountability for its results, adding impetus to its implementation, and fostering its use by an agency as a marketing tool. However, it also increases the possibility that the plan can end up in the 'wrong hands' and be used against the agency. As we noted earlier, some participants in one process became worried about this possibility. Use of the stamp 'DRAFT—NOT FOR CITATION' on each page of the final product helped alleviate this concern. Finally, the vagueness and/or difficulty of quantifying goals for many public organizations requires the strategic planning process to spend more time on this area. This characteristic indicates why examining existing organizational goals is an important step.

The participative approach highlights the significance of the process dimension of strategic planning. It reflects Marshall McLuhan's idea that 'the medium is the message'.[11] Participation in the process may be at least as important as the contents of the plan. It promotes the following among participants:

☆ *A common vision of the future and its implications for the organization, including any necessary changes.* Especially for middle managers, there may be no other opportunity to participate in this type of discussion during the year.

☆ *More effective group problem-solving skills.* These skills carry over to other decision making situations as well as to future strategic planning iterations.

☆ *Recognition that continuous planning is a management necessity.*

References

(1) For example, see Douglas C. Eadie, Putting a powerful tool to practical use: the application of strategic planning in the public sector, *Public Administration Review*, **43** (5), 447–452, September/October (1983), and Barry Selberg, Strategic planning and energy management, *Public Management*, **64** (4), 6–7, April (1982).

(2) John B. Olsen and Douglas C. Eadie, *The Game Plan: Governance with Foresight*, Studies in Governance, Vol. 1, The Council of State Planning Agencies, Washington, DC (1982) is an exception. It contains a few suggestions for handling the process.

(3) For instance, see Robert E. Linneman and John D. Kennell, Shirt-sleeve approach to long range plans, *Harvard Business Review*, **55** (2), 141–150, March/April (1977) and Olsen and Eadie, *The Game Plan*.

(4) We have used Linneman and Kennell, Shirt-sleeve approach to long range plans.

(5) See James Marshall, Daniel E. O'Toole and Francis Sargant, A visual approach to training plan development, *Public Administration Review*, **43** (2), 166–175, March/April (1983).

(6) Futures Research Division, Security Pacific National Bank, *Future Scan*, No. 362, p. 3, 16 January (1984) cites a study by the Wharton Applied Research Center that found that meetings are 28% shorter when information is presented in graphic form.

(7) For example, see Cortus T. Koehler, Product planning and management technique, *Public Administration Review*, **43** (5), 459–466, September/October (1983).

(8) The levers/elements draw upon material developed by the Futures Research Division of the Security Pacific National Bank of California.

(9) For instance, see Walter Kiechel III, Corporate strategists under fire, *Fortune*, **106** (13), 34–39, 27 December (1982); Richard T. Pascale, Our curious addiction to corporate grand strategy, *Fortune*, **105** (2), 115–116, 25 January (1982); and Research spotlight, *Management Review*, **72** (6), 55–56, June (1983).

(10) Paul Hersey and Kenneth H. Blanchard, *Management of Organizational Behavior: Utilizing Human Resources*, p. 5, 4th edn, Prentice-Hall, Englewood Cliffs, NJ (1982).

(11) See Marshall McLuhan, *Understanding Media: The Extensions of Man*, McGraw-Hill, New York (1964).

Futures Research—Working with Management Teams

David Sims and Colin Eden, University of Bath

This paper discusses ways of looking at the future, with particular emphasis on the future as a 'conscious dream', and discusses an approach by which conscious dreams can be represented as explicit models. A case study is given of the use of this method with three housing managers who were enabled by it to articulate their own images of the future and understand each others' images. The benefits to be gained from such a procedure are discussed.

The planning process has always involved making judgments about how the future is likely to unfold. The most evident ways of undertaking this task are through general discussion leading to a qualitative statement or description often called a 'scenario', or by the use of statistical forecasting methods. One or both of these approaches is used formally or implicitly by all groups concerned with making plans. In the context of the formal process of corporate planning in organizations these approaches can be identified as the use of the Delphi technique and trend extrapolation or computer simulation modelling. The work of Kahn and Weiner[1] used extrapolation extensively, even though the best known aspect of their approach to planning was the use of scenario building, that is 'hypothetical sequences of events constructed for the purpose of focusing attention on causal processes and decision-points'. This may be compared with the more formal and structured approaches which have the widest currency in the field of corporate planning.[2-4] Each of these proponents of the art emphasizes extrapolation of current variables rather than the consideration of presently unknown variables that might be relevant within an imaginative scenario. The activity is 'rational and scientific' and often uses a planner, operational researcher, or policy analyst. The direct involvement of the policy maker is relatively small for most methods which emphasize formal analysis.

By their very nature, highly mathematical, statistical, or computer based methods constrain the possibility of using creatively the subjective ideas and theories a group of people have gained from their individual experience of being a part of the world which is being considered. To some extent the Delphi technique was intended to attend to this shortcoming. When it was first introduced by Dalkey and Helmer[5] their intention was to get at the 'collective unconscious' of a group of people in such a way that they were not constrained in expressing idiosyncratic views. Their main concern was to encourage greater individualism by reducing the social pressures in group discussion which reinforce the singular views of powerful individuals, and which discourage conflict. Nevertheless their use of a questionnaire which is dominated by requests for numerical data reduces the chances that they will surface their collective unconscious effectively. In this article we shall give an example, and some discussion, of a new approach for releasing the idiosyncratic and subjective images of the world which are contained in the thinking of individuals. We shall show how the technique we use facilitates the exploration of subjective assumptions which are declared as theories about how the world has become the present and might change to become the future. The technique is designed to go beyond Delphi by being more amenable to handling non numerical data and collecting views in a non directive manner, and yet it has also been developed so that the qualitative scenario which unfolds can be the subject of analysis and a vehicle for shifting the group 'world-view'.

The Future as a Conscious Dream

Policy-making is a process of defining and treating ill-structured issues and problems, the tools of social science that have been applied largely to policy problems have been developed generally for well structured issues and problems. (Mitroff and Emshoff,[6] p. 1; see also Mintzberg, Raisingham and Theoret[7] and Rose.[8])

The authors are both Lecturers in the School of Management at the University of Bath, Claverton Down, Bath BA2 7AY.

As we have said, the established techniques emphasize the conceiving of problems as well structured entities, with dimensions of analysis that are established in advance of the collection of opinion and formal data. The approach we describe below attempts to emphasize the problem construction aspect of exploring possible futures. This means that the focus of the exercise is enabling policy makers to make explicit their 'world-taken-for-granted' (or 'assumptive world',[9]) so that a construction of a model of the future is allowed to be highly subjective, with content that may be conflictual, apparently illogical or contrary.[10] The process is designed so that the future can be conceived as ill-structured and confusing; but nevertheless amenable to analysis, extension and explicit exploration (see Eden, Jones and Sims[11] for a general appraisal of the use of similar models by individual decision makers).

Our aim can best be expressed through Warren Bennis and his apt notion of the future as

> an exercise of the imagination which allows us to compete with and try to outwit future events. Controlling the anticipated future is, in addition, a social invention that legitimizes the process of forward planning . . . most importantly, the future is a conscious dream, a set of imaginative hypotheses.[12] (p. 227.)

Recently Mitroff and Emshoff[6] have come closest to considering the planning process in a way which reflects this view. Their intention is to get at the underlying and possibly conflictual assumptions that reinforce current strategy. Like us, they consider that the process should encourage the explication of individualistic views and theories about the world of the organization. A process must be designed so that social requirements allow for thinking which is not constrained by the circularity and incestuousness of a single theory about the nature of the world. Organizational norms and culture encourage apparent consensuality about strategy and the theories that support it. After the first stage of 'assumption surfacing' Mitroff and Emshoff continue by establishing the negation of the spirit of the assumptions and then revealing counter strategies which would be supported by the assumption negation stage.

The picture we have tried to present of the relationship between different aspects of the way that planning can be approached is shown in Figure 1. The diagram emphasizes our own orientation to planning as a social process, and to persons' assumptive worlds; this is shown by the fuzzy diagonal boundary.

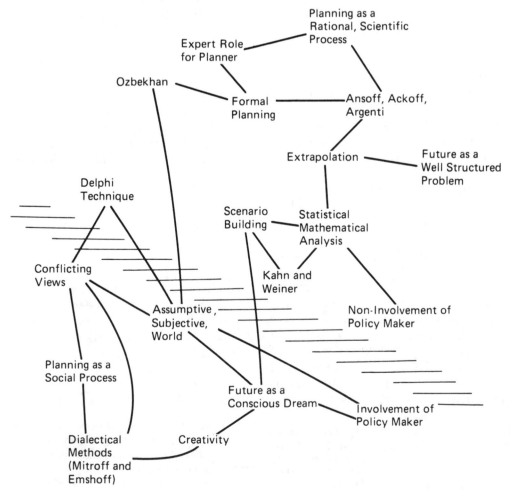

Figure 1. A map of planning

Building an Assumptive Scenario

Before describing a particular example of our approach to thinking about the future it may be helpful for us to describe how we go about building a model of peoples' ideas. Imagine somebody who has heard a few statements by different people at different times about the state of the economy! Suppose this person then decides to see how these statements relate to one another. The result of their building a representation could be a 'cognitive map'[13] such as that shown in Figure 2.

A cognitive map such as this is designed to store information in a straightforward and visual way. A map is based on the observation that most of the concepts we use when talking are, at least implicitly, stated with an opposite, and the opposite needs to be known, or implied, to know what the concept means. There are several examples in the map above; 'people receiving social benefits' has been contrasted with 'people with money', but another person could have contrasted it with 'people not relying on charity'. Concepts are linked together by an arrow to indicate that one concept is believed to influence another. So, for example, somebody believed that: 'government borrowing continually going up' may lead to 'government cutbacks'; or 'government borrowing not increasing' may lead to 'more government spending'. However, sometimes one side of a concept relates to the opposite side of another concept, and to distinguish this sort of relationship from the previous one, we show arrow heads with a minus sign rather than a plus sign. For example, the map expresses the belief that 'interest rates too high' may

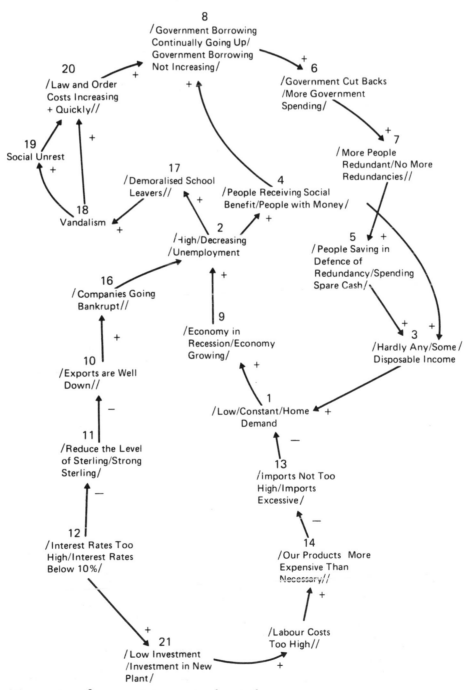

Figure 2. A cognitive map of some statements about the economy

lead to 'strong sterling'; whereas it may also lead through a positive signed arrow to 'low investment'. Sometimes the opposite is not readily apparent from our understanding of what somebody is saying. For example, the map shows uncertainty about the opposite of 'demoralized school leavers', but nevertheless shows the argument that 'high unemployment' may lead to 'demoralized school leavers'. Finally, it is sometimes believed that the opposites are 'an increase in . . .' rather than 'a decrease in . . .'; here, for convenience, the map shows the concept which increases or decreases. For example, the maps shows the argument that 'an increase in social unrest' may lead to 'law and order costs increasing quickly'. Note that arrows may also be read so that they suggest an explanation rather than a consequence. For example, 'an increase in social unrest' may be explained by 'an increase in vandalism'.

As this small map indicates, concepts may have multiple explanations and consequences. Considering a topic by looking at a map of this kind may, particularly for a person who cares about the topic, lead to wanting to add to the map, argue with its contents, analyse its structure by noting clusters of concepts, feedback loops, and to cases where a concept may lead both to another concept and to its opposite, by different strings of argument.

Using this approach to model building, combined with some of the requirements of the planning process which were illustrated in Figure 1, leads us to an approach something like that shown in Figure 3.

A Case Study in Housing Management

At the time of the events we describe here, we had been doing work for a number of years in a local authority housing department, including detailed work for the three most senior housing managers. One of their annual tasks is to prepare the Housing Programme for the forthcoming year, and the stage at which it seemed to them sensible to come together and talk about this coincided with a time when we had what they believed to be adequate and up-to-date models of each of their views, and also with a time when the most senior of them, Alan, was about to leave to take up another job. This meant that the next most senior, Richard, would be left in charge of a department which included the third member of this top team, John.

We had done different projects with each of the three, concerned with how they saw the situation of the Housing Programme. In addition to these

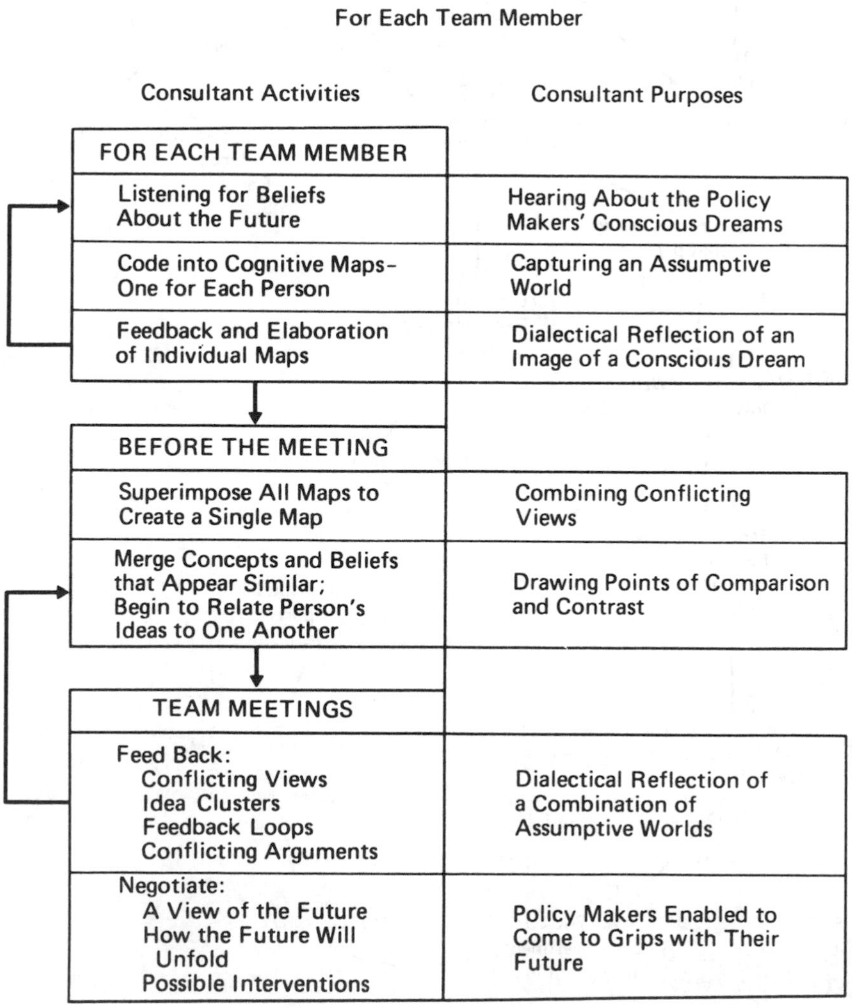

For Each Team Member

Consultant Activities	Consultant Purposes
FOR EACH TEAM MEMBER	
Listening for Beliefs About the Future	Hearing About the Policy Makers' Conscious Dreams
Code into Cognitive Maps— One for Each Person	Capturing an Assumptive World
Feedback and Elaboration of Individual Maps	Dialectical Reflection of an Image of a Conscious Dream
BEFORE THE MEETING	
Superimpose All Maps to Create a Single Map	Combining Conflicting Views
Merge Concepts and Beliefs that Appear Similar; Begin to Relate Person's Ideas to One Another	Drawing Points of Comparison and Contrast
TEAM MEETINGS	
Feed Back: Conflicting Views Idea Clusters Feedback Loops Conflicting Arguments	Dialectical Reflection of a Combination of Assumptive Worlds
Negotiate: A View of the Future How the Future Will Unfold Possible Interventions	Policy Makers Enabled to Come to Grips with Their Future

Figure 3. A scheme for the consulting process

personal models, we took the previous year's Housing Programme, as laid out in the document that had gone to the appropriate committee of the Local Authority concerned, and made the propositions contained in this document into another model. This included a few things that had not been mentioned by the individuals, and of course left out an enormous number of significant but 'illegitimate' issues that had been discussed by each of the individuals. We merged these four models to produce one big model, where points made by different people about the same topic were brought together.

Sharing and Developing the Dream

We started by asking them which of six topic areas they wanted to explore first. They went for the topic labelled: 'Demands, applicants, infill development, conservation, housing market', and within it they started looking at ideas to do with 'the use of existing stock'. At the same time they started talking about a current event in their authority, which was a report about a delapidated council housing area, with suggestions as to how it might be improved in the hope of breaking out of the cycle of delapidated areas attracting only tenants who do not care, or who can not go anywhere else, causing further delapidations to the areas and so on.

As the three of them started talking about these concepts, we created a map with the labels of the bits they were talking about, followed round the related concepts as they stood in the computer model, drew in new concepts that they raised, and searched around the model with a word finding device for concepts that we believed were related to what they were saying, and which one or other of us thought would help. They had each been given the opportunity to check their files and remove any concepts which they did not want their colleagues to know about.

For an example of how the conversation went, John mentioned 'those who are forced to apply', and within a few seconds we could check on the computer models to see what they had all said to us on other occasions about that group of people who are 'forced to apply for council accommodation, rather than deliberately choosing to apply'. We found that, for example, they had said that 'an increase in broken families who can not afford good accommodation' led to an increase in 'those who are forced to apply', and that 'an increase in the mortgage rate' led to 'an increase in those cut out by a mortgage increase', which led to 'a decrease in households' ability to afford purchase', which in turn led to 'an increase in those forced to apply'. They had expressed a great many more beliefs about both those questions to us, and we would put on a flip chart beliefs and relationships between beliefs that we could find that related to what was being said currently.

The appearance of such 'writing on the wall' has a dramatic effect on the process of the group whose views are being written. In particular, ignoring someone else's preoccupations simply because they are not the same as your own seems to be much harder if they appear on a diagram than if they are just stated in a meeting. Also, for questions of long-range planning, an even more significant difference is that this procedure seemed to relax the social norms which mean that one may not spend more than a fairly short period of time expounding views, even if the topic is arguably very complicated. Usually if a person thinks there are four main causes for some particular effect, he can not state more than one or at the very most two of them without feeling that he is boring his audience. Figure 4, for example, shows some of the reasoning around 'those forced to apply', which Richard and Alan saw worked through by John with our help as computer-assisted secretaries. John did not produce any ideas that were new to himself during this session, but he was enabled by the technology to lay out his ideas, make them explicit, argue for them, and show more of the connexions between them than he had ever been able to do in ordinary face to face meetings.

As we built up the maps on the flip charts, so all three housing managers would read what was going up, and start commenting and adding to what we were writing. This meant that instead of either accepting or rejecting John's ideas, they started relating them to ideas of their own. They found that they did not want to do anything so simple as accept or reject, but rather to explore the various different ideas in relation to one another. The ideas that were built during the day contained virtually nothing which had not been thought of before by at least one of the participants. However, there were four major trends which they came up with as having an important influence for everything they were going to do in their work for several years to come, and these were new to all of them, because they were built and strengthened by the interaction of the ideas of the different persons.

In brief, these trends were: firstly, there was a vicious circle around delapidated areas, which they reckoned produced people who further delapidated whatever areas they lived in. Secondly, they expected that in the future they would be handling a higher proportion of 'bad' tenants, as more private dwellings became available; on the presumption that council housing would be less attractive than other forms, their tenants would increasingly become those who could get nothing else. Thirdly, and related to the last, they thought that they would be moving increasingly into a 'social management' rather than a housing management role, as social dislocation produced people whom landlords would not have, and who therefore came to the council. Fourthly, they would increasingly deal with elderly applicants as the

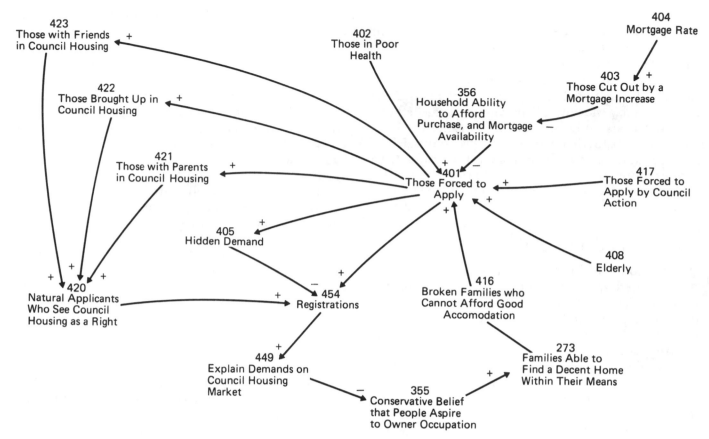

Figure 4. Some beliefs expressed about 'those forced to apply'

numbers of the elderly increased and it was found that they could not be serviced anywhere else.

Affecting the Assumptive World

In the afternoon, they chose a topic area labelled 'Political problems, conflict and management problems, stock with members'. Looking back on it we may say that this is the 'how' that goes with the 'what' that had occupied them for the morning. Richard and John would almost certainly not have felt able to ask, nor Alan to answer, the question 'What do we need to know about the organizational politics, then?' But by the same sort of process as had been employed in the morning, they ran through discussions about how the position of the department in the view of elected members was improved if some parts of the department were carrying out policies very well, but was also improved if some parts of the department were failing to carry out their policies perfectly (because otherwise you became almost frighteningly perfect).

In this session, instead of the three participants bouncing ideas off each other and gradually building up a notion more complicated and more complete than any one of them had had before, Richard and John would lead off with a few comments about some feature of their organization's politics, for example, 'how to gain stock with members', and then Alan would

comment on this and develop some ideas. We would note some of these ideas diagrammatically in the form of a 'cognitive map' on the flip chart, and as we did so all three of them would read what we had written, and would respond. As the afternoon went on, so things that were said later would gradually be related to things that had been said earlier and had been noted.

What was it about this event which enabled these three managers to take a look together at the future when they had previously found themselves unable to do so? The morning session revolved around the theme of how things in future would go, what it was that in the future they wanted to make happen, and what their expectations were about the future context in which they would have to make those things happen. There was thus a considerable amount of predictive activity, which was followed in the afternoon by a discussion of how they might effectively turn their expectations of future situations into situations which they would regard as more desirable. The afternoon particularly interested them because they had never thought of doing anything like this before—the topic was not a legitimate arena; and yet their view was that it was as crucial to the effective implementation of policy as the policy itself.

Planning as a Social Process

It was important to each of these three managers that they prepare their positions well for the discussions on the Housing Programme, and that the documents and Committee reports that were to be presented later should be sound and convincing ones that would produce the effects they wanted. However, each of the three had on different occasions, and with different levels of commitment, suggested to us that they should be looking further ahead than the next Housing Programme. We had thus expected the day that we were to spend with them to contain some reference to more fundamental and longer term housing issues, but also that they would feel that such discussion was a luxury at a time when Alan was about to leave and Richard was about to fill his role.

We were wrong. Quite early on in the morning, as the three of them started discussing the concepts, they started also working back to more and more fundamental concepts, and to major questions about the future of housing policy and Local Authority housing in the U.K. In this discussion, they seemed to be fascinated by what each other was saying; afterwards, when talking to us individually, they all made remarks about how 'this should have happened years ago'. Far from being reluctant to talk about the long term future, these three housing managers set off to discuss it as if a dam had burst; there was a furious rush of all the things they had been wanting to say and hear about the longer term future of housing for years. We had done nothing in particular to make such a conversation happen, nor even consciously to facilitate it happening. What we had done was to provide a mechanism, as these three saw it, for holding a conversation which they had been wanting to hold for a long time.

It is sometimes asserted that the urgent, even if unimportant, drives out the non-urgent, even if crucially important. The experience in this case suggests to us that one major reason why long term futures are not discussed as much as they might be is not lack of motivation, but is simply the lack of a mechanism for going about the business of discussing them in anything more than a simplistic way. Our mapping techniques enabled the participants to hold on to more complexity than they could have done in an ordinary conversation in their offices, and as soon as this aid to handling complexity was provided, they were able and keen to use it in discussing long term developments.

Locating the Case

We have now described one project among many in which we used the technique of cognitive mapping to facilitate creative thinking about the future. We stated in the introduction that the Delphi technique intends to facilitate getting at the collective unconscious. How does the approach we used in the above project compare to the Delphi technique? In our approach and that taken by Mitroff and Emshoff there has been a belief in the benefits that

can accrue by decreasing the commitment of a group of policy makers to what is taken to be the established group 'world-view'. Mitroff and Emshoff deliberately set out to introduce conflict because it 'is needed to permit the existence of maximally opposing policies to ferret out and to challenge the underlying assumptions that each policy makes . . . the methodology proposed builds on the very existence of such tensions'. In our case there are no such forcing characteristics in the method structure and yet it has always been the case that the opportunity to compare subjective views of the future has revealed complex and subtle conflicts which significantly affect conceptions of the future and views about strategy. Mitroff and Emshoff argue that 'commitment [to opposing policies] is also necessary if the proponents for each policy are to make the strongest possible case'. It seems to us more likely that commitment is achieved when alternative points of view are not seen within a conflict framework but rather are the outcome of being able to model individual ideas and complexity. As the above case demonstrates, alternative views only stand a change of surfacing and being taken seriously when their proponents have had the opportunity to declare the full complexity of their assumptions and also believe the model of their views belongs to them.

While all three approaches recognize the dangers of 'group-think'[14] to the possibility of capturing what we have called the 'world-taken-for-granted' the method Delphi employs only goes half way. The structure imposed by Delphi focuses attention on particular aspects of the future, indeed it was intended that this should be so. For our purposes it falls well short of enabling the construction of a 'conscious dream' which has any chance of creating a view of the future which is imaginative and contains variables and concepts which had previously been undeclared or related one to another. In the above case the three people involved thought they knew one another's views. This planning event surprised them because they each began to see one another's ideas in a new light and also more peculiarly (to them) found themselves seeing aspects of their occupational world which they had not either heard from their colleagues or thought about. The social dynamics and time constraints of meetings (however well chaired) are such that the context of points of view must either be presented in short formality with supporting 'evidence' or cannot be presented at all. The approach we use combats this problem in two ways: firstly the mapping approach is deliberately designed to model the structure (contextual meaning) of ideas, as well as representing the content. Thus context which would have been provided at best sequentially in discussion, or more likely at different points in the discussion is now represented in a single picture form. Secondly, the use of a computer to represent the complex interrelationships between one person's ideas and those of another facilitates more thoughtful consideration of the ideas. There is a reduction in the social demands made on each person to the extent that he can consider more slowly the content and its ramifications without feeling a need to respond immediately.

This process of seeing one another's views mapped together so that the complex ramifications of mixed and often contradictory beliefs about the nature of the world can be appreciated, discussed, elaborated, and modified is difficult to undertake without a method and technology for so doing. Yet to miss out this activity and go directly to the dialectic approach of Mitroff and Emshoff is to miss out on an exploration and evaluation of the beliefs that are currently influencing the decision making of each member of the group. There seems to us to be a case for considering moving on to their approach after the process we have described. In the case discussed above our clients were well pleased with their day and felt they had created a new 'conscious dream' of the future, which was one on which they needed to act. The notion of facilitating the making of dream into a conscious model is important partly because articulation changes the nature of the dream even without any further work on thinking about its content.

Using the Approach

In this article we have described a specific case study where a form of Futures Research was undertaken using the approach shown by Figure 3. How applicable is the process to other topics and other organizations? How does a planner use the approach? Is a computer necessary?

As we indicated earlier, we have developed and used the approach in a variety of organizations including publishing, printing, chemicals, engineering and furniture industries, as well as the probation service, national charities and a community action group. Many of these episodes have been documented.[15-18,21-24] These experiences suggest that it is the approach—its contribution to the management of debate, the facility it provides for sharing idiosyncratic beliefs, for negotiating conflict, and for analysis—that gives help to managers involved in a planning venture; rather than characteristics inherent in the topic or type of organization.

Successfully using the approach depends upon learning and developing 'listening' skills and the ability to code concepts and beliefs into a cognitive map which is 'owned' by the clients. Traditional skills in the management of team process are important for effectively facilitating team feedback and negotiation. These are all skills the planner is likely to claim, or are techniques that can be learned from reading and practice in low risk situ-

ations.[19,20,25] The approach is deliberately designed to be transparent and understandable to the clients.

Although we used a computer and specially written software (COPE) to help us in the project reported here, we do not and cannot always use this facility. The storing, manipulation, analysis and representation of networks of ideas and beliefs can be made simpler and less laborious using a computer; but it is both possible and sometimes helpful to construct and analyse models manually.

Acknowledgements—This work was undertaken with the help of grants to Colin Eden from the SSRC and Leverhulme Trust. We are also grateful to the participants of the project we have reported for reading and agreeing the contents of this article.

References

(1) H. Kahn and A. Weiner, *Toward the Year 2000—A Framework for Speculation,* Macmillan, New York (1976).

(2) I. Ansoff, *Corporate Strategy,* Penguin, Harmondsworth (1968).

(3) J. Argenti, *Corporate Planning,* Allen and Unwin, London (1968).

(4) R. L. Ackoff, *A Concept of Corporate Planning,* Wiley Interscience, New York (1970).

(5) N. C. Dalkey and O. Helmer, An experimental application of the Delphi method to the use of experts, *Management Science,* **IX** (1963).

(6) I. I. Mitroff and J. R. Emshoff, On strategic assumption-making a dialectical approach to policy and planning, *Academy of Management Review,* **4,** 1–12 (1979).

(7) H. Mintzberg, D. Raisingham and A. Theoret, The structure of 'unstructured' decision processes, *Administrative Science Quarterly,* **21,** 246–275 (1976).

(8) R. Rose, Disciplined research and undisciplined problems, *International Social Science Journal,* **28,** 99–121 (1976).

(9) K. Young, Values in the policy process, *Policy and Politics,* **5,** 1–22 (1977).

(10) H. Ozbekhan, Thoughts on the emerging methodology of planning, *Fields within Fields,* **10** (1974).

(11) C. Eden, S. Jones and D. Sims, *Thinking in Organizations,* Macmillan, London (1979).

(12) W. G. Bennis, Future of the social sciences, *Antioch Review,* **28,** 227 (1968).

(13) R. Axelrod ed, *Structure of Decision,* University of Princeton Press, Princeton, N.J. (1976).

(14) I. L. Janis, *Victims of Groupthink,* Houghton Mifflin, Boston (1972).

(15) C. Eden and S. Jones, Publish or perish? a case study, *Journal of the Operational Research Society,* **31,** 131–139 (1980).

(16) T. Smithin and P. Harrison, The third dimension of the two dimensional cutting problem, *Omega,* **10,** 81–87 (1982).

(17) D. Sims and T. Smithin, Voluntary operational research, *Journal of the Operational Research Society,* **33,** 21–28 (1982).

(18) S. Jones and C. Eden, OR in the community, *Journal of the Operational Research Society,* **32** (5), 335–345 (1981).

(19) C. Eden and D. Sims, On the nature of problems in consulting practice, *Omega,* **7** (2), 119–127 (1979).

(20) C. Eden, S. Jones and D. Sims, *Messing About in Problems*, Pergamon (1983).

(21) C. Eden, S. Jones, D. Sims and T. Smithin, The intersubjectivity of issues and issues of intersubjectivity, *Journal of Management Studies*, **18** (1), 37–47 (1981).

(22) C. Eden, S. Jones, D. Sims and H. Gunton, Images into models: the subjective world of the policy maker, *Futures*, **11**, 56–63, February (1979).

(23) T. Smithin, Maps of the mind: new pathways to decision-making, *Business Horizons*, **23** (6), 24–28 (1980).

(24) T. Smithin and C. Eden, A package that helps to cope with decisions, *Computer Weekly*, 19, 8 January (1981).

(25) D. Sims and S. Jones, Explicit problems modelling: an intervention strategy, *Group and Organization Studies*, **6**, 486–499 (1981).

PART SEVEN

Additional Tools

Foresight Activities in the U.S.A.: Time for a Re-Assessment?

Leonard L. Lederman, National Science Foundation, Washington DC

This article reports on a brief, informal, reconnaissance study of 'foresight' activities now being conducted in the private sector and the Federal government. Such activities include: external environmental assessment, internal organizational assessment, direction setting, definition, and selection of base and contingent plans, implementation, performance evaluation and feedback. The study involved the reading and analysis of the existing literature and discussions with over 50 people in diverse private and public sector organizations. The objective was to determine what foresight activities are being done, how, by whom, with what results, and what are the implications and options.

Some people (organizations) make change;
Some people (organizations) watch change being made;
Some people (organizations) don't seem to know that things are changing.
> Well known contemporary philosopher—Pogo

Introduction

The major findings of a reconnaissance study of foresight activity in U.S. organizations revealed that:

☆ There is a growing interest and involvement in foresight activities and a growing awareness of the need to carry out such activities on a broad as well as specific level as a part of strategic management.

☆ Such activities are most likely to be effective to the extent that: (1) they are supported by and involve the top management of the organization; (2) they are the responsibility of a top official of the organization and are directed by a line officer or manager; (3) they involve the active participation of line managers and staff in many parts of the organization; and (4) they are

used in the decision-making and operations of the organization.

☆ Current systems for carrying out such activities are relatively recent, still evolving, and are under review in the hope of improving their effectiveness.

☆ While the staff carrying out such activities are generally organized within specific central groups, the functions are not usually the sole responsibility of such groups. They are likely to be carried out more effectively if the staff is operating in a cross-functional matrix regardless of their administrative home.

☆ The breadth and degree of involvement in such activities seems to be much greater in the private sector than the Federal government. A growing number of private sector organizations are integrating foresight activities under a strategic management system. Public sector activities tend to be a part of budget and resource management and as a result are shorter-term and narrower with less top management involvement.

☆ Foresight activities are very much of an art; clear measures of benefits and costs and of success or failure do not exist. Despite this, most respondents were sure that the benefits were greater than the costs and cited examples of why.

The people interviewed provided information that is summarized in this report on a number of important topics:

☆ the extent to which their organizations engage in such activities;

☆ the scope and purpose of such activities;

☆ the mechanisms used;

☆ the cost of such activities;

☆ who gets the outputs;

☆ how outputs are disseminated;

The author is Director, Strategic Planning and Assessment, Directorate for Scientific, Technological and International Affairs, National Science Foundation, Washington DC 20550, U.S.A.

☆ what the benefits, successes, advantages are;

☆ what the liabilities, failures, disadvantages are;

☆ whether the results are worth the effort and how this is determined;

☆ what developments, issues, problems and opportunities in science, technology and education such activities identified early;

☆ what services are available from what organizations, at what cost, with what outputs, and who uses them.

It became clear during this study that much attention is being paid to foresight activities, that such activities and their organization are changing and that it is appropriate for organizations to reassess what they are doing and how it can be improved. Three generic options exist:

☆ continue doing what is now done with no change;

☆ incrementally improve the organization, co-ordination, communication, effectiveness and use of what is now done;

☆ make a major or dramatic change in what is now done and how it is done.

A discussion of each of these options and their implications is in the last section of this report.

Scope and Approach

Over the past few years attention has increased, especially in the business literature,* to activities that are sometimes described as 'foresight', 'strategic planning and management', 'environmental scanning/monitoring', 'issues management', etc. Taking cognizance of such activities, the Assistant Director and Deputy Assistant Director NSF/STIA asked the author to conduct an informal, selective reconnaissance study of the subject to determine: what's being done, how, by whom, with what results, and what are the implications.

Respondents were selected to reflect a range of perspectives from business, Federal government and organizations that provide input services, from the central management of the organizations to sub-units and business units, from broad societal monitoring to specific technical responsibilities, from R & D to marketing and public or government relations, from manufacturing to retailing and financial institutions, from the White House to subunits of larger federal agencies and organizations that serve the Congress. It should be clearly stated at the outset that no attempt was made to select a 'representative' sample of some larger group. First of all this would not have been possible because the 'larger group' is not known; and secondly, the purpose was to determine what the people and organizations in the 'foresight'* business were doing, why and with what outcomes. That there are many who do not engage in such activities is a known fact, but the focus of this project was to learn from a limited number of those who do. Because of this focus, results are expressed verbally and qualitatively. No attempt is made to present the results quantitatively because that would be inappropriate.

The scope of this inquiry is difficult to pin down precisely because different people and organizations use different terminology; even where similar terminology is used, it is often defined or described differently. One of the best overall descriptions of the area encompassed can be found in the recently published 'Foresight in the Private Sector: How Can Government Use It?'.† The 'Glossary of Selected Terms' from that document is reproduced in Figure 1, and selected charts from that document are reproduced in Figures 2, 3 and 4. Taken together these describe the scope of this report; the discussions, along with the literature, provide the basic information. A selected list of information sources are in the Appendix. These are by no means the bulk of the literature used as background for this study, but they are the references uncovered that list the major people and organizations involved as well as much of the identified literature.

Briefly, the subject matter includes activities that fall under what is generally called 'The Strategic Process' (see Figure 2) and include terms such as:

☆ External environment assessment: this is the principle area traditionally associated with foresight. Most of the organizations contacted indicated that the management is reasonably satisfied that they are on top of their many lines of business but is concerned that external forces are increasingly affecting future opportunities and threats. External environmental assessment involves judgement concerning alternative outcomes of existing trends (social, economic, political, technological, etc.) as well as speculation about emerging developments. It focuses on threats and opportunities and uses the techniques of scenario construction, premises quantification, media scanning, environment monitoring, and issues management.

☆ Internal organizational assessment: this involves self-assessment in which the organization

---

*See for example, Firms hiring new type of manager to study issues, emerging troubles, *Wall Street Journal*, 10 June (1983); The oddball forecasters, *Dun's Business Month*, March (1983).

*There seems to be some concensus that the term 'foresight' is as good as any to serve as a shorthand surrogate for the range of activities discussed and therefore it will be used in this report.
†Foresight in the Private Sector: How Can Government Use It? Report of the Foresight Task Force, prepared for the Committee on Energy and Commerce of the U.S. House of Representatives, January (1983), Committee Print 98–B.

BASE PLANS — The Base Plan is the Plan of Action Which is Consistent With the Most Likely Scenario and the Organization's Mission, Goals and Objectives

CONTINGENCY PLANS — The Back-up Plan to the Organization's Base Plan. The Plan of Action Taken Should the Most Likely or Probable Scenario Develop in a Pattern Different Than Expected

COST-BENEFIT — The Relation Between Social and Economic Benefits and Social and Economic Costs With the Operation of the System Under Study Including Direct and Indirect Effects

COST-EFFECTIVENESS — A Term Widely Used in Systems Analysis and Subsequently Carried Over Into Budget Analysis. It Signifies the Relationship Within an Explicit and Finite Period (Such as Product Life in Service), of Cost in Dollars and Other Tangible Values to Effectiveness

CROSS IMPACT ANALYSIS — An Analytical Technique for Identifying the Various Impacts of Specific Events or Well-Defined Policy Actions on Other Events. It Explores Whether the Occurrence of One Event or Implementation of One Policy is Likely to Inhibit, Enhance, or Have No Effect on the Occurrence of Another Event

DELPHI — An Analytical Technique Using Expert Opinion and Judgement. It Consists of a Carefully Designed Series of Interrogations Using Written Questionnaires, Personal Interviews and/or Variations of Computer Conferencing, Statistically Evaluated Information and Opinion Feedback, Inhibiting the Attribution of Particular Remarks to Individual Participants

ECONOMETRIC MODELLING — A Form of Modelling, Usually Done with Computers Which Explores the Components and Interactions of a Given Economic System

EXTERNAL ENVIRONMENT — All Relevant Elements or Forces (Social, Economic, Political, Technological) External to and Impacting on the Organization

INTERNAL ENVIRONMENT — All Relevant Elements or Forces Within an Organization that Impact on its Components

SCENARIOS — Narrative Descriptions of Alternative Futures Based on Specific Assumptions About Relevant Social, Economic, Political and Technological Forces and Their Interactions

STRATEGIC BUSINESS UNIT — Within a Corporation, an Independently Managed Cluster or Grouping of Products With One or More Markets That Share Similar Competitive, Growth and Other Risk and Earnings Potential Characteristics

STRATEGIC PROFILE — A Set of Characteristics Describing the Critical Qualities of an Enterprise Within its Field of Industry (its Opportunities, Geographic and Product Line Coverage, Resources, Costs Competitive Standing, Special Circumstances, etc.), and How Those Characteristics Relate

TREE DIAGRAM — An Analytical Tool Sometimes Referred to as Relevance Tree. It is a Diagrammatic Technique for Analyzing Systems or Processes in Which Distinct Levels of Complexity or Hierarchy can be Identified. It May be Used to Provide a Hierarchical Representation of the Mission, Goals, Objectives and Policies of a Corporation

TREND IMPACT ANALYSIS — An Analytical Technique for Evaluating the Potential Effect of a Set of Chosen Events Upon a Designated Trend

WILD CARD SCENARIO — A Scenario With Very Low Probability of Occurrence, But High Impact

Produced from *Foresight in the Private Sector: How Can Government Use It?* Report of the Foresight Task Force, Prepared for the use of the Committee on Energy and Commerce, U.S. House of Representatives, Print 98-B, January, (1983)

Figure 1. Glossary of Terms

evaluates its human, financial, technological, and structural/informational capacities and potentialities. It focuses on the organization's strengths and weaknesses.

☆ Direction setting: the strategic process is usually embedded within a vision which provides guidance for the organization. Direction setting seeks to render this vision concrete in terms of defining an operational mission, goals and objectives of the organization (see Figure 3).

☆ Definition and selection of base and contingent plans: this part of the process involves identification of alternative courses of action under alternative future conditions. It includes strategic, long-range, and operational plans.

☆ Implementation: usually this involves the carrying out of the programs and strategies to achieve the objectives of the plans and includes accountability and execution.

☆ Performance evaluation and feedback: performance evaluations compares actual with expected results and identifies the reasons for and magnitude of differences. It is a part of management control systems and should feed

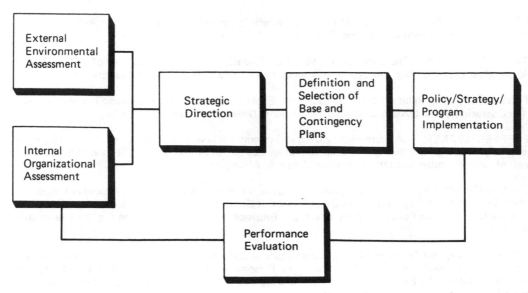

Figure 2. The strategic process

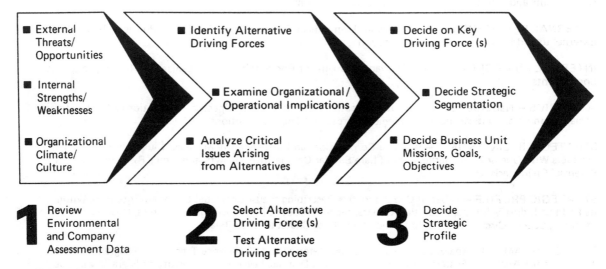

Figure 3. Direction setting

back on the other parts of the process in order to make them more realistic with the passage of time.*

A number of recent occurrences have highlighted the growing interest in understanding this strategic process better and improving how it works in both private and public sector organizations. Already mentioned, is the growing attention paid to such activities in private companies. In addition, considerable Congressional attention is being paid to such activities as exemplified by: the Congressional Clearinghouse on the Future, the activities and publications of the House Committee on Energy and Commerce,† inclusion of foresight and reporting functions in legislation authorizing the activities of some federal agencies and the introduction of a number of bills such as HR 3070

by representatives Gore and Gingrich of the 'Critical Trends Assessment Act', introduced 19 May 1983. Among other things this bill would:

☆ Establish in the Executive Office of the President an Office of Critical Trends Analysis, with a $5m annual budget.

☆ Authorize this office to advise the President 'of the potential effects of government policies on critical trends and alternative futures'.

☆ Authorize the office to produce every 4 years, beginning in 1986, an 'Executive Branch Report on Critical Trends and Alternative Futures'.

☆ Authorize the Joint Economic Committee of Congress to produce every 2 years, beginning in 1987, a 'Legislative Branch Report on Critical Trends and Alternative Futures'.

☆ Establish an Advisory Commission on Critical Trends Analysis with Executive, Congressional and private sector representation.

---

*Definitions of the terms used and greater description of what is involved may be found in Figures 1 and 2 and the document from which they are taken.
†See the Appendix for references.

As a result of this growing interest in the private and public sectors, an increasing volume of activity in service organizations is devoted to providing information inputs to foresight. These range from frequent, inexpensive newsletters to public opinion polls, trend data and analyses and broad, continual and fairly expensive subscription programs.

Finally, there has been significant growth in the membership, publications and attendance at meetings of professionals who practice the art of foresight. This ranges from organizations such as the World Future Society (started in 1967) to the less than 2-year-old Issues Management Association which has over 500 members.*

Major Results, Findings and Differences

The major results, findings and differences uncovered during the course of this study are highlighted in the following points:

(a) The growing interest and involvement in foresight activities as well as a growing awareness of the need to carry out such activities on a broad as well as specific level was empirically confirmed. To date the breadth and degree of involvement in such activities seems to be much greater in the private sector than in the Federal government.

(b) Such activities are most likely to be effective to the extent that: (1) they are supported by and involve the top management of the organization; (2) they are the responsibility of a top official of the organization and are directed by a line officer or manager; (3) they involve the active participation of the line managers and staff in many parts of the organization; and (4) they are used in the decisionmaking and operations of the organization. Respondents stated over and over the need for both a top–down and bottoms–up approach if such activities are to be successful.

(c) Many of the respondents indicated that their system for foresight activities is relatively recent and still evolving. Some indicated that their system and activities are currently under review in the hopes of making improvements.

(d) While the staff carrying out foresight functions are most often housed within a department, division, branch, office, etc. the functions are usually not the sole responsibility of a centrally organized group. Respondents frequently

stressed that the functioning of such activities need to be broad and integrated covering the range of activities described above. While individual people and groups are often responsible for particular functions (e.g. strategic planning, policy analysis, issues scanning, monitoring and management) they are most often successful if operating in a cross-functional matrix that utilizes the professional skills of people from each of these groups on specific projects regardless of administrative structure.

(e) A growing number of organizations, especially in the private sector, are integrating foresight activities under the strategic process system model shown in the charts reproduced above. In the Executive Branch such activities tend to be a part of the budget and resource management system; in the Legislative Branch they tend to be part of oversight functions. This difference, in part, explains the broader and longer-term orientation of private sector organizations than Federal government organizations to such activities.

(f) The need for appropriate career identification, adequate professional rewards, and organizational incentives for people engaged in such activities was stressed by a number of respondents. Such activities are unlikely to be successful if they are viewed as expendable, reducible 'overhead costs' when resources are tight.

(g) There is general acknowledgement that such activities are more of an art than a science. Clear measures of benefits and costs do not exist. Neither do generally accepted standards of success.* Despite 'soft' measures of success or failure most respondents were sure that the benefits were greater than the costs and cited examples of why. This included responses from users of the outputs (e.g. top and line managers) and not just the suppliers of foresight services. There was a little more doubt about this in government organizations, often thought to be due to the fact that in planning there is less strategic and more short-term budget oriented than in private organizations.

Responses to Specific Subjects

In some cases the people interviewed provided a general description of their organization's foresight approach, activities and organization; some supplied written background material which was then supplemented by a telephone conversation which

---

*Much more information was collected on the breadth, output and excitement of foresight activities in individual organizations than can be reported in this summary report. Readers who are interested in any of the publicly available details are encouraged to contact the author who is now a part of a growing network of people interested in exchanging ideas and information.

---

*For example, there was an interesting debate at a recent meeting of the Issues Management Association as to whether the banking industry had dealt with the issue of withholding taxes on interest very successfully or whether they may have 'won a battle but in the process lost the war'.

filled in information in response to a series of questions. In other cases the respondents answered the series of questions by phone and then added any additional information they thought important. The following summarizes responses under the generic subjects discussed.

(1) Does your organization engage in activities that seek to determine important social, economic, political, educational, scientific or technological changes?

In all cases the answer was yes, although, as expected, with different degrees of emphasis. In the business organizations there was usually some kind of 'management system' that ranged from strategic and operations planning through issue monitoring and management. In all but one case in the Executive Branch of government this was also true, although the range of activities tended to be narrower and frequently shorter-term. In the organizations serving the Legislative Branch this tended not to be the case, because they were primarily responsive to specific requests from Congressional Committees and members. In the various service organizations, the activities ranged from broad scanning activities and regular ongoing services to subscribers to more specific special studies in response to individual clients.

(2) What is the scope and purpose of such activities?

In most cases foresight activities involved a broad attempt to identify changes mentioned above as well as a more specific attempt at one or more of the following:

(2.1) Social and/or economic forecasts at the macro (e.g. country) or micro (e.g. industry, product) level.

(2.2) Specific science and technology developments and outlooks.

(2.3) Market opportunities or problems.

(2.4) Specific issue management, identification, and early warning (e.g. legislative, regulatory). See for example Figure 4.

Obviously, different organizations were focused more or less on different purposes. As expected, business organizations were more focused on market opportunities or problems; high technology business organizations were more concerned with science and technology; virtually all organizations were concerned with tracking specific issues and management and with social and/or economic forecasts. Some of the broadest, most sophisticated and long-term efforts were reported by business organizations (e.g. long-term demographic and economic trends) while federal government efforts tended to be somewhat narrower and oriented to the shorter-term. A high proportion of the business organizations were also

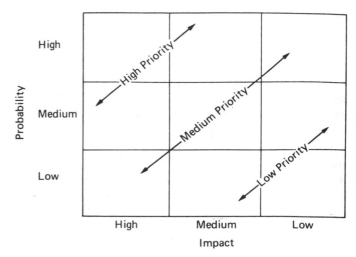

Figure 4. Issues priority matrix

concerned with defensive issues and problems (e.g. government regulation) although in some instances this was balanced with offensive opportunities as well.

In most organizations foresight activities are both systematic and continual, as well as specialized and reactive to specific requirements, and served broad, overall strategic planning as well as operational purposes.

The geographic focus of foresight activities varied depending on the organization—from a focus on a single country and its regions (generally U.S.) to groups of countries and, in a few cases, the world. The time horizon of such activities varied from 1 to 2 years (e.g. operational plans), to 3 to 5 years (specific issues), to 5 to 10 years or longer (strategic planning). Business capital investment and other planning tended to be more long-term (frequently more than 20 years), whereas Federal government activities tended to be more short-term, because of (1) belief that longer-term planning was less realistic, and (2) in many instances a preoccupation with the next 1- to 3-year budget cycle or the more immediate interests of Congressional committees. There are, of course, important exceptions to these general trends.

(3) What mechanisms are used?

In almost all cases the regular line staff of the organization, including the operating heads of business units, is heavily relied on for foresight activities. In most cases, a special staff group in the central organization has leadership and co-ordinating responsibilities, often reporting to one of the top officials of the organization. In almost all such cases, significant stress was placed upon the need to involve operational management as well as key officials. In business organizations there is frequent use of cross-cutting committees of top officials, staffed by the head of a special central group, with inputs provided by *ad hoc* groups of operating staff. Stress on the active support and involvement of top management (and sometimes board members) was common in business organizations. Indeed this was often stated as a necessary condition for success, along with the active participation of line staff. At the Spring 1983 meeting of the Issues Management Association, Margaret Stroup, Director, Strategic Issues Analysis at Monsanto gave an insider's look at how issues management developed in her company. It first started in public affairs, but evolved into a branch of planning. Monsanto has established an extensive system directed by the Emerging Issues Committee of senior executives.

In many instances, work by the organization's staff was supplemented with consultants, subscription services, and outside groups doing specially commissioned studies. The use of regular subscription services (e.g. for environmental monitoring, media scanning, public opinion polling) was viewed by the business organizations with differing degrees of utility. While almost all of the organizations contacted used such services, especially for early identification, some said they were cutting back such use because in their experience the services were not particularly useful to their business interests. One firm indicated that they had recently done away with their central planning unit and were relying instead on a decentralized system at the business unit level, while another firm had recently eliminated its special issues management director. Top management interest in, and attention to, foresight activities seemed to be greater in business organizations than in government.

(4) What is the cost of such activities?

All respondents indicated that it was difficult if not impossible to estimate the total organizational costs of foresight activities, especially those carried out by line staff at the operating level. In most cases they were able to estimate the cost of the central staff, which generally was in the range of 2 to about 15 professional people. Some had a rough estimate of the amount of money spent on special external services, consultants and special contracts which ranged from about $20k to $250k, and in a few instances amounted to several millions a year. However, in the business organizations there were frequent comments that the cost is not significant; what is more significant is whether such activities were viewed as a vitally necessary function or as an overhead luxury to be cut back during times of poor business. In government organizations there was frequent mention of stringent personnel and budget limits, although the use of external services through special contracts were both more extensive than in private organizations and at higher cost than in the private sector. Service organizations, some of which rely heavily upon government funding in other areas (e.g. research), frequently indicated that in foresight activities, working for business organizations tended to be more rewarding both financially and intellectually than working with government. This was due to more continuity and greater breadth.

(5) Who gets the outputs of such activities?

In business organizations, the output of foresight activities tends to go to a high level executive group or committee. It is generally headed by the CEO or a Senior Vice President, and in some cases includes all or parts of the board of directors as well as the operational heads of business units. On occasion some parts of the output (e.g. policy with regard to a specific issue) were communicated to the general staff. In Executive Branch organizations, agency heads, deputy and assistant agency heads, and operational managers received the output. In organizations that serve the legislative branch, outputs went to the Congressional Committee or Member who made the request and frequently became publicly available. The active involvement of top officials in making decisions based upon these outputs seemed to be greater in business organizations than in government.

With regard to issues monitoring and management, most frequently brief staff analyses of a large number of issues, including some prioritizing based upon likely impact and probability of occurrence, went to a top level committee. After review, such a top level committee determined which small number of issues needed their attention, determined the corporate policy for each, and reviewed implementation plans. Less important issues were dealt with at lower levels of the organization. Such prioritizing and specific assignment of issues based upon importance was less common in public organizations where multiple levels were involved in most issues.

(6) How are outputs disseminated?

Generally the outputs of foresight activities take the form of written documents ranging from a volume of comprehensive plans to brief papers on specific issues. In almost all cases this was accompanied by extensive briefings aided by visuals. In a few organizations electronic conferencing, video tape and other aids (e.g. newsletters) were used to communicate to geographically dispersed parts of the organization. In some cases company sponsored courses or seminars were used to disseminate results and techniques used. In all cases stress was put on the need for continual and close communication with users or clients. In some cases certain outputs (e.g. trends analyses) were made available to people outside the business organizations. In government organizations outputs are often available to anyone in the public requesting it. Outputs in service organizations (reports, briefings, etc.) were disseminated to sponsors and, for the more academic service organizations, outputs were often to the professional community via professional literature and/or special reports.

(7) What information inputs are used (e.g. newspapers, magazines, scientific publications, trade publications, government documents, trade or industry association publications)?

Organizations use the full range of publication inputs to a greater or lesser extent. How useful individual publications are depends upon the subject matter or issue under consideration. Business organizations appear to be broadening their use of general literature as a part of their horizon scanning activities, including local newspapers in the locations where they have operations or interests. Some scanning services are employed; however, attitudes concerning their utility vary greatly. Most government organizations rely heavily on 'news clips' that are prepared for their broader organizations as well as other sources already noted.

[Note: (8), (9) and (10) were the focus of conversations with the users of foresight activities.]

(8) What are the benefits, successes, advantages?

A broader realization of trends that may effect future opportunities and problems is the most frequently cited benefit of foresight activities, along with continuing education of management and a feeling of greater control of, and preparedness for, the future. In private organizations, positive outcomes relating to specific issues and opportunities are frequently cited. There are numerous examples of firms that expanded into new areas of business in part due to foresight activities (e.g. new insurance and financial services, biotechnology, personal computers and consumer electronics). In addition, such activities are resulting in some firms broadening their enlightened self-interest in matters as diverse as: released time with pay for teaching in local schools, more flexible fringe benefit plans that enable employees to select packages that best suit their needs, and the design and advocacy of broader social programs to deal with unemployment and employee displacement by placing more emphasis on continual education and retraining before unemployment. One firm has engaged in a serious study of people in their late teens and early 20's to determine their interests and concerns, and to help guide the design of future products and services.

Government organizations seemed to be more depressed about their ability to deal with problems and opportunities they have not raised themselves but have found 'thrust upon them' although there are examples of positive benefits from foresight activities. Greater appreciation of and involvement by both top management and line staff in issues that will affect the organization is a frequently cited benefit of foresight activities by most organiz-

ations, both private and public. Another benefit sometimes mentioned is that foresight activities challenge the organization's values and assumptions. As examples of current issues of concern such things as: sex discrimination in insurance, pre-employment medical screening and genetic testing of employees, and video display terminal effects on employees were some of the many explicitly mentioned.

(9) What are the liabilities, failures, disadvantages?

There was less consensus about this. Being treated as an overhead cost that might not be valued, especially during times of great resource constraint, was the most frequently mentioned liability. This was inversely correlated with the degree of top management support for and involvement in such activities. In addition, the problem of getting the attention and involvement of operating officials and staff who were preoccupied with day to day problems and fire fighting was also a significant factor. The fact that some emerging issues and opportunities, that later turned out to be important, were missed was mentioned as a failure. Examples include: missing the implications of electronic banking and the potential value of satellite communications and data system links (this latter one by a government organization that had previously predicted and became an early user of the dramatic increase in microelectronic capabilities at reduced cost and space). The difficulty of doing such work, and the lack of good rules or paradigms for its conduct was mentioned, as was the need to track implementation and determine progress.

(10) Are the results worth the effort thus far? How do you determine this? What indicators or index of success or failure is used?

These questions were recognized as most difficult to pin down by most respondents. No real clear 'bottom line' indicator(s) appeared. The degree of acceptance by top management and line operating staff was most frequently mentioned as an indicator, as were changes in organization's policy and plans, and organization's increased flexibility. A greater or lesser allocation of resources by top management to foresight activities was frequently mentioned, especially by executive branch organizations. In many private sector organizations foresight activities have been allocated increased resources despite cutbacks in other activities during poor economic conditions. While these were stated as 'soft' measures, most respondents cited a growing interest in and commitment to such activities; in this regard, private sector and Legislative Branch respondents were far more positive than Executive Branch respondents. An expanding role and scope of such activities was noted as a positive indicator; so were a number of 'correct calls' that were against conventional wisdom. Examples of this include the forecast that broader fringe benefit options for employees would lessen costs and forecasts of the instability of certain foreign governments despite the assurances and encouragement of the U.S. Government (e.g. Iran, Mexico) and as a result the decline of investment opportunities.

(11) What, if any, science, technology and educational developments, issues, problems and opportunities have activities in this area provided early identification, of and where did such early identification come from?

There were many and very different responses to this subject, ranging from scientific breakthroughs (e.g. DNA and biotechnology) to technological requirements (e.g. greater production efficiency). A number of private sector organizations expressed growing concern about declining educational achievement (especially in mathematics and science), inadequacy of college and technical training and the need for continuing education. A number of private organizations expressed concern for the likely increase in structural unemployment given technological change, not only in production work but especially in white collar and middle management positions. In fact, several private firms expressed the view that their foresight activities were increasingly indicating that federal and some non-federal employment forecasts were too optimistic.

As to where such early identification came from there was no clear answer, because, by the time some clear consensus was achieved, publications, staff and regular channels were in some agreement. Yet a number of organizations could and did cite specific scientific, technological or educational problems or opportunities they felt they got started on early. This was less common among government organizations which seemed to be more reactive to such problems or opportunities after they had surfaced. Although the government respondents frequently stated that it was increasingly necessary to get out in front of such matters, they seemed to have difficulty coping beyond the time horizon of the next budget cycle.

A special set of subjects were addressed to organizations who supply services for foresight activities. This included:

(11a) What services do you provide?

(11b) For specific, generally available services, describe
  ☆ the nature of the service
  ☆ the nature of the outputs
  ☆ the cost
  ☆ to whom the service is available
  ☆ names of organizations using the service.

(11c) A similar set of questions, about any special services that might be provided in response to specific requests, was discussed.

It is difficult to describe the responses in summary form because of the diverse nature of the many service organizations and the many different kinds of services available. These range from free or low cost newsletters (e.g. concerning trends or abstracts of literature) to expensive ($10–$20K per year) multiclient forecasting, public opinion, technological forecasts, etc. In addition, virtually all of the service organizations are available to provide specially commissioned seminars, studies and micro forecasts (e.g. for particular products, markets, geographic regions). All responding service organizations were quite willing to describe the services available, the cost, and the names of some of the organizations who are subscribers or sponsors. Many of the organizations supplied extensive descriptive material. A file of such material is available for consultation.

Implications and Options

It became clear during this study that much attention is being paid to foresight activities, that many changes are occurring in them and that it is appropriate for most, if not all, organizations to reassess what they are doing and how it can be improved. Based on the interviews conducted, which included a discussion of the organization's previous 'system' as well as the current one and why a change was made, it is possible to suggest reasonable options. Any organization seeking to reassess its current system is faced with the following three generic options with obvious intermediate possibilities:

(a) *Continue Doing What is Now Done With No Change*. This is an obvious choice if the organization, and particularly its top management, is convinced that what is now being done is good and is comfortable with how it is done. 'If it isn't broke, don't fix it.' applies here. However, if there are important dissatisfactions with the current 'system', consideration should be given to the two remaining generic options and intermediate possibilities.

(b) *Incrementally Improve the Organization, Co-ordination, Communication, Effectiveness and Use of What is Now Done*. This is generally a consideration in cases where the current system is a distributed or decentralized system. The natural question raised is, will things improve if in addition to having all or many parts of the organization involved in scanning, monitoring, analyzing, planning and managing potential problems and opportunities, a focal point for co-ordination and communication in the form of a single person or small group were established?

Such a move could involve the sending of copies of relevant material to such a person(s) who would be responsible for reading across and summarizing the more important trends, problems and opportunities and communicating the results to the top management and to the broader organization. Such communication can take the form of informal, regular newsletters and/or more formal trends and issues analyses, plans and contingency plans, policy analysis, etc. Often this option, as well as the others, is supplemented by the purchase of external services in the form of consultants, subscriptions, membership in group programs and special studies.

The incremental improvement option should be actively considered if the top management of an organization is generally happy with what is going on and believes the organization is generally exercising appropriate foresight but that some more central focal point is needed to pull such activities together in a form that will direct attention to necessary decisions and actions. Many of the organizations involved in this study indicated they were now at this stage.

(c) *Make a Major or Dramatic Change in What is Now Being Done and How it is Done.* This is generally a consideration when the top management of an organization wants to focus foresight activities and organize them in one or more centrally located and co-ordinated groups. Frequently such a move is made if there is general dissatisfaction with how such activities are handled and/or top management wants to pay more concerted attention to such matters in order to be better prepared for future changes. Models for better organization of foresight activities are provided in the report of the private sector Foresight Task Group, cited earlier.[3] This Task Force believes that the report presents good models of the best practice of 'Foresight in the Private Sector'. In considering options it would be useful for any organization, public or private, to consider the models presented here. A major advantage of these models is that they make the process more explicit and put the various components of foresight activities (e.g. strategic planning, issues management) within the broader context of a 'system'.

Decision Rule

Which of these options, or intermediates, is most advantageous depends to a critical degree on the culture and history of the organization considering the options. There is obviously no one best option for all organizations. To a considerable extent the option chosen should reflect the predilections of the

organization's management. None of the options or models will work well without the support and active involvement of the organization's management—both top and operating line management. Any of the options or models is likely to be more or less satisfactory to the extent it matches the style and preferences of the organization's management. The key decision rule is, match the foresight strategic management system and organization to:

(a) the strategic needs of the organization,

(b) the interests and support of the organization's management at all levels, but especially top level management, and

(c) what will be used for decisionmaking and operations.

Given a realistic assessment utilizing this decision rule, a specific organization should be able to plot a sensible way of conducting appropriate foresight activities.

Appendix

Selected List of Information Sources

(1) *The Study of the Future: An Agenda for Research*, Boucher, Wayne I., editor, NSF RANN, Washington DC, July (1977).

(2) *The Future: a Guide to Information Sources*, second edition, World Future Society, Bethesda, Maryland (1979).

(3) Robert C. Stuart and David Weaver, *Strategic Planning in Federal Agencies: A Directory*, USGS, Reston, Virginia, June (1981).

(4) Strategic Issues: Historical Experience, Institutional Structures and Conceptual Framework. A report for the Committee on Energy and Commerce, U.S. House of Representatives, Washington DC, July (1982).

(5) Public Issue Early Warning Systems: Legislative and Institutional Alternatives, Hearings and Workshop by the Subcommittee on Oversight and Investigations and the Subcommittee on Energy Conservation and Power and the Committee on Energy and Commerce, U.S. House of Representatives, Washington DC, October (1982).

(6) Congressional Foresight: History, Recent Experiences, and Implementation Strategies. A report for the Committee on Energy and Commerce, U.S. House of Representatives, Washington DC, December (1982).

(7) Foresight in the Private Sector: How Can Government Use It? Report of the Foresight Task Force, for the Committee on Energy and Commerce, U.S. House of Representatives, Washington DC, January (1983).

Realistic Planning for Transportation—A Flexible Approach

Ata M. Khan

Substantial progress has been made towards the development of a systematic framework and associated methodology for supporting transport policy and planning decisions with long-term consequences. However, a critical difficulty that still remains is that, frequently, such reliance is placed upon answers, without a treatment of the uncertainties in forecasts. This paper advances flexible approaches to the analysis and evaluation of transport policy and planning decisions. Forecasting elements in methodology used for typical transport decision making contexts are described, and sources of uncertainties are identified. Examples of methodological deficiencies in actual decision cases are covered. Innovative planning methodology based on group assessments, Delphi studies and the use of systematic framework based on decision theory are described and practical benefits for the use of such approaches are discussed.

Transportation, as a major sector of the economy, competes for limited resources at all levels of government. Also, both the short- and long-term impacts of transportation system changes are felt widely. In the practice of transportation planning over the past two decades or so, quantitative analyses of increasing complexity have gradually become available as aids to policy and planning decisions. However, the outcomes of analyses, although of questionable accuracy, are accepted as exact answers even though forecasts are made for up to 20 or 30 years into the future. Lessons learned from past practice suggest that decisions involving billions of dollars in transportation are frequently based on inadequate information.[1,2,3]

Techniques for transportation planning have become complex but are highly deficient in underlying theory.[4,5] Furthermore, inputs into these techniques are often unreliable. Consequently, uncrtainties exist in the estimates of such factors as future demand, technical performance of systems, costs of construction and operation, and regional socio-economic impacts. It is not suggested here, however, that long range forecasting for transportation planning could become an exact science. The availability and quality of data coupled with shortcomings of the concepts or theories of human behaviour and economic performance serve as constraints.

Two families of possible approaches can be used to deal with uncertainties in long range planning. Firstly, through research, reliability in forecasts should be sought through methodological advances. This approach, although highly desirable from a long range perspective, is, however, time consuming and may not be of immediate assistance. The second approach resorts to subjective assessment of uncertain factors through group assessments, Delphi studies and decision-theoretic approaches.[6] It is essential to foster better planning and decision making capabilties which can effectively develop and utilize improved information. This paper assesses the existing planning approach, including forecasting methods and recommends improvements in the form of flexible approaches to transport policy and planning decisions from a long range perspective.

Planning Process and Methodology

Decision Making Contexts

Transport policy and planning decisions frequently result in major additions or changes to the transportation system of a region or a country. Examples of past and future decisions include: whether to build a new high speed rail system in a well defined intercity corridor (e.g. Toronto–Ottawa–Montreal), building a new (second) airport in a region

The author is Professor of Civil Engineering at Carleton University, Ottawa.

(e.g. Mirabel, Montreal Region), whether to build a third airport in the region (e.g. London, England), whether to expand capacity of the St. Lawrence Seaway–Welland Canal system, and whether to increase the capacity of Western Canadian railway tracks for the transportation of mostly bulk commodities. In all these and numerous other cases, major investments of scarce public or private funds are required. How are such decisions supported in terms of their information needs?

Typically, the planning process of a transport system in its progressive planning mode takes a hierarchical form[7,8] (Figure 1). It consists of:

(1) the preliminary analysis,

(2) the detailed analysis and design,

(3) the partial implementation, and

(4) the full implementation.

Taking the example of urban transport system planning, in the preliminary analysis phase, the most likely economic, regional and urban development pattern is predicted for the future years of interest. Transport system alternatives to serve the economic and social activities (expressed as transportation demand) that are implicit in the development scenario are generated and analysed. By using transport analysis models, the impacts of system

alternatives are forecast. The estimated impacts (i.e. forecasts), which include costs and benefits/revenues are evaluated by using economic efficiency or cost-effectiveness or other techniques. The results of this evaluation form the basis of policy and planning (including investment) decisions.

The detailed analysis phase attempts to refine the concept in the preliminary phase of the process. Detailed analyses are usually carried out which are model-based or take the form of market surveys designed to measure the market potential of the service under consideration. The information obtained is used to reassess the adequacy of the preferred system development option without implementing it.

In most types of transportation systems, investments can be made sequentially. Whenever appropriate, protection or acquisition of the right-of-way is the first step towards partial implementation. There is, however, a tendency on the part of many transportation planners to prepare detailed and inflexible master plans (with staging schedules) which offer little opportunity to change the course of system development should circumstances necessitate such a change.

It has been argued by this author that the performance of a partially implemented system can be studied on a demonstration basis.[8] The resulting information can be utilized for further policy and planning decisions. Examples of urban and intercity transportation demonstrations include: the Government of Ontario's Lakeshore Rail Transit Service in the Toronto Region, and the demonstration of passenger train services in the North-East Corridor of the U.S.A. The Toronto demonstration led to the implementation of similar services in other corridors in that region. The North-East Corridor demonstration was considered instrumental in track upgrading decisions in the corridor.

Transportation demonstrations could also have a wider role to play in terms of yielding information on poorly understood factors such as technical performance and user acceptance of new or innovative services. An outstanding example is the Air Transit Short Takeoff and Landing (STOL) Service specifically implemented as a demonstration between Montreal and Ottawa in the early 1970s. Experience gained from this demonstration has been very useful in planning and implementing the present STOL services linking Toronto with Ottawa and other cities.

A number of further observations can be made which characterize the context in which transportation policy and planning decisions are made. These include:

(1) uncertainties in forecasting demand, performance and costs,

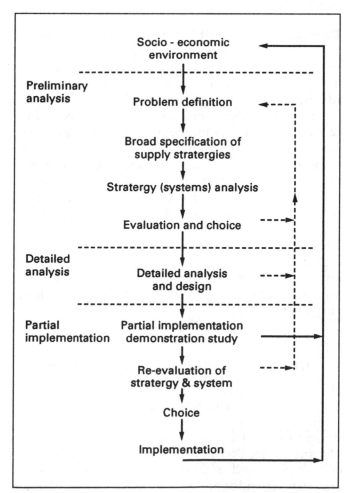

Figure 1. The progressive planning approach

(2) high costs of new systems or capacity expansion of existing systems,

(3) high congestion costs in case of insufficient capacity, and high economic losses in case of the provision of excess capacity,

(4) a shift in emphasis from the traditional approach of expanding capacity primarily through more facilities to less capital intensive means (i.e. more efficient use of existing facilities through better management and reorganization of operations), and

(5) an emphasis on societal costs and environmental and energy factors.

The economic consequences of insufficient capacity as well as excess capacity are illustrated in Figure 2.

A number of transportation decisions can be cited which, due to the factors named above, have resulted in inadequate facilities and/or economic losses. Examples are provided here. The plan for Mirabel Airport (Montreal Region) was based on high projections of traffic which never materialized. Mirabel is well recognized to have excess capacity at a high cost to the public. In the planning of Dulles Airport (Washington, D.C.), the forecasters did not anticipate the effect of aircraft size on aircraft traffic and competition from other airports on its air travel market. Consequently, for over a decade in the late 1960s and early 1970s, Dulles Airport did not serve the market that was forecast for it.[3]

There are also examples of underestimation of traffic. Air transportation policy planners in the U.S.A. have come to realize that air traffic growth response to deregulation of the industry has been much beyond expectation. Consequently, airport and air traffic control system capacity deficiencies have become evident in the form of congestion-induced delays. There are also increasing concerns for aviation safety that arise from the imbalance of traffic demand and capacity of major hub terminal areas.

Transportation decisions in some cases have had to be reversed due to unanticipated circumstances. For instance, in the process of locating sites for new airports for Toronto, New York City and London (England), the importance of environmental impacts (e.g. perceived noise and devaluation of property) was underestimated. There are of course numerous examples of urban freeways that were never completed due to public opposition.

Forecasting Methodology
Transport systems analysis, which is a key component of transportation planning, requires a methodology for forecasting a large number of interrelated factors. Major forecasting elements include: user acceptance as indicated by demand for transportation, system performance (in technical terms) including operating and maintenance costs, costs of constructing facilities and acquiring vehicles, etc., and system impacts on the socio-economic environment. Since most of these forecasting elements relate to estimating future traffic in temporal and spatial terms, much of this discussion focusses on demand forecasting methodology.

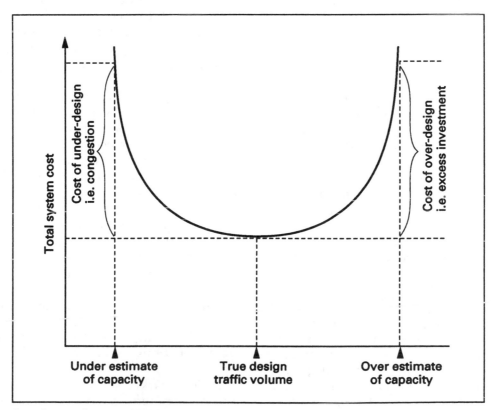

Figure 2. Cost of under and over design

Formal methods for forecasting transportation demand can be categorized into trend extrapolation, market disaggregation, statistical and econometric aggregate type of models, disaggregate models, and disaggregate mode choice models. In the case of new technologies, forecasting goes beyond demand estimation. Technological forecasting is used as a broad framework for estimating the market potential for new systems, as well as the technical performance and cost of such systems, especially in circumstances where prior experience with such systems is largely absent.

Two forecasting approaches are employed depending upon the agency and purpose of the forecastng. For long range strategic planning, the 'top down' approach to forecasting is used. That is, national level forecasts are developed first, and from these regional and local level estimates are arrived at. On the other hand, 'bottom up' forecasting is preferred by many planners for estimating traffic changes at specific locations in response to socio-economic (including demographic) and transport system changes.[9]

Past trends were extrapolated in many planning studies. In such cases, anticipated developments or changes in the socio-economic environment were used subjectively as a basis for adjusting trends.[10] Although, in recent years, passenger demand forecasting techniques have improved in the case of urban transportation and intercity passenger transportation, such simple approaches are still used for forecasting air freight as well as surface and marine traffic.[9,11,12] As another example of oversimplification of a complex forecasting problem, a major research study relied upon the use of growth factors for establishing the feasibility of high speed ground transportation systems (i.e. trains, magnetically levitated vehicles) for the Toronto–Ottawa–Montreal Corridor.[13]

Disaggregate market segmentation and projection of trip propensities is a more advanced and expensive version of the extrapolation technique.[4,6,14] Market segments are defined by user attributes that are believed to affect their propensity to travel (e.g. age, education, trip purpose, etc.). Trends for each market segment are projected. Basic information or statistics on individual travel behaviour are obtained through market surveys.

Recent developments in forecasting methodology have focussed on the general family of statistical and econometric (aggregate type) models and disaggregate mode choice models. The statistical and econometric modelling approach involves the definition of mathematical expressions that resemble common econometric models. While econometric models are based on economic theories of growth and consumer behaviour, transportation demand models, even at their best, are based on crude analogy with physical systems (e.g. the gravity model) or economic systems (econometric models of travel demand).

A rationale for the application of the statistical and econometric models is that they are able to reproduce (or simulate) known travel decisions. Calibration of the models is achieved through survey data which are put through numerous transformations so as to achieve the best fit. Frequently, the choice of a model for preparing travel forecasts is based on how well a given model fits the known data rather than its conceptual appeal (i.e. underlying theory), ease of application, and confidence in the forecasts of model inputs.

A number of observations about the aggregate type models were made by the author in another paper.[6] The major points raised are summarized here. Analyses suggest that demand elasticities are sensitive to the mathematical form assumed for the demand function. In practice, in the absence of a convincing conceptual basis, numerous forms are tried by forecasters and the 'best' results are retained. In the transportation planning profession, there is much scepticism about demand elasticities obtained from various studies that used arbitrarily selected functional forms. Also, specification errors are generated by the use of incorrect functional forms. The functional forms of aggregate type models have other effects including parameters effects, distribution of residuals, and significance of variables.

The disaggregate mode choice prediction techniques involve the development of mathematical functions from survey data (e.g. logit function) which are used to calculate the probability of travel by a given mode. These models are based on a behavioural theory, although largely unsubstantiated, that individuals maximize the 'utility' or value that they place on travel service attributes and that utilities are additive.

The disaggregate approach to modelling travel demand has been regarded as a major advance over the aggregate model types. These models have a relatively sounder behavioural foundation and use relatively more powerful statistical estimation methods than the aggregate models. However, their development has not been carried out far enough since existing models of this type are based on a limited number of readily quantifiable attributes (mostly time and cost) for the creation of different mathematical functions (multinomial probit, generalized logit, etc.) out of a limited number of variables. The need for research has been stressed by the author in developing models which incorporate the essential attributes affecting travel decisions, interrelationships between attribute dimensions and value functions applicable to the attributes.[6]

Detailed market surveys are carried out in cases where more refined estimates of new transportation services are required. Such surveys are very costly but at the same time provide an extensive database on the attitudes of potential users about a large number of service attributes. Models of consumer acceptance can be developed from such data.

The cost of forecasting logically increases with the increasing complexity of the methodology and the extent of the data requirements. Also, it is an expectation of the planners that costlier forecasting techniques should reduce inaccuracy of forecasts and therefore reduce the cost of under or over capacity. A research goal worthy of immediate attention is the development of behavioural models of travel demand at reasonable cost capable of producing forecasts of acceptable reliability (see Figure 3).

Uncertain Forecasts

Transportation planning requires the estimation of location-specific transportation growth and the composition or nature of traffic. Such forecasts are required for planning the level and timing of transport system changes involving substantial investments. Realistically, predicting future traffic demand is a difficult task. Our understanding of the critical factors that influence travel and modal choice decisions is deficient. It is hardly surprising that comparisons of predicted and actual traffic reported by previous authors suggest systematically large errors.[2,15] For instance, forecasts of traffic growth for even a decade into the future could be over 20 per cent in error.[3]

Forecasts are also unreliable in terms of the estimates of elasticity of demand. An examination of fare and income elasticity predictions and actual experience shows significant variations.[16,17] Furthermore, location-specific forecasts of traffic demand characteristics are subject to even more uncertainty than aggregated national projections.

In addition to traffic demand, estimates of system construction, operation and maintenance costs are also highly uncertain. Reasons include the difficulty of predicting traffic, inadequate knowledge of technology, and uncertain cost factors. Frequently, the construction costs of capacity expansion to existing systems or building new systems are well over 30 per cent higher (even in constant dollars) than original estimates.[1] Similar observations apply to operation and maintenance costs, technical performance of the system, and socio-economic impacts. Clearly, forecasting future values of key planning factors is fraught with substantial uncertainties.

Deficiencies in the Planning Process

The planning process has not so far seriously recognized that transportation forecasts are commonly inaccurate. A process has to be adopted which is more appropriate for transportation systems. A step in this direction is to define the deficiencies in the current methodologies and the planning process. A list of such deficiencies could

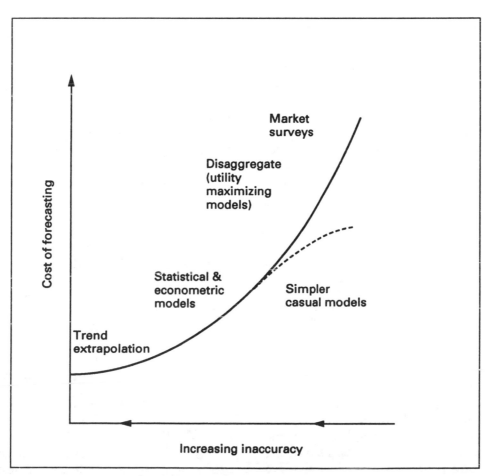

Figure 3. Cost of forecasting vs increasing inaccuracy (case of under estimation of capacity shown)

indeed be very long. Here, only major ones are noted.

(1) Transportation planning (including forecasting) has become highly procedure-oriented. Presently, excessive reliance is placed on available methodology with recognized deficiencies. Such a tendency renders the long range planning process rather narrow and ineffective. The analyst rarely questions the accuracy of forecasts, and major components of systems that are implemented are arrived at by mechanical procedures. Clearly, heavy reliance on a set of techniques alone is unreasonable since these are of limited accuracy and scope.

(2) A high level of confidence attached to forecasting models is inappropriate. It is wishful thinking to believe that current models can forecast the salient features of the behaviour of passengers (and shippers of freight) and the exact level of future traffic for 20 or more years into the future.[18] Although a number of recent methodological developments have resulted in structural and behavioural models for forecasting transportation demand, their success in actual planning studies is hardly proven. Also, the application of such models is viewed as an end in itself, rather than as means to the generation of probable forecasts.

(3) The selection of forecasting models for practical applications is based on the criterion of the ease of calibration. It is much more important to favour models which have convincing underlying theories and whose inputs can be projected reliably.

(4) In the development of cost estimates, there is little attempt made to calculate and use risk factors. Considering that significant uncertainties are encountered in transportation investment decisions, the use of factors that account for risk and uncertainty would be very appropriate.

(5) Estimates of capacity requirements are based on traffic forecasts and a mathematical definition of capacity. A closer examination of the techniques for estimating future capacity requirements indicates substantial sensitivity to the nature of the traffic, and its spatial and temporal characteristics.[11,19] Narrow technological projections and the absence of a 'systems' perspective render transportation infrastructure development strategies ineffective.

(6) Decisions to expand facilities are usually based on forecasts which contain hidden assumptions about the value of time and other value functions. Also, forecasts of the acceptance of system development decisions by various socio-economic groups are not based on the consideration of differential impacts. That is, the questions of 'who pays' and 'who benefits' are not explored since the narrow criterion of

maximum net (aggregate) benefits is often used. In such instances, evaluation of strategies such as economic (benefit–cost) evaluation, if used rather narrowly, may turn out to be smokescreens rather than serving as instruments to clarify issues.

Flexible Approaches to Planning

Methodological Improvements

Planning methodology in support of transport decisions can be improved in terms of the methodological framework, techniques and quality of information. Clearly, it is difficult to analyse complex systems thoroughly without the proper tools (techniques), systematic linkages between these and reliable data used by these tools. A number of requirements that are to be met by the improved methodology are: the recognition and treatment of uncertainties, flexibility in the supply of services, and the incorporation of the value structure of the affected interest groups.

In this direction, the first step was taken through the use of systems analysis in transportation and its attendant philosophy that good analysis be applied with the use of expert knowledge of sources of uncertainty, an appreciation of the difficulty of placing economic values on a number of planning factors, the absence of objective measures for some impacts, and the requirement of balancing individual preferences and social values.

From a long range planning perspective, it should be recognized in the planning process that the consequences of any plan cannot be forecast precisely. It is therefore extremely risky to choose a system development option for any specific location for 20 or more years into the future. Clearly, rigid master plans that define what projects to implement at what future time are inappropriate. A flexible planning process incorporating the features of group interaction, the use of expert panels and decision theory would be more appropriate.

As a part of any transportation system plan development process, the test of contingency measures for coping with a wide range of probable developments should be a requirement. Through such tests, system plans would be made flexible enough so that they can be altered to suit changing circumstances.

On a more theoretical level, methodological improvements are also required.

(1) For any forecasting element (such as demand for travel, construction costs, etc.) all the relevant risks must be assessed and their probable effects should be taken into account.[21]

(2) In defining simulation requirements, testing of critical combinations of important factors

should be emphasized at the system and subsystem level. For example, wide fluctuations in the rate of traffic growth combined with rapid expansion of traffic could pose serious difficulties for expanding infrastructure.[3]

(3) Demand forecasting models can be improved by enhancing their conceptual and behavioural base. In the development of innovative models with a strong conceptual base, statistical analyses would be required to enhance our understanding of the determinants of travel or freight transportation demand and to estimate calibration constants.

(4) Another improvement that could be affected relates to the extrapolation of basic factors which are included in the transportation forecasting model. It is equally important to obtain realistic forecasts of these factors (e.g. population, fuel prices, etc.).

(5) For major projects, technological forecasting based on the Delphi technique or modified versions of this technique is a worthwhile activity. However, such an activity could be assisted by appropriate modelling.

A number of approaches are described below and benefits from their practical application are noted.

Group Interaction, Technological Forecasting, Delphi Technique

In a number of situations where uncertainties are involved, simple benefit–cost analyses cannot be relied upon to establish the best course of action due to multiple interest groups and the absence of a market mechanism to resolve conflicting objectives. In such cases, shared decision making could be gainfully applied. Participation in decision making, before a particular alternative policy or plan is selected for implementation, has been successfully used by Transport Canada in order to decide on the national airspace system plan for the next two decades. On many aspects of the plan, interests overlapped sufficiently for the parties to come up with a consensus view that made sense.[22] A similar study was carried out by the Federal Aviation Administration (U.S.A.) on air traffic regulations, navigation aids and facilities, meteorological services and communications requirements.[23]

Technological forecasting is another approach for estimating technical performance, cost and future market share for new systems. Since there is little past or meagre current experience with novel transportation systems (e.g. magnetically levitated vehicles), this approach is a reasonable way to arrive at estimated values of uncertain factors such as market level, costs and performance.

The process of implementing the technological forecasting framework requires the use of a panel of experts as well as selected forecasting methods.

Through Delphi (described below) and other panel approaches, estimates of the likelihood or timing of critical developments are arrived at. Following this step, plausible scenarios for the future are defined. The strength of this approach lies in the fact that it serves as a mechanism for bringing crucial expert judgements on the forecasting elements. This author has reviewed a number of technological forecasting studies that were carried out on the interaction of telecommunications and travel. The review confirms the usefulness of this approach.

The Delphi method is an approach for acquiring and refining the opinions of groups of experts. The use of 'expert judgement' in forecasting under uncertainty has been investigated by a number of planners. In recent years, several investigators have experimented with the use of this approach as a technique for urban and regional planning. For example, the Delphi approach was used for forecasting land use, regional industrial land use, and for predicting the impacts of alternative transportation programmes.[25–27]

Members of the Delphi panel draw upon past experience with events similar to the one under study, and also upon their in-depth knowledge about the items being forecast and the context within which the forecasts are being made. Forecasts resulting from the informed opinions of experts are more likely to cover a realistic range of possibilities rather than a single forecast obtained from a model. Transportation planning decisions that ultimately evolve from this approach are likely to be flexible in adapting to a range of future requirements.

Decision-Theoretic Approach

Statistical decision theory can be used as a basis for the development of approaches to the treatment of risk and uncertainty in long range planning. Also, principles of utility theory can be used to quantify the value structure of decision makers. Decision-theoretic frameworks that combine these two theories are very attactive for long range transport system planning. An experimental application of decision theory to airport site selection was reported by DeNeufville and Keeney.[28] Khan developed and applied decision-theoretic approaches to regional transport plan selection and highway improvement programming problems.[7,8,20]

In the U.K., in forecasting for highway planning and design, the Department of Transport study group acknowledged that the accuracy implied by point estimates was spurious. This group recommended that the Department of Transport should indicate the likely range of uncertainties involved in the forecasts and demonstrate the consequences of selecting different values within that range. For the combined treatment of various future states, the use of a probabilistic approach to highway planning was illustrated. Also, another innovation that has been tried is that of combining the Delphi approach and the probabilistic approach. A Delphi poll among experts formed the basis of obtaining 'high', 'low' and 'most likely' estimates of forecasts. These were combined with different assumed probability distributions fitted to the estimates. It was acknowledged that further research is required to incorporate risk aversion satisfactorily through utility function specification.[29]

This brings up a widely recognized issue in transportation dealing with the resource constraints upon procuring information. The availability and quality of information affects the quality of the analyses that support the decision making process. As previously noted in the literature, constraints on information acquisition have traditionally been fairly severe (see for example Shallal and Khan[30,31]). This becomes quite apparent when investment in information acquisition strategies is compared to the costs and benefits of providing transport facilities. Commonly, only a small fraction of 1 per cent of the total cost of the system is accounted for by planning studies. The addition of design and construction supervision costs could raise it to 4 or 5 per cent. In support of business decisions, investments in planning (including forecasting) tend to be on the order of 7 or 8 per cent. During a planning horizon (say 20 years), capital outlays for transport facilities may be between 1000 and 2000 times as much.

Logically, better information costs more to acquire but could result in greater reduction in uncertainty. This suggests that information collection in transport planning can be studied on a trade-off basis. It is desirable to have complete detail on every aspect of a transport system that can possibly have a bearing upon investment decisions. On the other hand, it is essential to keep the cost of information as low as possible.

It should be recognized that an additional sum spent on information acquisition may well lead to investment decisions which realize savings several orders of magnitude greater than that sum. As most transport systems involve a substantial magnitude of expenditure (in social and economic terms), even a relatively small saving due to improved information will be large in absolute terms. However, it is also likely that, eventually, a point will arrive when the social saving in terms of better planning is worth less than the resources invested in additional information acquisition. Logically, in such a case, the expenditure of scarce revenues in information acquisition cannot be justified.

As pointed out earlier in this paper, a decision-theoretic framework could be gainfully used for establishing the value of information from detailed studies, market surveys and demonstrations prior to making system development decisions. This approach in essence is the answer to an outstanding issue in transportation, namely that of a rationale for

investment in information acquisition. That is, the transport planner, among other factors, has to determine the feasibility of investing resources in planning studies and other information acquisition strategies.

Concluding Remarks

(1) Planners and decision makers should view transportation forecasts with much caution since substantial uncertainties are involved.

(2) Rigid master plans with horizons of 20 or more years cannot be regarded as realistic. Flexible strategies should be devised for coping with unexpected developments in such factors as traffic demand. This necessitates a planning process which is sequential in nature and enables an examination of alternatives in the light of a broad range of possible futures. Also, in order to be prepared against unforeseen circumstances, elements of flexibility (e.g. contingency plans) should be included in system development strategies.

(3) Transportation forecasting methods at present span from simple projection types to reasonably sophisticated models. Projection methods are inappropriate for long range planning. In general, the available models are deficient in underlying theories. The statistical and econometric models are data-intensive. In relative terms, behavioural disaggregate type models and market analysis methods, although costly, are attractive due to their information content about demand characteristics and consumer preferences. However, projecting these involves uncertainties. Uncertainties are also encountered in forecasts of costs and other planning factors.

(4) Research is required in the development of innovative and cost-effective models with less demanding data needs than existing econometric and statistical types of models.

(5) Depending upon the importance of projects and the level of innovation involved (e.g. new technology, new applications of existing technology), planning agencies could gainfully combine modelling approaches and judgemental types of methods involving group assessments. It is important to anticipate major technological, demographic, and socio-economic changes which could alter the desirability of the type and level of service. For major system changes, technological forecasts involving panels of experts is attractive. Through such forecasting endeavours based on the Delphi/modified Delphi technique, consensus of expert opinion on uncertain forecasts can be reached.

(6) A systematic framework based on the principles of statistical decision theory appears attractive

for supporting transport planning and policy decisions. Such a framework will enable planners to incorporate their best estimates of the probability of different futures, their expectations of future costs and benefits associated with different alternatives, and the value of additional information. It is contended that such a framework in association with other methodological improvements will enable transport systems to successfully adapt to future conditions and events.

Acknowledgements—The research reported in this paper was supported by the Natural Sciences and Engineering Research Council of Canada. An earlier version of this paper was presented at the Third International Symposium on Forecasting held in Philadelphia, U.S.A. in June 1983. An abstract of the paper was published in the Conference Programme.

References

(1) G. E. Germane, *Transportation Policy Issues for the 1990s,* Ch. 1, Addison-Wesley (1983).

(2) J. L. Carroll, Great Lakes/St. Lawrence Seaway Season Extension—who needs it?, *Canadian Transportation Research Forum Proceedings,* **1,** May (1982).

(3) R. De Neufville, *Airport System Planning, A Critical Look at the Methods and Experience,* MIT Press, Cambridge (1976).

(4) Charles River Associates, *Policy Evaluation with Travel Behaviour Models: Methodological Issues and Case Studies,* Boston (1979).

(5) Charles River Associates, *Methods for Analyzing Fuel Supply Limitations on Passenger Travel,* National Cooperative Highway Research Program No. 229, Washington, D.C. (1980).

(6) Ata M. Khan, Towards the development of innovative models of intercity travel demand, *Transportation Quarterly,* **XXXIX** (2) (1985).

(7) A. M. Khan and M. C. Poulton, Decision theory, transportation planning and evaluation process, *The Logistics and Transportation Review,* **15** (3) (1979).

(8) A. M. Khan, Transport policy decision analysis: a decision-theoretic framework, *Socio-Economic Planning Sciences,* **5,** 159–171 (1971).

(9) Transport Canada, *Aviation Forecasts 1986–1996,* Ottawa, TP7960E (1986).

(10) Airport Inquiry Commission (Canada), *Report of the Airport Inquiry Commission,* Information Canada, Ottawa (1974).

(11) Transport Canada, *CATA's National Aviation Forecasting Models and Other Forecasting Methods,* Ottawa, TP2046 (1979).

(12) D. Rubin and N. D. Lerner, Forecasting for Aviation System Planning, Transportation Research Board Annual Meeting, Washington, D.C., 15 January (1987).

(13) Canadian Institute of Guided Ground Transport, *Alternatives to Air: A Feasible Concept for the Toronto–Ottawa–Montreal Corridor,* Queen's University, Kingston, Ontario, Report No. 80–84 (1980).

(14) Charles River Associates, *On the Development of A Theory of Traveller Attitude–Behaviour Interrelationships,* Transportation Systems Centre, U.S. D.O.T., Cambridge (1978).

(15) St. Lawrence Seaway Authority, How is it that the Welland Canal continues to meet increasing tonnage demand? *Canadian Transportation Research Forum Proceedings,* **1,** May (1982).

(16) C. H. Glenn, Fuel Efficiency of Canadian airline fleets, a simulation of intra-Canada jet operations, *Proceedings of Transportation Research Forum,* **XXIII** (1) (1982).

(17) C. A. Lave *et al.,* Price elasticities of intercity passenger travel, *Proceedings of Transportation Research Forum,* **XVIII** (1) (1977).

(18) N. Ashford, Problems with long term air transport forecasting, *Journal of Advanced Transportation,* **19** (2) (1985).

(19) D. H. Pickrell, Airline Deregulation and Air Traffic Congestion at Large Airports, Transportation Research Board, Annual Meeting, Washington, D.C. (1982).

(20) A. M. Khan and P. L. LaFontaine, The management of highway infrastructure rehabilitation: a forward look, *WCTR '86, World Conference on Transport Research,* Vol. 1, pp. 459–479 (1986).

(21) D. E. Raphael, U.S. Airline Financial Future, Transportation Research Board Annual Meeting, Washington, D.C. (1982).

(22) J. Macbeth, Participating before the fact, *Transpo/85,* Transport Canada, Ottawa, Vol. 8/2 (1985).

(23) Federal Aviation Administration, *The Federal Aviation Administration Plan for Research, Engineering and Development, V. 1, Plan Overview,* Washington, D.C., August (1986).

(24) A. M. Khan, *Transportation and Telecommunications: An Examination of Substitution and Stimulation,* Prepared for Research Branch, Canadian Transport Commission, Ottawa, WP60-84-12 (1984).

(25) J. M. Davis, *Land Use Forecasting: A Delphi Approach,* Thesis Presented to the University of Georgia, at Athens, GA (1975).

(26) O. L. Ervin, A Delphi study of regional industrial land-use, *Review of Regional Studies,* **7** (1) (1977).

(27) V. Cavalli-Sforza and L. Ortolano, Delphi forecasts of land use–transportation interactions, *Journal of Transportation Engineering,* **110** (3), May (1984).

(28) R. DeNeufville and R. L. Keeney, Use of decision analysis in airport development for Mexico City, in DeNeufville, R. and Marks, D. (Editors), *Systems Analysis and Design,* Prentice Hall (1974).

(29) A. Jessop, Forecasting for Highway Planning and Design in the U.K., Third International Forecasting Conference, Philadelphia (1983).

(30) L. A. Y. Shallel and A. M. Khan, Predicting peak hour traffic, *Traffic Quarterly,* **34** (1) (1980).

(31) L. A. Y. Shallel and A. M. Khan, A decision-theoretic framework for urban transport design and investment decisions, *Transportation Quarterly,* **36** (2) (1982).